THE BRESSONIANS

THE BRESSONIANS

FRENCH CINEMA AND
THE CULTURE OF
AUTHORSHIP

Codruța Morari

berghahn
NEW YORK · OXFORD
www.berghahnbooks.com

First published in 2017 by
Berghahn Books
www.berghahnbooks.com

© 2017, 2024 Codruța Morari
First paperback edition published in 2024

All rights reserved. Except for the quotation of short passages
for the purposes of criticism and review, no part of this book
may be reproduced in any form or by any means, electronic or
mechanical, including photocopying, recording, or any information
storage and retrieval system now known or to be invented,
without written permission of the publisher.

Library of Congress Cataloging-in-Publication Data

Names: Morari, Codruța, author.
Title: The Bressonians : French cinema and the culture of authorship / Codruța Morari.
Description: New York : Berghahn Books, 2017. | Includes bibliographical references and index.
Identifiers: LCCN 2017014767 (print) | LCCN 2017024867 (ebook) | ISBN 9781785335723 (e-book) | ISBN 9781785335716 (hardback : alk. paper)
Subjects: LCSH: Bresson, Robert--Criticism and interpretation. | Motion pictures--Aesthetics. | Motion pictures--Production and direction--France.
Classification: LCC PN1998.3.B755 (ebook) | LCC PN1998.3.B755 M67 2017 (print) | DDC 791.4302/33092--dc23
LC record available at https://lccn.loc.gov/2017014767

British Library Cataloguing in Publication Data
A catalogue record for this book is available from the British Library

ISBN 978-1-78533-571-6 hardback
ISBN 978-1-80539-310-8 paperback
ISBN 978-1-80539-424-2 epub
ISBN 978-1-78533-572-3 web pdf

https://doi.org/10.3167/9781785335716

Contents

List of Illustrations	vi
Acknowledgements	viii
Introduction	1
1 *"Il faut un auteur!"*: Robert Bresson and the Making of the Author	23
2 An Elusive Style	58
3 Kinsmen	86
4 The Ethics of Duplicity	119
5 Working Artists	150
Conclusion	177
Bibliography	181
Index	193

Illustrations

Illustration 2.1	Mouchette Lights Up	74
	(*Mouchette*, dir. Robert Bresson, 1967)	
Illustration 2.2	Muddy Shoes	75
	(*Mouchette*, dir. Robert Bresson, 1967)	
Illustration 3.1	Isabelle Weingarten, as Gilberte	87
	(*La Maman et la putain*, dir. Jean Eustache, 1973)	
Illustration 3.2	Alexandre Bressonian	87
	(Jean-Pierre Léaud and Isabelle Weingarten in *La Maman et la putain*, dir. Jean Eustache, 1973)	
Illustration 3.3	Françoise Lebrun, as Véronika	90
	(*La Maman et la putain*, dir. Jean Eustache, 1973)	
Illustration 3.4	Daniel à l'église	93
	(*Mes petites amoureuses*, dir. Jean Eustache, 1974)	
Illustration 3.5	Petite Mouchette	94
	(*Mes petites amoureuses*, dir. Jean Eustache, 1974)	
Illustration 3.6	Daniel Pickpocket	96
	(*Mes petites amoureuses*, dir. Jean Eustache, 1974)	
Illustration 3.7	Daniel Pickpocket Hand 1	97
	(*Mes petites amoureuses*, dir. Jean Eustache, 1974)	
Illustration 3.8	Daniel Pickpocket Hand 2	97
	(*Mes petites amoureuses*, dir. Jean Eustache, 1974)	
Illustration 3.9	Pickpocket at Work 1	98
	(*Pickpocket*, dir. Robert Bresson, 1959)	
Illustration 3.10	Pickpocket at Work 2	99
	(*Pickpocket*, dir. Robert Bresson, 1959)	
Illustration 3.11	Arduous Walk	106
	(*Sous le soleil de Satan*, dir. Maurice Pialat, 1987)	
Illustration 3.12	Erotic Encounter	107
	(*Sous le soleil de Satan*, dir. Maurice Pialat, 1987)	

Illustration 3.13	Priest in Church	108
	(*Sous le soleil de Satan*, dir. Maurice Pialat, 1987)	
Illustration 3.14	Mouchette Enters Room	108
	(*Sous le soleil de Satan*, dir. Maurice Pialat, 1987)	
Illustration 3.15	The Dead Priest	109
	(*Sous le soleil de Satan*, dir. Maurice Pialat, 1987)	
Illustration 3.16	Death Mask	110
	(*Sous le soleil de Satan*, dir. Maurice Pialat, 1987)	
Illustration 4.1	Index	125
	(*Les Photos d'Alix*, dir. Jean Eustache, 1980)	
Illustration 4.2	Infinite Frames	126
	(*Les Photos d'Alix*, dir. Jean Eustache, 1980)	
Illustration 4.3	Jean Douchet	127
	(*Une sale histoire*, dir. Jean Eustache, 1977)	
Illustration 4.4	Michael Lonsdale	130
	(*Une sale histoire*, dir. Jean Eustache, 1977)	
Illustration 4.5	Jean-Noël Picq	130
	(*Une sale histoire*, dir. Jean Eustache, 1977)	
Illustration 4.6	Jean-Noël Picq 16mm Frame	131
	(*Une sale histoire*, dir. Jean Eustache, 1977)	

Acknowledgements

I am grateful to a number of colleagues whose council and conversation proved to be essential as I thought about and wrote this book. I owe a debt of immense gratitude to Tom Conley whose keen mind and unfailing enthusiasm played a crucial role in conceptualizing this project and articulating my thoughts. Profound thanks to Scott Durham who helped me clarify my thinking on authorship and cinephilia in the context of contemporary French theory and philosophy.

Research for this book was conducted in France with the aid of funding from my home institution, Wellesley College. Wellesley's Newhouse Center for the Humanities provided a happy forum for dialogue when it hosted a manuscript workshop during which Dudley Andrew, Tom Conley, and Eric Rentschler offered invaluable insights and suggestions. A special thank you to Vincent Amiel, who shared his inimitable book on "Lancelot du Lac" before it was commercially available, and to François Thomas for his collegial support. Konstanze Baron's workshop on "authorship and self-exegesis" provided an ideal opportunity to test ideas in the company of passionate scholars of authorship across disciplines.

Thank you to Chris Chappell from Berghahn for his receptiveness to my project and the remarkable ease with which he guided this book into production. Thank you to Melina Mardueño (Wellesley Class of 2018) who provided the drawing for the book's cover.

During the last year of the manuscript's completion, my friend and colleague Lamia Balafrej listened to weekly updates and provided feedback. Over the past decade, Camille Tauveron has supported my intellectual initiatives. A big thank you to Fanny Gribenski for her generous ear and engaging dialogue during the various stages of the project and to Corina Olteanu whose friendship made months of painful writing a lot easier. This book is for Sorin, as a thank you for his constant and unfailing encouragements and support.

Introduction

An Embattled Discourse

What, I want to ask, is a film author? Why is it that the notion has become so central to our thinking about cinema and yet remained so fraught? The film director is recognized as the film's *auteur* insofar as she or he acts as a centering creative force, an ordering intelligence who controls and choreographs the multiple voices at work in any given production. The film author demonstrates marks of individuality, a recurring set of themes and patterns, as well as a singular way of shaping space and time. This unique manner of organizing film worlds, which French auteurist critics spoke of as *mise-en-scène*, is said to provide a distinct vision, indeed a distinctive world view.[1] "The auteurist idea at its most basic (that movies are primarily the creation of one governing author behind the camera who thinks in images and sounds rather than words and sentences)," Kent Jones recently argued, "is now the default setting in most considerations of moviemaking, and for that we should all be thankful. We'd be nowhere without film auteurism, which boasts a proud history: the lovers of cinema did not just argue for its inclusion among the fine arts, but actually stood up, waved its flag, and proclaimed its glory without shame."[2]

Although there were noteworthy earlier pro-auteur mobilizations by European film critics and filmmakers, auteurism gained its definitive form and focus as the *politique des auteurs*, a polemical method of criticism practiced by contributors to the *Cahiers du cinéma* during the mid-1950s. Imported from France and transformed by Anglo-American film critics into the so-called *auteur* theory, the *politique des auteurs* would become highly resonant, shaping the ways in which cinema is appreciated, criticism is framed, and careers are established. Indeed, the notion of the *auteur* would assume an auratic luster. Both suggestive and influential, it would nonetheless cause occasion for sustained debate. Despite serious misgivings about the concept's ability to account for the collaborative nature of film production, self-branding, and marketing, or alternative modes of production both within and outside the film industry, film theorists and historians have not been able to dispense altogether with the figure of the author.[3] Although the question of the "author" constitutes a site of ongoing controversy, the notion remains an inordinately resilient category. Auteurism still retains a great amount of cultural capital, even in the wake of discourses that have declared the author dead and superseded by cine-structures, texts, and readers.

Accounting for modes of authorship associated with Hollywood cinema, Stephen Crofts emphasizes the use value this concept enjoys across a wide range of institutions, from film production and distribution to film criticism and academic film studies.[4] Throughout its long history, auteurism has prompted waves of criticism; the appearance of new cinemas, new filmmakers, new discourses, and new social conditions has repeatedly given rise to interventions that urge us to question this paradigm. Mindful of the entrenched status of authorship in discussions about cinema, we would do well to "locate the rules"[5] that formed this concept, to recall the conditions that brought about its triumph, as well as rehearse the arguments that have challenged it. Given its highly persuasive presence over many decades and still now in the age of digital media, it makes sense both to review and reassess its considerable legacy. That is the project of this book.

Reconsidering film authorship in ways that might allow us to work beyond the uneasy face-off between conceptual discomfort and critical consensus, this study pursues three main endeavors. First, it interrogates the ideas that have dominated discourse on authorship: the authority of the filmmaker, the celebration of genius, and the affirmation of an inimitable style generally referred to as *mise-en-scène*. It then extends the discourse of authorship beyond the veneration of directorial style by scrutinizing and laying bare the dynamics of the director's status as a professional and a worker; by broadening the discourse of authorship beyond the dominant paradigm of singularity, this study probes the workings of communities of authors and examines them as "communities of the senses" to use Jacques Rancière's term. Beyond that, this book confronts the two most dramatic challenges to discourses of film authorship: claims regarding the "death of the author" (and the implications of these claims for our understanding of film authorship) and the so-called "end of cinema" thesis that laments how personal filmmaking—which is to say *auteur* cinema—is a thing of the past.

Taking its cue from Michel Foucault, this study scrutinizes the question of the film author within the longer Western history in which authorship figures as "a privileged moment of individualization." Foucault urged that we examine *how the author became individualized in a culture like ours, what status he has been given, at what moment studies of authenticity and attribution began, in what kind of system of valorization the author was involved, at what point we began to recount the lives of authors rather than of heroes, and how this fundamental category of "the-man-and-his-work criticism" began.*[6]

He spirited us back to the late eighteenth century, at which time a strong tie was established between "the juridical construction of authorship and the legal definition of the bourgeois conceptions of the individual and private property,"[7] a link that would circulate in various permutations during the next two centuries and have a fundamental impact on the constitution of film authorship and its critical discourse. In order to understand the importance of this legacy, let us take a slight detour in the form of a flashback.

The Author's Lawful Rights

In the midst of heated exchanges between dramatists and actors during the 1770s, the French playwright Pierre-Augustin Caron de Beaumarchais made a heartfelt appeal to Louis XVI: "Is not the foremost of all honors, Sire, to assure to dramatic authors, by a law, the ownership of their work and the just fruit of their labors?" He requested that the King recognize *by law* the intellectual property of authors in matters of copyright and financial remuneration. Authorship should have a legal basis, argued Beaumarchais in his letter; it should not just be an empty concession, a form of lip service accorded to artistic endeavor. After the success of his *Barber of Seville* in 1777, Beaumarchais sided with other playwrights and received from the Duke of Duras permission to present a reform plan, which, after extensive negotiation on many fronts, gained approval in 1780. "It is very strange that it has taken an express law to attest to all of France that the property of a dramatic author belongs to him and nobody has the right to run off with it," stated Beaumarchais in his petition to the Committee on Public Instruction on 23 December 1791:

> *This principle, taken from the first rights of man, went so much without saying for all the other property of people acquired through labor, gifts, sale, or even heredity, that it was believed derisory for it to be established in law. My sole property, as a dramatic author, is more sacred than all other kinds because it*

comes to me from nobody else and is subject to no contestation for fraud or seduction. The work coming from my brain, like Minerva fully armed with the work of the gods, my property alone had need of a law to pronounce that it belongs to me.[8]

The debate leading to the legislation was both memorable and symptomatic. And Beaumarchais's victory would be substantial; its impact was strong and its legacy would be lasting. The law of 1791, with a few minor alterations, still regulates French copyright to this very day. It confirmed, quite dramatically, that French discourse of artistic sovereignty had crystallized at the end of the eighteenth century. This discourse figured centrally in the legal battle for the recognition of artistic creation as a professional practice, conferring upon its "makers" social legitimation and material rights. One immediately recalls John Locke's theory of property which holds that a man, as the proprietor of his own person, is also the owner of the products of his labor. As these perspectives on authorship and property over time assumed even clearer shape, a specific aesthetic category, namely originality, would acquire a crucial importance. To grant originality central significance in the appreciation of literary compositions ensured that they would be subject to their own criteria of evaluation and no longer judged by the policies used for mechanical inventions (which were subject to patents). "Literary compositions were not identified with any of their material forms," argues Roger Chartier in a study about scientific and literary authorship in the seventeenth and eighteenth century. "Their identity was given by the irreducible singularity of their *style, sentiment and language* present in every duplicate of the work. The inalienable right of the author was thus transformed into an essential characteristic of the discourse itself, whatever the vehicle of its transmission might be."[9]

Beaumarchais's petition arose from and resonated at a moment when, as Foucault observed, the social order of property within French culture had become codified. In the wake of Beaumarchais's intervention, a system of ownership and strict copyright rules gained official sanction and, as a result, a modern understanding of authorship took shape, which Foucault would later speak of as the author-function.[10] The law of 1791, slightly revised in 1794, constituted a revolutionary mutation in the institution of art. For all its lasting values, it also became the site of further conflicts, among them an ongoing disagreement about the egalitarian promise of a new working field and the elitist principle of singularity and originality known as talent.

This tension between workers within the creative community and original artists would find an especially dramatic enactment in the field of cinema. The collective nature of film production, as well as its technology that relied on mechanical reproduction, made it particularly difficult to assign authorship and authority to a single individual. Early film critics who relied on interpretive models used for the other arts, especially for literature and painting, could not agree whether the rightful author should be the director or the scriptwriter, or perhaps even the producer. Banking on the privileges granted to them by the copyright law of 1794 that recognized writers as the proprietors of their creations, scriptwriters discredited directors, describing the latter's endeavors as the mere application of technique and the deployment of technology rather than the creation of original art.

As early as 1920, in the pages of *Ciné pour tous*, the critic Pierre Henry insisted that the film author is "the person who conceives the film from beginning to end and *thinks* cinematically."[11] Louis Delluc and Marcel L'Herbier concurred.[12] In Germaine Dulac's film from 1927, *Invitation au voyage*, we see the director literally stake her claim to authorship, displaying her hand as she signs her name at the end of the credits. Taking a theoretical step further, Jean Epstein assigned to the filmmaker's vision the property of "photogénie," the capacity to reveal the "inner nature of things" that are mechanically captured by the lens. Although "the lens alone can sometimes succeed" in this endeavor, Epstein wrote in 1926, "the proper sensibility, by which I mean a personal one, can direct the lens towards increasingly valuable discoveries. This is the role of an author of film, commonly called a film director."[13] A few years later, in 1930, in the *Panorama du cinéma*, Georges Charensol envisioned a "complete" work (that would even include films deemed to be "quite marginal") organized according to national production and the category of *auteurs*.[14] Heated debates about the rightful author would continue, but would not find resolution until much later. Interrupted by the war years and complicated by the switch of film production from the jurisdiction of the Ministry of Art and Culture to that of the Ministry of Industry, the discussion concerning copyright and authorship would assume renewed prominence after the Liberation.

Numerous professional associations and organizations, among them the SACD (La Société des Auteurs et Compositeurs Dramatiques), AAF (L'Association des Auteurs de Films), and SRF (La Société des Réalisateurs de Films), would wage a successful battle for legal recognition that produced new legislation enacted on 11 March 1957.[15] At the same time, celebrating the postwar success and popularity of films by Jean Renoir, Charlie Chaplin, Carl Theodor Dreyer, and

Roberto Rossellini, a group of young film critics and cinephiles drafted polemical theses regarding film authorship in what became consecrated as the *politique des auteurs*. To be sure, the assessments of these critics who would become the leading lights of the Nouvelle Vague, the most prominent being Claude Chabrol, Jean-Luc Godard, Jacques Rivette, Eric Rohmer, and François Truffaut, did not seem at all burdened by or even aware of the professional debates raging around them in the French film community. For the so-called Young Turks, there was no doubt where authentic authorship resided. The filmmaker alone was the master of cinematic creation, using the camera to create a unique sense of time and space and, in so doing, a singular world. In this way they reiterated the claims of Alexandre Astruc's essay of 1948, "The Birth of a New Avant-Garde: *La Caméra-Stylo*": "The film author writes with his camera just like the writer with his pen."[16]

Distinguishing *auteurs* from the lesser likes of *metteurs-en-scène* or "mere filmmakers," the young critics at *Cahiers du cinéma* formulated a *"politique des auteurs"* that raised directors to a higher power, positioning them as the organizing principle in any understanding of single films as well as any informed appreciation of film as an art. By the early 1950s, critics and spectators alike would in large measure come to think of the director as the film author. Indeed, over time the *politique des auteurs* would succeed to such an extent that the term *auteur* would almost exclusively find use in reference to cinema. The impact of the *politique des auteurs* has been so strong and compelling that subsequent history has all but overlooked, even forgotten, the numerous discussions in postwar France that gave rise to and attended it, the heated exchanges among professionals, journalists, and filmmakers regarding the rehabilitation of cinema as the seventh art and the valorization of the film artist.

The principal concern of the *politique des auteurs* was not as much the legitimation and recognition of French directors, whose superiority to the mere *metteurs-en-scène* remained uncontestable.[17] Hollywood studios, the often decried site of industrialized fantasy production, would become the primary ground on which the young critics would wage their campaign. In the words of Derek Schilling, they sought to revive "the romantic notion of artistic genius in a domain largely defined by economic and institutional pressures."[18] In spite of constraining circumstances, the *auteurs* defended by the *Cahiers* critics were considered capable of conveying themes and obsessions in a distinctive fashion that was the equivalent of a signature. The practitioners of the *politique* formulated standards of evaluation that would assure even popular features by American directors a place within the established arts. To grant Hollywood productions the status of art was a bold move—and a decidedly discriminating one as well. For by linking the medium's industrial hegemony to the West's aesthetic, the *politique* critics excluded from consideration vast stretches and far reaches of film history.[19]

The heyday of the *politique*, especially between 1955 and 1965, diminished any lingering sense of inferiority that cinema might have harbored vis-à-vis the other arts. In the estimation of film director and critic Olivier Assayas, the success of this enterprise was so substantial that *auteur* would come to mean first and foremost *film auteur*.[20] The triumph of the *politique des auteurs* provided much cause for celebration; it brought aesthetic recognition to the cinematic medium, and sealed the victory of, in Jean Renoir's words, "the *auteur*'s fight against the industry."[21] But at the same time as it reproduced the romantic cult of personality and celebrated the filmmaker's singularity and genius, its practice over the following decades became conventionalized, reducing the author to a useful, albeit predictable function within a critical and theoretical discourse. Indeed, a reciprocal relation between what determines authors and what authors determine would play a shaping role in the evolution and practice of auteurism.

Towards an Archeology of Film Authorship

As it celebrated individual artists, the *politique des auteurs* foregrounded the author-function, to employ Foucault's famous category. Indeed, the film author fulfilled the role ascribed to an individual author within the modern episteme. The author's crucial function, maintained Foucault, was to grant unity to a body of work, to provide a "means of classification," to "differentiate" and "establish forms of relationship" between films and authors. In this way, one might say that the author-function serves to "guarantee the authenticity" of a film as well as to "characterize the existence, circulation and operation of certain discourses within a society."[22] Especially during the 1960s, in the wake of political and ideological challenges to authority that led to the events of May 1968, the place and function of the film author would come under serious attack. Among the critical interventions which argued for the irrelevance of the author, Foucault's archeology is no doubt the most famous. In *The Order of Things*, his method presents the work of individual thinkers as entirely determined by epistemic configurations; in this dynamic, individual authors above all become functionaries of these epistemes.

Since the overarching project of Foucauldian archeology is to analyze discourses as epistemic configurations subordinate to impersonal forces, one might well assume that "What is an Author?" is no less adamantly anti-authorial than Roland Barthes's famous essay, "The Death of the Author." Indeed, "What is an Author?" begins with a phrase by Beckett—"What does it matter who is speaking?"—and concludes with the answer that it should not matter at all. Nonetheless, Foucault's essay provides an incisive—and most compelling—example of why the question *does* matter. The key passage of his argument comes after a number of preliminary and schematic observations on the author-function:

> *I seem to have given the term "author" much too narrow a meaning. I have discussed the author only in the limited sense of a person to whom the production of a text, a book, or a work can be legitimately attributed. It is easy to see that in the sphere of discourse one can be the author of much more than a book—one can be the author of a theory, tradition, or discipline in which other books and authors will in their turn find a place. These authors are in a position which we should call "transdiscursive." This is a recurring phenomenon—certainly as old as our civilization.*[23]

Foucault maintains that the principle of authorship exceeds the bounds of the body of texts bearing an author's name. Thus the idea of an author exercising his jurisdiction over his own texts has not only been accepted in principle but is also considered to be too narrow and restrictive in particular cases. It is easy to see how in such an understanding one might well ascribe a transdiscursive status to a number of authors. Indeed, whenever an 'ism' attaches itself to a proper name, one might say that some degree of transdiscursivity has arisen. Nonetheless, in Foucault's view, transdiscursive authors are not a set of exceptional individuals or schematic models. Rather, they should be seen as "founders of discursivity,"[24] because they "have produced something else: the possibilities and rules for the formation of other texts." The notion of "founder" has, not without justification, earned Foucault much disapprobation, putting him in a position diametrically opposed to an archeological endeavor dedicated to uncovering the discourse's epistemic strata. As he seeks to analyze discourses as configurations of knowledge entirely subordinate to impersonal forces, he in fact proves why it does matter who is speaking—especially if the speaker is the founder. Foucault recognizes that there is an "inevitable necessity for a 'return to the origin',"[25] but is careful to stress that this return, which is part of the discursive field itself, never ceases to inflect our understanding.

The present endeavor, in rethinking the conceptual and historical shapes of film authorship, takes an essential impetus from Foucault's notion of a "transdiscursive" authorial position. Who, among the authors of French cinema, can claim a "transdiscursive" status and what precisely lends itself to this transposable and transmittable category? We could look at the original distinction between the Lumière Brothers' project of documenting everyday life and Georges Méliès's animated world of fantastic stories and magic tricks. But to position them as "transdiscursive" authors would require first that we ascribe to them the role of authors, which would be anachronistic, especially since they thought of themselves as inventors rather than artists. Film critics and scholars of French cinema have often reflected on who might be thought of as cinema's founders. "There have always been in the French cinema two great movements," argues the influential critic Michel Ciment, "the source Renoir, and the source Bresson. Whatever one might think or say, there are no others." Any others, he insists, come from other countries, from the United States, from Sweden, Asia, Iran, and elsewhere.[26]

The two defining French legacies, the Bressonian and Renoirian, are well-known to film historians and cinephiles alike. Additional attempts to position other directors as points of origin have involved earlier filmmakers like Jean Epstein or Jean Vigo, or Nouvelle Vague luminaries such as Jean-Luc Godard or Alain Resnais. Bresson constitutes an obvious example, and yet is full of surprises and challenges; his career provides a particularly effective vehicle to study the dynamics of authorship, its canonization as well as its influence, within the context of French cultural history. Unlike the very popular Jean Renoir, whose retreat to Hollywood during the war generated an altogether different career that made him an ideal object of focus for *politique* critics eager to defend the American features of European film directors, Bresson appears to be a typically French artist. Bresson's formidable Frenchness, as well as the longevity of his career, enable an understanding of the various discursive formations around authorship over half a century, from the striking victory of the notion both in film criticism and copyright legislation to the internationally acclaimed crisis of the "death of the author" and the reactions that ensued in its wake. In ways that are self-evident, but also elusive, the director's estimable heritage exemplifies the essential factors that have shaped both the French film canon and the access of filmmakers to the Pantheon of French culture. The choice of Bresson has shaped the analysis of film authorship that this book offers; another choice, say Renoir or Resnais, much less the usual suspect Godard, would without question have prompted us to take different paths and involved a quite different cast of players and constellations.

The Trans-Position of the Author

Bresson's uncompromising cinema of restraint, inordinately poignant in its style, and inflected by the artist's own interpretation and promotion as the sole creator of a visionary art, has provided an imposing model of authorship. No single phrase describes Bresson's art and life better than his own declaration: "I am a maniac of truth." His modest, minimalist style is both eccentric and exemplary, at once intense and subdued. How could someone so seemingly elitist and elusive become a French *auteur* par excellence? How do his imperatives of artistic excellence and creative singularity function within the pluralistic community of the film profession? Addressing these questions, my book examines Bresson's legacy as a transdiscursive model of authorship. Within such an approach, the notions of style and signature, so central to classical auteurism, might seem insufficient, related as they are to a conception of the film *auteur* as an indivisible entity. Authorial signature and style often serve to justify the artistic status of individual filmmakers, but such a circumscribed focus occludes our appreciation of artistic communities and their historical determinations.

From the extended list of filmmakers working in the wake of Bresson, I will particularly focus my attention on Jean Eustache and Maurice Pialat. One might argue that they should be accompanied by the likes of Jacques Rozier, Philippe Garrel, Bruno Dumont, to name just a few of those who might be said to share Bresson's attitude towards the medium. Had this study aimed to gather all the Bressonians and to account for their work, the scope and shape of this book would have increased exponentially. My interest here, however, is not encyclopedic. Above all I want to see how a community of Bressonians might be constituted and how it can work, or, as Jean-Luc Nancy brilliantly put it, can become "operative."[27] Within this community, as well as in the history of French cinema, Eustache and Pialat have played an influential and to this day not adequately appreciated role. They presented far different and decidedly more unsettling images of French life than their renowned counterparts such as Alain Resnais, François Truffaut, and Jean-Luc Godard. The cinemas of these Bressonians arose outside of, and in crucial ways despite, the Nouvelle Vague, while nonetheless confronting the political and economic imperatives of French cinema. In order to find a place in the history of French authorship for these figures, whose remarkable films are both striking and haunting, we need to consider their precarious operating base and tenuous professional status.

With this in mind, my book revisits the terms "signature" and "style" and theorizes them as dynamic concepts enmeshed in both aesthetic and political formations. Rather than the mark of an individual, style, in this assessment, has in fact the potential, indeed the property, to differentiate cinema from the other arts, granting it autonomy, but also emphasizing the consequences of such differentiation, especially in the creation of new aesthetic values and communities. Style is not only a filmmaker's unique vision, but a modality bound to the community of the senses. Bresson's clear vision of what cinema should and could be provides us with a striking example of the new art's autonomous place next to and among the arts of painting, literature, and theater. In addition to his formal prowess, Bresson's legacy has taught generations of filmmakers moral lessons in maintaining the integrity of the cinematic art.

Following Foucault's cue and providing a more specific elaboration of the larger dynamics at play here in the form of a case study of "Bressonianism," this project examines the ways in which filmmakers position themselves in relationship to their "master" and to their peers and form communities bound by a shared formal and moral attitude towards the medium. What I will be referring to as the "maniacs of truth" constitutes such a community. Neither a school nor a movement, it is rather a rubric that unites filmmakers and spans generations. Driven by a fierce embrace of filmmaking as a personal and professional vocation, the directors I will be discussing remain uncompromising in their pursuit of film as a form of truth-revelation. That pursuit, however, is complicated and conflicted; it would be better defined by the "manic" commitment to truth than by any actual truth possession. The "mania of truth" is an ethos and, in crucial regards, also a pathology.

Authenticity and truth are terms often invoked in discussions of Bresson and comparisons of his work with that of filmmakers who defer to him, like Eustache and Pialat. "Despite their very different approach to actors and to the act of filming, Pialat was no less obsessed with authenticity than Bresson," writes Marja Warehime in her monograph on Pialat. "Yet where Bresson aimed to arrive at truth through the discipline of rehearsals," she presses on, "Pialat worked more instinctively."[28] In developing a highly personal approach to filmmaking, the two film directors, argues Warehime, are linked by "an obsession with a particular kind of cinematic truth, each representing a different kind of absolute." Here, as in much auteurist discourse, these terms remain taken for granted as signifiers of profundity and deeper meaning without being clearly defined or carefully questioned. What, after all, is truth or authenticity? Such usages resemble what Theodor W. Adorno has called the "jargon of authenticity," a mode of discourse that employs a "Wurlitzer organ of the spirit" to extol existential adventure and imbue it with metaphysical authority and grant it cultural currency.[29] Clearly, authenticity and truth are slippery terms, especially when they lack a historical ground and a concrete point of reference. That these categories so frequently appear in auteurist discourse at the very least confirms the power and authority ascribed to them and, for that reason, provides a good reason for us to consider their use with care and caution. This book does not celebrate the discourse of truth, but rather tries to comprehend its operations and its consequences. In this sense, the study offers neither a general overview of film authorship, nor a circumscribed case study of an individual film author. Rather, it provides a conceptual model for a communitarian understanding of film authorship.

The demystification of truth has motivated my endeavor to elucidate the constitution of discursive formations of authorship and to lay bare the complex mechanisms that led to the promulgation of *auteur* theory in film criticism, film studies, and film spectatorship. This book's methodology might be described as archeological: it aims to uncover the various layers that led to the constitution of the author as a function of the work. The author-function, writes Foucault, "is not formed spontaneously through the simple attribution of a discourse to an individual. It results from a complex operation whose purpose is to construct the rational entity we call an author."[30] Although these complex operations vary according to "the period and the form of discourse concerned," he continues, "there are nevertheless transhistorical constants in the rules that govern the construction of an author."[31] The present book locates precisely these rules and in this sense traverses crucial aesthetic dimensions of French film authorship while paying equally close attention to its socio-economic, political, and legal determinants.

Postwar discourses on authorship stressed individual volition while downplaying the collective character of film production, exhibition, and reception. The inextricable bonds between vocational concerns and professional constraints, long considered to be of central importance within French understandings of authorship, figured less notably in the Nouvelle Vague's conceptual renegotiations.

The agency of the author, a key element within cinema's own legitimation as an art, seemed in this construction to function outside of—or apart from—film's institutional operations, particularly in regard to economic and legal factors. Indeed, previous film scholars have repeatedly overlooked the seminal French copyright law of 1957. Still in place today, this law grants the "droit d'auteur" not only to the film director, but also to the producer, scriptwriter, and sound track composer. Any understanding of authorship in France, my book argues, must take into account the economic, legal, and political considerations that are essential factors in its constitution.

My approach dwells on the attributes that made auteurism so controversial: the very notion of cinematic style and its reliance on the vague term "mise-en-scène," the anti-historical, anti-social, and anti-economic penchants that put the auteur in an ivory tower and films in a dusty Cinémathèque, the opposition between *auteurs* and *metteurs-en-scène*, the notion's failure to transcend the pamphlets of a critical discourse and give rise to an aesthetic theory, and most especially the contradictory destiny of a revolutionary concept carrying a promissory democratic flag only to become an elitist discourse with an international reach.

Although scholars of French film have in recent years reconsidered the many myths attending the Nouvelle Vague,[32] the legacy of the *politique des auteurs* has yet to be reevaluated in the light of expanded discussions in aesthetics, epistemology, and sociology. In this book, the essential questions about film authorship—originality, signature, *mise-en-scène*, and the question of truth in artistic matters—are examined from philosophical, socio-economic, and legal perspectives. The study ponders in particular the interplay between the singularity of individual filmmakers and the plurality of the professional community, talking about film authors not as solitary geniuses but as working artists.

While the conceptual questions at the heart of this study are informed by discourses of film authorship, they also derive from a sweeping view of French film history and my deliberate choice of certain films and filmmakers to the detriment of others. Strongly aware of the numerous factors that affect the work of filmmakers, I want to avoid the commonly travelled roads and to traverse other routes that might afford us a wider view. From a methodological point of view, sociological perspectives regarding the conditions of authorship and professional organizations complement the examination of the discursive formations that led to the legitimation of the director as the film author, both aesthetically and legally.

The first and last chapters are especially concerned with elaborating these determinants and drawing more general conclusions about authorship as a function of both creative endeavor and material circumstance. In addressing key concepts in the study of authorship, this book relies on close analyses of exemplary films. The materials under discussion reflect significant factors in previous assessments of film authorship—authorial signature and style (chapter 2), legacy, originality, and influence (chapter 3), the crisis of authorship or the so-called "death of the author" (chapter 4), and responses to critical discourse proclaiming "the end of cinema" (chapter 5)—and reenact the evolution of the category of authorship from celebration to crisis.

The Road Ahead

The opening chapter employs Robert Bresson as a point of reference in the study's reflections on the history of French film authorship. His long career (1934–1983) inspired great veneration among the country's filmmakers and filmgoers, and later international cineastes. This chapter augments existing scholarship on Bresson's work, paying careful attention to the social, economic, and legal conditions of film authorship that informed his career. Caught between the liberal arts (scriptwriting) and the mechanical arts (photography), French cinema waged a long struggle for both cultural regard and legal legitimacy. Subject to antiquated authorship laws dating back to 1794, French filmmakers applauded new legislation in 1957 that nominally recognized the filmmaker as *auteur*. This breakthrough, however, would prove to be at best a partial victory, for attempts to implement the new law would catalyze challenges on a variety of fronts. Reflecting this history and its vicissitudes, Bresson's career—from his artistic elitism to his professional commitment, from his quest for a personal style to his prominent role in the 1958 defense of the Society of French Auteurs—provides a compelling instance of self-conscious film authorship equally informed by creative impulses and driven by political determinations. Bresson's track record as a film activist complicates the framework of the Nouvelle Vague's *politique* and compels us to reconsider it in light of a larger archeology of authorship in post-Liberation France and well into the 1960s.

The second chapter turns to the aesthetic categories that served to consecrate auteurism, and reconsiders them in the light of active tensions between individual vocation and membership within a community of artists. In their early writings, auteurist critics claimed that what distinguishes an *auteur* is the ability to think in audiovisual terms, a capacity they deemed to be the mark of elevated style in contrast to the mere mechanical exercise of technique. Like the careers of many recognized filmmakers, Bresson's offers a privileged object for the investigation of critical categories like style, technique, cinematic writing, and montage. In particular, his example allows an opportunity to understand these categories in their ardent endeavor to free cinema from the influence of theater and literature. Why is Bresson's "transdiscursive" position more transparent than that of other filmmakers? Using the tools of aesthetics, my demonstration turns to the arguments of the philosopher Jacques Rancière. In *Les Écarts du cinéma* (*The Intervals of Cinema*), Rancière suggests that Bresson's cinema constituted more than a singular style, indeed that it provided a new "distribution of the sensible." For Rancière, Bresson envisioned the cinematograph as an experience that might offer individual citizens and their communities both a new world of art and a new sense of life. Within this specific approach, the second chapter focuses on three aspects that render Bresson's style singular and exemplary: his project of literary adaptation that negotiated cinema's autonomy in the artistic field; the signature iconography of his expressionless, unaffected *models*; and the spare economy of his cinematic means, particularly in his use of ellipsis.

Film critics and scholars have raised Bresson to the status of a saint, in the words of one critic, the "father of this land we call the Cinematograph."[33] He is praised not only for the invention of a new, original, and powerful filmic form, but also for providing a point of departure for a distinct cinematic tradition, for creating the very possibility of this tradition. Bresson's legacy and influence, reflected in the indelible traces he has left in the history of cinema, play as much a role in his creative position as in his actual films. Focusing on the prominent French directors Jean Eustache and Maurice Pialat, the third chapter examines Bresson's remarkable influence on the world of cinema and how the reverence for an *auteur* role model legitimates the new creators in their own quests to become singular artists. What unites these filmmakers and indeed links them to Bresson is their understanding of filmmaking as an existential necessity. As *auteurs*, these remarkably difficult and fiercely uncompromising figures at once seek to maintain their personal singularity while nonetheless sustaining their predecessor's legacy. They attempt to become Bresson's equals in terms of film style and aesthetics, both acting in accordance with his example and yet, in crucial regards, acting out against it. The Bressonian iconography of Eustache's films includes an anti-

Bressonian dramatic structure, while Pialat's use of ellipsis outdoes and, in the process, undoes Bresson's inimitable narrative fragmentation. In adapting Georges Bernanos's *Under the Sun of Satan*, Pialat writes his way into French film history, at once with and against Bresson. The impact of these two directors, who are often mistakenly seen as extensions of the Nouvelle Vague, is unthinkable without Bresson's example, both as an artistic legacy and a creative burden with which each director reckoned in different ways. These exemplary instances provide novel case studies of French film authorship in the wake of Bresson.

The first three chapters examine the discursive formation of the film *auteur*, from the making of the author to the negotiation and recasting of authorial legacy. They elucidate the factors that determine how individual filmmakers are raised to the status of *auteur*, as well as the dialectic between individual originality and collective artistic endeavor. This discourse of auteurism, as we know, would play—and still does play—a central role in the creation of film studies curricula, the writing of *auteur* monographs, and the programming of film festivals. For that reason, film scholars faced significant challenges when the "death of the author" was declared by leading theorists in the late 1960s and had a seismic impact on subsequent discussions within the humanities and social sciences. The demise of the author would figure within a larger crisis of a cinematographic medium deemed to be essentially visual; it would also impact on larger discussions about the denigration of vision.[34] The Bressonian tradition plays an important role in these conversations, for his defense of cinema as "the art of the image where one must lose the notion of image"[35] inspired what Eustache declared to be his anti-auteurist project, one that Pialat embraced as well. In the wake of the author's loss of authority and power, Eustache deliberately installed the narrator as the master on the set. This replacement was motivated by an ethical impulse and a sense of duty: the narrator could articulate the "truth" while the image could not help but conceal it. In order to account for this major negotiation of the moral dilemma created by the absence of the author and allow for a related but in crucial ways different perspective, the fourth chapter will position Eustache's late films vis-à-vis another cinematic project preoccupied with ethics, that of Eric Rohmer.

Responding to auteurism's penchant for ocularcentrism, filmmakers like Eustache and Rohmer drew on an important Bressonian legacy: the director's singular negotiation of sound and silence. Both make elaborate use of dialogue and diegetic sound to accentuate their narrators' duplicity and dissimulation, employing the spoken word to quite different ends. Eustache sees language as the only possible recourse in the face of the image's corrupted access to truth and knowledge. Rohmer's moral tales transform speech into a diversion from and a supplement to the camera's capacity to show things as they are. Often described as literary in its constitution, Rohmer's cinema challenges the possibilities of language and sound as well as the most hallowed premises of *mise-en-scène* criticism, reassessing the role of literature in the making of the film *auteur*. Both directors feature narrators afflicted with doubt, ignorance, and falsehood, and inscribe them in their films' formal framework. The moral weight of these projects lies in their appeal to the audience and the opportunity granted to viewers to find truth within the maze of the narrators' prevarications. While Eustache succumbs to despair and humiliation, questioning cinema's ethical values, Rohmer trusts in the power of the image and grants to it an ethical authority; truth, he submits in the venerable *Cahiers* tradition, is recorded by the eye of the lens, and that lens is objective.

Bresson's extreme artistic singularity ensured his status as *auteur* within and beyond the realm of the *politique des auteurs* that as a rule privileged directors working in the American studio system. Capitalizing on the romantic notion of the film *auteur* as genius, saint, or hero, classical auteurism paid far less attention to the undeniable fact that their hallowed *auteurs* were also professional artisans. The fifth chapter illustrates the fraught and contradictory legacy of the artist-artisan opposition in the larger discourse about the "end of cinema." European cinema at the end of the 1980s and the beginning of the 1990s seems to perform a sacrificial model of the artist; film narratives are organized around characters of struggling individual artists who are subject to financial constraints. Relying on the specific case study of Cannes's official selection of 1991, I will examine two key French features in that year's competition, Maurice Pialat's *Van Gogh* and Jacques Rivette's *La Belle Noiseuse*. In quite different and very striking ways, both Pialat, the often-embattled employee of Gaumont, and Rivette, the Nouvelle Vague exponent, reflect on the question of art appreciation and the place of the artist in the working world. Their two productions enhance our appreciation of the ways in which *auteurs* are also workers and subject to the laws of the market, as well as members of professional communities.

While film scholarship positions *auteur* cinema in striking contrast to the dominant sphere of commercial film production, the relationship between art and the market requires more nuanced conceptual models. By probing the professional identity of the artist, these two films reveal how artistic endeavor inhabits various sectors of the working world. Engaging with recent sociological research, this chapter elaborates the identification of the artistic activity with the "métier" whose exercise is deeply individual, as well as the profound professional inequality that governs the work of artists. Rivette's and Pialat's films afford us a deeper appreciation of the intrinsic link between film authorship and a notion of art as an "expressive" pursuit that issues from and figures within the realm of labor.

While recent publications devoted to film authorship have provided useful overviews of the subject, this book seeks to be at once broader and, in its use of paradigmatic examples, more focused.[36] It is broader in that it incorporates into the study of film authorship more careful attention to the socio-economic determinations of a society facing successively the Second World War as well as the anti-bourgeois (and anti-auteur) revolution of May '68. It is also broader insofar as it apprehends the continuity between film authorship and other discourses of the author-function, from discussions that go as far back as the eighteenth century to others that reach into the new millennium. Although English-language film scholarship includes a number of estimable studies on Bresson, as well as several monographs on individual directors like Rohmer, Rivette, and Pialat, the work of Eustache has been woefully overlooked, all the more since access to his films has been blocked by his heirs. Despite their undeniable international cachet as *auteurs*, maverick filmmakers like Eustache and Pialat have not received the penetrating analytical attention that their rich and stirring work deserves. This book reconsiders their accomplishments, engaging with their films and putting them into dialogue with the works of more critically acclaimed contemporaries such as Rivette and Rohmer in order to find useful points of comparison and contrast as well as to appreciate significant moments in the history of French film authorship. Throughout I review critical commonplaces and problematic constructions within this singular history.

While it revisits the formation of modern French film authorship, both historically and conceptually, this book does not propose a counter-model of authorship. Nor does it offer a comprehensive history. Rather, it reviews an important legacy of thinking about authorship and provides much-needed additional augmentation, especially in regard to the relations between the singularity of the individual filmmaker and the plurality of the professional community. In examining a "situation" of what I call Bressonianism, my book negotiates larger conceptual stakes within the framework of a concrete case study.

Notes

1. This account follows John Caughie's presentation in *Theories of Authorship* (London: Routledge & Kegan Paul, 1981).
2. Kent Jones, "Critical Condition: From the *Politique des Auteurs* to the *Auteur* Theory to Plain Old *Auteurism*. How Clear of a Picture of Actual Movies Are We Receiving?," *Film Comment* 50.2 (March–April 2014): 40–41.
3. In this regard, a marked tension between film criticism and film theory has continued and catalyzed some refreshingly novel contributions to authorship studies. See Dana Polan, "Auteur Desire," *Screening the Past* 12 (March 2001). Recent endeavors, such as Tom Gunning's magisterial monograph on Fritz Lang's films, seek to counter the *politique*'s hagiographic discourse with the "more progressive assumption that meaning is made by readers and viewers in an ongoing interaction with texts whose energy should not be frozen by being referred back to an authoritative source." See Tom Gunning, *The Films of Fritz Lang* (London: British Film Institute, 2000), 3.
4. Stephen Crofts, "Authorship and Hollywood," in *American Cinema and Hollywood: Critical Approaches*, ed. John Hill and Pamela Church Gibson (New York: Oxford University Press, 2000), 84–98.
5. Michel Foucault, "What is an Author?," trans. Donald F. Bouchard and Sherry Simon, in *Language, Counter-Memory, Practice*, ed. Donald F. Bouchard (Ithaca, New York: Cornell University Press, 1977), 114.
6. Foucault, "What is an Author?," 124.
7. Roger Chartier, "Foucault's Chiasmus: Authorship between Science and Literature in the 17th and 18th centuries," in *Scientific Authorship: Credit and Intellectual Property in Science*, ed. Mario Biagioli and Peter Galison (New York: Routledge, 2003), 13.
8. Maurice Lever, *Beaumarchais, A Biography*, ed. Jean-Pierre Thomas, trans. Susan Emanuel (New York: Farrar, Straus and Giroux, 2009), 180. Cited from the "Petition to the National Assembly," a statement against the usurpation of the authors' property by theater directors, presented by Beaumarchais to the Committee on Public Instruction on 23 December 1791 and published shortly afterwards.
9. Chartier, "Foucault's Chiasmus," 17–18.
10. See Antoine Compagnon, *Qu'est-ce qu'un auteur? Cours de M. Antoine Compagnon* (Cours de Licence LLM 316 F2, Université Paris IV–Sorbonne, 37–39: http://aphelis.net/wp-content/uploads/2012/03/Compagnon-Auteur.pdf).
11. Pierre Henry, "L'Évolution de l'art de l'image animée," *Ciné pour tous* 55 (17 December 1920): 5–6.
12. See Christophe Gauthier, *Cinéphiles, ciné-clubs et salles spécialisées à Paris de 1920 à 1929* (Paris: AFRHC, 1999), 289.
13. Jean Epstein, "On Certain Characteristics of *Photogénie*," trans. Tom Milner, *Afterimage* 10 (1981): 23.
14. Georges Charensol, *Panorama du cinéma* (Paris: Éditions du Sagittaire, 1930).
15. See the text of "Loi sur la propriété littéraire et artistique, Loi du 11 mars 1957:" http://www.wipo.int/edocs/lexdocs/laws/fr/km/km003fr.pdf.
16. Alexandre Astruc, "La Naissance d'une Nouvelle Avant-Garde: La Caméra-Stylo," *L'Écran Français* 144 (30 March 1948): 22.

17. See for example François Truffaut, "Crise d'ambition du cinéma français," *Arts* (30 March–5 April 1955). Truffaut suggests four categories to classify the French filmmakers in 1955: 1) the ambitious (*Ambitieux*), a mere 17 filmmakers, among them only half the writers of their own scripts; 2) the semi-ambitious (*Semi-ambitieux*) in number of 15, having made 52 films in ten years; 3) the honestly commercial (*Commerciaux honnêtes*), 27 with 190 films shot in ten years; and finally 4) the 30 deliberately commercial directors (*Délibérément commerciaux*) who "executed" 247 films in ten years.
18. Derek Schilling, *Eric Rohmer* (Manchester: Manchester University Press, 2007), 79.
19. Ibid., 78.
20. Olivier Assayas, "Que d'auteurs, que d'auteurs! Sur une politique," in *La Politique des auteurs: Les Textes*, ed. Antoine de Baecque and Gabrielle Lucantonio (Paris: Cahiers du cinéma, 2001), 172–75.
21. Quoted by the French Prime Minister Lionel Jospin during the closing ceremony of the conference "Le Cinéma à venir," at Cannes on 10 May 2000: http://discours.vie-publique.fr/notices/003001179.html.
22. Foucault, "What is an Author?," 119–24.
23. Foucault, "What is an Author?," 131.
24. This is a category that has emerged in the modern episteme, and more particularly in the nineteenth century.
25. Foucault, "What is an Author?," 132–33.
26. Michel Ciment, "Editorial: Bresson et Kubrick," *Positif* 468 (February 2000): 2: "Il y a toujours eu dans le cinéma français deux grands courants, la source Renoir et la source Bresson. Quoi qu'on en pense ou en dise, il n'y a pas eu d'autres. Le reste vient d'ailleurs, d'Amérique, de Suède, d'Asie, d'Iran, etc., et cela risque de continuer encore longtemps, même si Godard, Resnais, Pialat commencent peu à peu à constituer eux aussi des pôles magnétiques assez puissants."
27. Jean-Luc Nancy, *The Inoperative Community*, ed. and trans. Peter Connor (Minneapolis: University of Minnesota Press, 1991).
28. Marja Warehime, *Maurice Pialat* (Manchester: Manchester University Press, 2006), 11.
29. Theodor W. Adorno, *The Language of Authenticity*, trans. Knut Tarnowski and Frederic Will (Evanston: Northwestern University Press, 1973), 17. See Scott Durham, "On the Authenticity of Jargon: From Barthes and Adorno to Godard," *The World Picture* (2008).
30. Foucault, "What is an Author?," 127.
31. Ibid.
32. In this sense, see particularly Geneviève Sellier, *Masculine Singular: French New Wave Cinema*, trans. Kristin Ross (Durham: Duke University Press, 2008); Richard Neupert, *A History of the French New Wave Cinema* (Madison: The University of Wisconsin Press, 2002); Jill Forbes, *The Cinema in France: After the New Wave* (Bloomington and Indianapolis: Indiana University Press, 1992).
33. Thierry Jousse, "Bresson souffle où il veut," *Cahiers du cinéma* 543 (February 2000): 30–31.
34. See Martin Jay, *Downcast Eyes: The Denigration of Vision in Twentieth-Century French Thought* (Berkeley and Los Angeles: University of California Press, 1994).
35. See Robert Bresson, "Entretien avec François-Régis Bastide," *Le Masque et la plume*, 30 April 1966, reprinted in *Bresson par Bresson: Entretiens (1943–1983)*, ed. Mylène Bresson (Paris: Flammarion, 2013), 165.

36. In addition to edited volumes gathering seminal essays, recent studies have updated the scholarship on film authorship. C. Paul Sellors, *Film Authorship: Auteurs and Other Myths* (London: Wallflower, 2010) and Sarah Kozloff, *The Life of the Author* (Montréal: Caboose, 2014) justify the relevance of the concept of film *auteur* and supply an overview of the most important moments in the concept's development.

CHAPTER ONE

"Il faut un auteur!"
Robert Bresson and the Making of the Author

"The Lonely Giant of the French Cinema Is Dead"

Robert Bresson died on 18 December 1999 at the age of 98, in his home southwest of Paris. "My husband, author of films, will be buried in private," wrote Mylène Bresson in a sober announcement. The funeral was discreet, very much in keeping with the reclusiveness of the filmmaker's life. Quickly, however, the news of Bresson's death got caught up in the widespread discourse about the so-called end of cinema. That Bresson "who was practically born with the century of cinema [in 1901] did not outlive it, seems almost natural, like the moonrise follows the sunset," assessed Kent Jones in the *Cahiers du cinéma*.[1] The encomium for the director became a eulogy for cinema and "the beauty of the world."[2] In this unconditional work of mourning, "death alone from death can save."[3]

As the announcement of Bresson's funeral made the rounds, the private event would become the object of substantial discussion and public spectacle. Around the world, hundreds of obituaries mourned the loss of "one of the greatest artists of the century,"[4] a "single-minded filmmaker of unique vision,"[5] a "master of precise gesture and cinematic emotion,"[6] a "genius in search of inner passion and complexity."[7] Bresson, the filmmaker who "distilled the motion picture narrative down to a particular essence,"[8] allowed us to "enter the realm of pure cinema,"[9] redefining the seventh art as a "continuous quest for perfection."[10] "Filmmaker of the spirit," he was "prophète à son insu."[11]

Genius, master, prophet: the words of devotion celebrating the filmmaker's life and work echoed the hagiographic terminology that had become common parlance during his lifetime. In a moving tribute, Paul Schrader lamented the departure of a figure that "has seemed like God himself, distant, beyond communication. Now, like God, Bresson is dead."[12] Striking in its poignant intimacy,

Schrader's eulogy acknowledged the visceral link between the man and his œuvre. The loss of a filmmaker to whom Schrader owed so much prompted a reaction of "disparity," the very term he had employed in his book *Transcendental Style in Film: Ozu, Bresson, Dreyer* to characterize the omnipresent tensions in Bresson's films, especially those that stress human solitude. Schrader's monograph argued that the director's indelible signature and inimitable style abide in the dialectic between "disparity" and "stasis." In addition to the continuum of disparity, i.e., the unrelenting tension between the abstract and the concrete, between the soul of the world and the gravity of the body, Bresson allowed occasional glimmers of resolution, or moments of stasis.[13]

Reiterating formulations from his influential analysis, Schrader commemorated Bresson in Bressonian terms, extending the "transcendental" signature of a personal style to the posthumous aura of the deceased master. The touching tribute celebrated the filmmaker's œuvre as "a 'new' world in which the spiritual and the physical can coexist, still in tension and unresolved, but as part of a larger scheme in which all phenomena cohere in a larger reality," which Schrader terms "the Transcendent."[14] A moving contribution to the international celebration of Bresson's life and work, Schrader's obituary culminated in a moment of silence that sealed, with the unmistakable force of "stasis," Bresson's canonization. His persona, claimed Schrader, possessed the allure of a physical property, similar to "the charred stake in *The Trial of Joan of Arc*," but also "the spiritual expression of ... martyrdom." In short, "*an icon.*"[15] Buried in private, and now all spirit, Bresson, the reclusive "author of films," became sanctified before the eyes of the world as he entered the *Panthéon des grands hommes*. As the rhetoric bears out, Schrader's eulogy offered both a religious act of consecration and a secular homage.

In the Pantheon of Great Men

"In France, Robert Bresson never leaves our screens, our imaginations, our culture: since *Les Anges du péché*, whether the tone has been one of controversy or veneration, Bresson has always appeared as the superego for France's cinematic *auteurs*, just as Pascal or Racine do for writers." Speaking as a French film scholar and a representative of the Cinémathèque Française, Nicole Brenez contributed these words in response to a transatlantic symposium on the filmmaker's work and reputation. In a round table that brought together film scholars and critics, curator

James Quandt, the driving force behind major North American retrospectives of Bresson's films, spoke of how the filmmaker's endeavors deserved exhaustive, careful, and nuanced attention. From Bresson's spirituality to his politics, from his take on existentialism to his place within (or against) modernism, from his relation to the culture of May '68 to his aesthetics and artistic legacy, the discussion led to "exciting and accurate exchanges," whose quality and richness, Brenez maintained, ensured that Bresson's work would be of lasting importance.[16]

Wherein exactly does the importance of Bresson's work lie? A closer glance at the obituaries confirms that Bresson's canonization in the Pantheon of such great men as Pascal and Racine was very much in keeping with a venerable French tradition of constituting authority and authoritative figures. Well-known rhetorical patterns emphasize his genius, invoke his saintly aura, and glorify his grand achievements, his uncompromising devotion to what he called the cinematograph, his formidable theological themes, and his experience as an imprisoned *résistant* during World War II.[17] Throughout the tributes one notices a conspicuous insistence on the "transcendental" nature of his cinema; this emphasis potentially complicates Bresson's heritage insofar as it would seem to suggest that his work lacked a political or historical foundation. In 1972 Schrader said as much when he spoke of Bresson's personality being at odds with the profound meaning of his work. As an artist alienated from his cultural environment, he appeared to be "morbid, hermetic, eccentric, obsessed with theological dilemmas in an age of social action." The culture in which he lived, maintained Schrader, "has had virtually no influence on his work."[18]

The filmmaker's relationship to the problems of his time is of course a major point of contention among Bresson scholars. Some pay attention to the inward grace and austerity of a profoundly "spiritual style,"[19] others emphasize the social and political charge and commitment that such a singular style could not but embrace. The French critic René Prédal is well aware of this disparity in his claim that an artist of Bresson's stature could not operate outside a deep engagement with his time. "What's more," insists Prédal, "in other countries, Bresson is seen to be 'typically French,' which means that while some of us do not wish to recognize him as one of our own, the distance of the *outsiders'* gaze results in their seeing him as characteristic of our state of mind and our cinema."[20] The heart of what Prédal calls the "Bresson phenomenon" rests upon a virulent contradiction between the passionate investment of "cinephiles and moralists" and the disinterested responses of historians and sociologists. The members of the first party tend to affirm that even in the invocation of figures such as Joan of Arc or Lancelot, Bresson is confronting his times. Not wanting to side with either group, Prédal is keen to emphasize the deep ideological motivations of a filmmaker who "speaks to his age rather than of his age; a visionary, not an echo, he inspires more than he draws inspiration; a vision, not a sponge, he paints what he understands, leaving to others the simpler task of filming what they see."[21]

Along similar lines, Schrader's comments point to the existence of an intrinsic dialogue between Bresson and French history. For all his idiosyncrasies, Bresson should not be perceived as an anomaly, "a suicidal neurotic or an eccentric genius," but rather the incarnation of "a different and older culture," even if this might not be readily apparent to modern viewers. The culture of which Bresson was a part embraced theology and pursued art in a manner mindful "of the role of the individual artist, but also of the function of art in a universal, multicultural sphere." Seen in this light, Bresson set "himself a near-impossible task: to update an older aesthetic into a contemporary form."[22] In this understanding, Bresson is not a point of origin, but rather an artist who worked within, and extended the historical framework of certain aesthetic conventions. Is it Bresson's visionary art that which secured him a place in the canonical film tradition, in spite of his work's alleged lack of historical or sociological resonance? Does Bresson's work, as Prédal laments, have no appeal for historians and sociologists? These questions bring to a head the problem of the filmmaker's legacy and his place in the critical Pantheon. More generally, they bear out the tensions at work in the constitution of canons and their function within the larger institution of authorship.

Bresson's ascension to a canonical status might be said to have come at the risk of imputing to this singular filmmaker social and political values that might not have been his own. "From a French perspective," elaborates Brenez, as if responding to Prédal, "we should recall that Bresson's spiritual values belong to a specific tradition: an aristocratic culture which is the class-based product of a formerly dominant ideology." In so doing, she echoes Schrader's claim that Bresson's "concern for spirituality, free will, predestination and grace is an oblique comment on contemporary French society."[23] "Since the form used to represent these values reveals an aesthetic autonomy, and the films contain a gallery of outcasts in revolt," argues Brenez, "it is easy to invest these vestiges of aristocratic culture with all kinds of critical aspiration, including those of Marxism and Maoism."[24] Reflecting the pertinence of Brenez's observation, Brian Price's recent book on Bresson seeks to transform the spiritual and transcendental artist into an exponent of "radical politics,"[25] in this way recasting the prophet as a political genius and activist. Although this revisionist exercise and critical intervention challenge the influential readings of Schrader, as well as of Susan Sontag and Amédée Ayfre,[26] it nonetheless maintains a high regard for the filmmaker's influential status.

Seen as alienated from his political environment by some critics, reprimanded for the "political limits of his spiritualism" by others, Bresson is nonetheless consecrated as "a herald of (aesthetic) resistance."[27] In the words of Godard, he remains to French cinema "what Mozart is to German music and Dostoevsky to Russian literature." There is no doubt that Bresson's films catalyze in many audiences a hypnotic fascination, and the author has seemingly allowed these viewers to invest him with their own values and ideals. In 2001, while reflecting on Bresson's life achievements, Schrader confided that "I am no longer sure if I ever saw Bresson in the glass of his films; I only saw my own reflection."[28] Indeed, Bresson has served as a site of projection for a variety of critics; his work, likewise, has come to serve altogether different agendas.[29] From René Briot's 1957 monograph to Jean-Michel Frodon's half a century later, from analyses by Philippe Arnaud and Michel Estève to ones in English by Paul Schrader, Tony Pipolo, and Brian Price, to mention just a few, these studies, despite their different perspectives and critical approaches, all leave us to wonder how one is to write a book on Bresson without resorting to hagiography. Securing the film director a place among the distinguished company of French titans, Bresson's consecration complies with the process of the authorship formation in post-revolutionary France. The examination of this process will guide us in our attempt to unveil (and demystify) the hagiographic impulse, the strategies and dynamics behind the making of the artist, and the specificity it acquired with regard to cinema.

It is appropriate that we probe the intricacies of this critical consecration and dismantle the rhetoric that argues for Bresson's singularity. That Bresson would be made into a saint is not altogether surprising, given the theological subjects explored in his movies, his often-repeated quest to capture the essence of things (what he called the "soul," the "truth of the world") by stripping physical reality of its familiar trappings and conventional shapes and molding it into a denuded and raw material countenance. This model of sainthood surely reinforces all the clichés about Bresson's work, especially the ones surrounding his persona; it promotes the values of singularity and exemplarity at the cost of tremendous sacrifice.

In spite of the longstanding struggle to abolish the individualism of the master, "aristocratic ideals, though unidentified as such, provide an irresistible mirror for artists eager to achieve independence and sovereignty," suggests Brenez, before concluding that "the cinema of Robert Bresson transmits to us, in an anthropological sense, the legacy of an ideology once dominant, now more and more deviant."[30] To be sure, aristocratic ideals and poetic singularity are easily recognizable when one speaks of authorship in literature and the fine arts. But how are we to assess the presence of these elements in cinema, given its prominent place within the culture industry? Bresson cultivated the image of an esoteric artist more inclined to sacrifice his popular success than to compromise his aesthetic convictions. He surely never missed a chance to affirm the singularity of cinema as art, and vigorously defended it against the influence of other arts. As such, his case is perplexing; it seems at once obvious and yet exceptional.

The Maniac of Truth

How are we to confront the clichés, the standard points of reference, the obligatory examples found in assessments of Bresson's work, much less the overarching tendency to see his endeavors in absolute terms? Bresson, both as filmmaker and interlocutor, complicates the task, for in great part he laid the foundation for his own monument. Enacting the principles recorded in his booklet of *Notes* and reiterated in numerous interviews,[31] his work as a whole seems almost frightening in its absolute unity of content and form. The director's clarity is compelling and persuasive, at times even hypnotic. "Master precision. Be a precision instrument myself,"[32] we read on the first page of *Notes*, as Bresson sets himself up for a rigorous endeavor that requires that he "rid himself of errors,"[33] become sure of his resources and develop his project like a "military art."[34]

For Bresson, the act of filming brings together that which is intuited, desired, and anticipated: "Shooting is going out to meet something. Nothing in the unexpected that is not secretly expected by you."[35] What does Bresson secretly expect from these "wonderful chances, those that act with precision?"[36] He is looking for some sort of encounter,[37] for "a flash/fulguration of truth,"[38] for a moment of grace, nothing less than a revelation of the world in its true being, or rather in its being true. Within a perspective that rejects ideas, concepts, and formalistic concerns, and one that views cinematographic writing as a form of feeling, how does or can truth figure? Reading the *Notes* and Bresson's many interviews, it becomes soon obvious that neither naturalism, nor realism, much less historical veracity can possibly be the goal of his uncompromising and uncompromised pursuit marked by a clear distrust of intellectualism that leaves no room for philosophical digression: "Not to shoot a film in order to illustrate a thesis,"[39] warns Bresson, but rather "hide the ideas … . The most important will be the most hidden."[40] Elsewhere, he writes, using stark block letters: "IN THIS LANGUAGE OF IMAGES, ONE MUST LOSE COMPLETELY THE NOTION OF IMAGE. THE IMAGES MUST EXCLUDE THE IDEA OF IMAGE."[41]

Cultivating the interplay of chance and predestination, Bresson's method is both tenuous and fragile; it hangs on a thread. A shrinking frame is chosen for the immodest project of revealing the world as both symbolic and intensely concrete, both abstract and yet possessed of a weighty materiality. The precision of framing and editing makes viewers dizzy, leaving them intoxicated and enthralled as they experience the films' stunning unity of form and content, the result of Bresson's singular resolve. "I am a maniac of truth," he maintained in an interview conducted by advocates of the "politique des auteurs" at *Cahiers du cinéma*.[42] In qualifying the notion of "truth" in neat technical terms ("A false use of lighting is just as dangerous as a false word or a false gesture"), he offers a practical explanation of what appeared so enigmatic in the *Notes*. Elaborated in the interview's dialogical form, Bresson's reflections revolve around the imposing question of truth, approaching it from different angles and with a variety of inflections. The fixation on this term, the way in which he granted it such inordinate gravity, attest to his addictive embrace of such an authoritative concept, indeed his mania.

Rigorous in its execution, Bresson's cinema is conceived as an ascetic practice, an art of purification. The director distills and refines, doing away with the inessential and the superfluous. "One does not create by adding," he stipulates, "but by taking away."[43] Elsewhere he writes that "to create is not to invent persons and things. It is to tie new relationships between persons and things which are, and *as they are*."[44] Prefilmic objects and living beings do not dispose of any predetermined meaning, let alone a "true" identity. The images of persons and objects assume a semblance of truth only after "you set them together in a certain order" and, in that way, confer on them a certain "reality," [45] which is altogether foreign to the project of so-called realist representation. Rather, this reality is the state of objects and characters as they are brought to life by a filmmaker who seeks nothing less than to make visible the existence and activity of the soul: "Cinematographic films made of inner movements which are seen."[46]

The quest to reveal the "truth of the real" and to deliver the "absolute truth" in its material gravity traverses, of course, an entire mythology of creation.[47] Bresson does not think of this as a quixotic pursuit; he positions himself not as the keeper of some mystic truth, but as the mediator (although we might add a chosen one) of a message that awaits its delivery. The revelation of the real, as Bresson imagines his practice, can only come about instantaneously, in a fulguration, in a moment of "stasis," that emphasizes the unfaltering intensity of the pursuit. Driving this semi-mythological project is the technical potential of the cinematograph, this "wonderful" invention, which Bresson refuses to call an art, a concept that he deems inadequate (and insufficient) for such a vital enterprise.[48] The camera possesses the ability to grasp and record inner thoughts and make them palpable; its "incommensurable field" allows the filmmaker an "unlimited power of creating."[49] The camera enables one to probe a reality that would otherwise remain unseen. It makes visible "what, without you, might never have been seen."[50] In this truth-seeking enterprise, the filmmaker assumes ultimate responsibility for the creative endeavor: "Many people are needed in order to make a film, but only one who makes, unmakes, remakes his images and sounds, returning at every second to the initial impression or sensation which brought these to birth and is incomprehensible to other people."[51]

At first blush, Bresson's conception of the filmmaker's creative power seems ambiguous. On the one hand, he requires the discerning judgment of the artist to create a world from images and sounds; on the other, he celebrates the felicitous invention of the machine. His thoughts about the impetus behind *Pickpocket* offer some helpful clarification. "I would like the spectators to witness an actual birth," claims the director, "and not something that had already happened, a genesis that already took place."[52] While Bresson is adamant about effacing the traces of camera movements or anything that would point to the camera as a mere medium of reproducibility, he also stresses its role in capturing "the real, and nothing but the real."[53] A few years later, in a radio conversation about *Au hasard Balthazar*, Bresson reiterated that the camera be used as "an instrument of creation,"[54] manipulated by the vigilant filmmaker, the one endowed with judgment. The camera

> does not think, it is an eye, a "cow's eye" in Cocteau's words. It captures the real as it flies past. It offers in an instant what the writer, the painter, the sculptor cannot manage to grasp. It registers what our spirit could not retain... We hunt the rare instant, that which happens in the moment and won't be reproduced.[55]

Wielding a miraculous tool, the filmmaker recognizes and acts on the difference between sight (*vue*) and vision (*vision*), between what the spectator notices on the screen and the film's engine of visuality. For Bresson, this means mastering both the realm of the visible and the invisible.[56] If one puts it to careful and sensitive use, deems Bresson, the camera not only becomes a magnifying glass for physiognomies and gestures, but it also allows the filmmaker to penetrate the "soul" of people as well as objects. This process, he insists, differs from the work of the *metteur-en-scène*, a denomination from which Bresson wants to distance himself. "I don't design sets and settings. I am a director, if you wish, but I don't direct actors, I only direct myself and my contacts with my models are telepathic. It is a sort of divination."[57]

"It Would Not Be Ridiculous to Say to Your Models: I'm Inventing You As You Are"

Nothing is perhaps more singular about Bresson than his conception of what he calls models and his work with them. The director's systematic rejection of professional actors in favor of carefully chosen amateurs is a crucial component of his method. Only someone who is screen-innocent and unspoiled by previous dramatic experience could become a vessel for Bresson's "truth." The model does not emote or evoke identification; indeed it denies viewers the vicarious opportunity to partake of and thus share the feelings of others. The donkey in *Au hasard Balthazar* provides the clearest and most poignant enactment of this entity. He is, according to Michael Haneke,

> *a projection screen, a blank sheet of paper, whose sole task is to be filled with the viewer's thoughts and feelings… The animal Balthazar, along with the knights in the director's later* Lancelot du Lac, *locked up in their clattering suits of armor to the point of being unrecognizable, are Bresson's most convincing "models" simply because they are unable to pretend.*[58]

In portraying someone, it is essential that the model not act. The script suffices to define the figure, the model does not play any role in the elaboration of the character, for this is the writer's responsibility. The models, in this radical sense, do not deliver the truth as the opposite of falsehood, but position themselves in that realm before the "fall from grace," before they had any knowledge that there would be any truth.

In a letter to the *Cahiers du cinéma*,[59] Roland Monod, who played the priest in *A Man Escaped*, wrote that it would be impossible for professional actors to work with Bresson, for he strips his players of all intention and volition. Bresson, said Monod, wants to remain the sole creator of his movies, the only master on the set. Seen in this light, the professional actors' propensity for "expression" potentially undermines the voice of the master: "When I am in front of an actor," admits Bresson, "the more his power of expression augments, the more mine diminishes. Or, what matters to me is that I express myself, not him."[60] Elsewhere, he insists that the freedom to exercise his will as an author is the fundamental principle and guiding impetus of his work; it allows him to be a practitioner of the cinematograph and not an agent of "photographed theater."[61] Only the cinematograph ensures the total expression of the author's volition; it affords total improvisation[62] within the "premeditated, strict frames" imposed by the camera and the sound recorder.

In spite of repeated elucidations of his theory of the model, Bresson's relationship to his cast remains nonetheless elusive: "Between them and me," he says with characteristic terseness, "telepathic exchanges, divination."[63] The closest he comes to an elaboration is when he depicts this dynamic as a rigorous form of self-direction: "The important thing is not to direct someone else, but to direct oneself. The rest is telepathy."[64] For Dominique Sanda who played the main character in *Une femme douce*, working with Bresson involved a certain disorientation; "acting" takes place only after the model enters a trance, a state of mental confusion and intoxication akin to dizziness. Bresson becomes a "revelator" of the true character of his models, allowing to surface dimensions of their being which they themselves did not know they possessed. "Model: Withdrawn into himself. Of the little he lets escape, take only what suits you."[65] Bresson considers this to be "a strange mix, a mixture of them and of me, a sort of light exuding from them towards me and from me towards them, a kind of amalgam obtained not through the direction of actors or through *mise-en-scène*, but through a kind of divination, a mutual agreement, an intimate friendship, but in no case, I insist, a direction of actors or *mise-en-scène*."[66]

Such gnomic comments lead one to surmise that Bresson is not just describing his practice, but also forging a myth of his creative power. His theory of the model bears out Thomas Hobbes's famous understanding: "Of person artificial some have their words and actions owned by those whom they represent and then the person is the actor, and he that owns his words and actions is the author."⁶⁷ By relegating his characters to the status of disoriented and hypnotized entities, Bresson invents not only a new type of acting, but also a novel type of representation, one that divests and disembodies, reducing the human figure to its own literality. Indeed, by neutralizing the acting, Bresson fosters a new project of cinematographic figuration, not in the theatrical sense of the term, but in the sense of *figura*, i.e., a molding of the material that brings it to life. This method allows him to avoid the conventions of *mise-en-scène*.

Bresson dismissed such terms as "cineaste," "metteur-en-scène," "director" or "filmmaker," and instead stressed his formation as a painter. "I am a painter; I no longer paint, but once a painter, always a painter."⁶⁸ Being a painter is to

> *know exactly what you want to achieve plastically and do what is necessary to have it. The image that you have in mind* (en vue) *must be foreseen* (prévoir), *that is to say, seen in advance, literally seen on the screen (while taking into account the fact that there is the risk of a disparity, and even a strong difference, between what you see and what you will present), and you must make that image exactly as you want to see it, as you see it with your eyes shut.*⁶⁹

In what might be the most often cited pronouncement about his method, Bresson maintains that the cinematograph is not a matter of images alone, but of relations between images, of rhythms whose sole master must be the author. In such an enterprise, the filmmaker resembles the painter insofar as he is the only agent endowed with intention, volition, and agency; like the painter, the filmmaker breathes life into amorphous matter and animates an otherwise static world.

Bresson's observations about his work as a painter and the impact it exercised on his cinematograph are revealing in another significant way. It is not unconceivable that Bresson stopped painting because he felt that everything possible in the art had been achieved and expressed. "I haven't painted for a long time," he said in an interview with Michel Ciment:

> *I believe that painting is over. There is nowhere to go. I don't mean after [Pablo] Picasso, but after Cézanne. He went to the brink of what could be done. Others may paint because they are of a different generation, but I felt very early on that I must not continue. When I stopped, it was horrible. At first, cinema was only a stop-gap, to occupy my mind. It was the right choice, I think, because cinema*

can go beyond painting... [It] is tomorrow's writing or painting, with two kinds of ink, one for the eye, one for the ear.[70]

For Bresson, filmmaking was akin to painting; it was a physical activity that allowed the artist to mold and shape his materials, that is, recorded images and sounds, into bearers of truth. He thought of himself as a worker and mediator and above all the enabler of the higher energy vested in the cinematograph. This abstract conception of the cinematographic art, described and defended as a divination and magical creation, obscures the filmmaker's uncompromising struggle to preserve the purity of his art by prohibiting other agents from intentional action. He is the mastermind on the set. Everything else must be automatism.[71]

In 1994, François Weyergans presented an episode from the series *Cinéastes de notre temps*, "Robert Bresson ni vu, ni connu," an hour-long interview, originally broadcast in 1965, that covered questions of keen interest to the filmmaker, from the specificity of cinematographic art to his relationship with his models, from his early days as a painter to his reliance on Pascal and Dostoevsky. Many of the director's comments in this exchange would take on written form in the *Notes sur le cinématographe*. As Weyergans pointed out, the original format of the show was largely altered because the production team had to follow Bresson's lead:

> I find it funny to remember that Bresson had directed me for these questions. There are questions that he had more or less written himself. We made up all the questions after the answers, in order to somehow clarify his arguments and these are therefore questions that he has somehow rewritten himself because he likes answering questions that he himself asks.

In the conversation, Bresson spoke about the relationship between producer and filmmaker: "It is not always desirable that the producer adopt towards the filmmaker the attitude of this famous art trader who, after he became famous, required a tone of blue where the painter put red."[72] This tendency of the director to position himself within the professional field, to define himself "objectively in the relation to his work, and conflictually in his relation with the producer, was the mark of the modern author."[73] If Bresson is "*à part dans ce métier terrible*,"[74] in the words of Jean Cocteau, this special status is very much a consequence of his own strategic self-construction and self-promotion. Bresson's thesis that the cinematographic art bears a sole creator, virulently expressed in his master classes and media interviews, and rigorously practiced in his films, provide a quasi-manifesto for the *auteur* before the polemical interventions in the *Cahiers*. What is more, Bresson knowingly exercised a self-exegesis and a self-promotion as film author, and for that reason, one might well say that he set a critical tone that anticipated and fully blossomed with the *politique des auteurs*.

Bresson, Auteur of the Politique des Auteurs

With resolute consistency, Bresson remained true to his idiosyncratic approach. It is hardly surprising to find him among the filmmakers celebrated by the *politique des auteurs*. If his films stand somewhat outside of the *politique*'s temporal frame, they readily lend (and have lent) themselves to auteurist appreciations, especially as auteurism evolved over the years and until the present day. His last feature, *L'Argent*, provides an ideal object for this type of reading. The film recapitulates Bresson's themes, motives, and tropes; it attests to the continuities and emphases that make the director such a compelling example of the *Cahiers*' critical method. The culmination of a magisterial career, *L'Argent* returns to the early trilogy of imprisonment (*A Man Escaped* [1956], *Pickpocket* [1959], *The Trial of Joan of Arc* [1962]), reiterating images, objects, and sounds, from the apertures at the bank through which cash passes to the unnerving squeak of a laundry cart.

James Quandt's exemplary auteurist reading[75] shows well how single images from *L'Argent* resonate strongly in their studied revisitation of privileged scenes and moments from Bresson's entire œuvre: the radiating ripples on the surface of a pond (*Mouchette*), the lantern that lights the murderer's way (*Au hasard Balthazar*), the spy hole through which a policeman peers at his captive (*The Trial of Joan of Arc*), the prison soup cart (*The Angels of Sin*), the presence of pornography in a holy place (*The Devil, Probably*), and the look of complicity that binds criminal and victim (*Pickpocket*). *L'Argent* encapsulates the motifs and figures of an entire career: the trial and the prison (*The Trial of Joan of Arc, A Man Escaped*), the theft and the money (*Pickpocket*), the argument for an alternative ethics concerning the chosen ones (*Pickpocket, The Devil Probably*), the irreparable injustice of humanity (*Au hasard Balthazar*), and especially the figure of the innocent being preyed upon by inescapable evil (*Mouchette*). Employing his trademark motifs, enacting his radical anachronism, and indulging his fondness for casting nonprofessionals who are related to celebrities (in this case, Caroline Lang, daughter of then minister of culture Jack Lang, who helped get the movie funded), Bresson's last work offers a comprehensive précis of a career.

Speaking about *L'Argent* with Serge Daney and Serge Toubiana, Robert Bresson reiterated the principles of his cinematic project, acknowledging the way in which the film displays a gradual maturation in the treatment of sound and image, but also looking forward to achieving at long last the "adaptation" project of *The Genesis*.[76] It is a project he sought to realize on several occasions; it remained particularly important to him because he believed that it contained the essence of his style.[77] Although the adaptation of the Bible's first book would remain an unrealized plan, the undertaking would give rise to productive reflections on the unity of form and content, on the cinematographic genesis at the heart of Bresson's œuvre as a body: the "ejaculatory force of the eye," or, in other words, "the power to create. The eye demolishes what it sees and reconstructs it according to the idea it has of it: the eye of the painter in keeping with his taste or his ideal Beauty."[78] As Serge Daney put it, with Bresson "each shot is a genesis"[79] thanks to "this gift from heaven able to capture the Truth, that is the real."[80]

If Bresson's work presents an ideal object for auteurist interpretation, his role in what became the *politique des auteurs* would be even more significant. As stated, Bresson articulated similar premises already in the 1940s. Not only did he formulate the thesis of the *camera-stylo*, he also defended the author as a film's sole creator, possessor of a world view that opens up to and welcomes the spectator. "Il faut un auteur," he insisted:

> *There should be an author: We are pushing the love for style to mania, for film is the type of work that requires a style, that needs an author, a writing. The author is writing on the screen, he expresses himself through photographic shots of variable duration, of variable angles. For an author worthy of this name must make a choice, dictated by his calculations or his instinct, and not by chance.*[81]

The cinematograph, he submitted years later, is a means of novel expression that can only become the equal of other constituted arts if the authority of the filmmaker is recognized: "We will welcome the day when we express ourselves with the cinematograph like we do with the pen and the brush. The film has to be the work of one sole man, and absorb the audience in the world of this sole man, I mean a world that is his own."[82]

For the young French film critics writing in 1955, there was no doubt that Bresson deserved the status of *auteur*. Bresson's presence at the margins of cinema seems nonetheless out of keeping with a movement that above all focused on the epicenter of film production, the Hollywood studios.[83] This aristocratic film director, disdainful of big studio productions and star vehicles, was different from other *auteurs*, masters on lavish sets and successful employees within a commercial industry. Bresson's role in the development of the *politique des auteurs* seems to have been marginal,[84] but his method provided an intriguing variation and a compelling counterpoint.

Bresson, like other chosen *auteurs*, was asked to offer his perspectives about authorship in what would become a famous *Cahiers* interview. Conducted by Michel Delahaye and Jean-Luc Godard after the premiere of *Au hasard Balthazar*, the exchange[85] followed the format employed in the journal's dialogues with Jean Renoir, Alfred Hitchcock, Fritz Lang, and Roberto Rossellini. Focusing initially on a single feature, in this case *Au hasard Balthazar*, the interview would go on to address the key concerns of the *politique des auteurs*, namely *mise-en-scène*, the thematic and stylistic consistency of a filmographic trajectory, and, of course, the range of references used by the filmmaker. The interview format proved to be extremely effective for the hosts, so much so that Delahaye and Godard managed to make their own points without having to engage with Bresson's "method." Bresson did not possess Renoir's verve and polemical élan, nor Lang's zesty eloquence. Like his films, his interviews are exercises in precision, pontificating interventions imbued with a discernible uneasiness, even dismay, in the presence of the young critics who, although concerned with Bresson's singularity, pushed their own agendas as they sought to create their own community of authors.

Godard, at the time no longer a working film critic,[86] pressed the point of a continuity that seems to run through Bresson's work. "I have the impression," surmised Godard, "that this film, *Balthazar*, reflects something that goes back a long time, something you have been thinking about for fifteen years, perhaps, and to which all the films that you have made then were tending." For Godard, the girl in *Balthazar* appears as a synthesis of a lifetime quest that had found expression in previous films: "I mean that, with it, one meets, too, the pickpocket, and Chantal... Consequently your film seems the most complete of all. It is the total film. In itself, and in relation to you."[87] Bresson granted that working from his own original script forced him to "put myself into this film, still more than in my other films."[88] At the same time, he wanted to make clear that this should not be seen as an intellectual pursuit, that he avoids strict (conceptual) systems, and aspires to what he calls "intuitive" work, which for him is a form of grace.[89]

Bresson's cinematic vision issued from the unique link between a set of precise tools (the models' presence, the ellipsis, the formal composition, etc.) and the filmmaker's intuitive engagement with his material. In this interview Bresson openly conceded that he is a maniac of truth, someone possessed by the belief that what appears on the screen should appear as life itself and not be mistaken for a facsimile or a reproduction of life. As such, the filmmaker disposes of a form of grace that liberates viewers from the tyranny of simulation and falsehood (for instance, in photographed theatre), and engenders their admiration and, yes, "love." "You must leave the spectator free. And at the same time you must make yourself loved by him. You must make him love the way in which you render things."[90]

Such claims about spectatorial volition (or the lack thereof), especially when coming from the ultimate tyrant, were sure to generate a response from the young critics. Committed to the idea of *mise-en-scène* as the most hallowed incarnation of the director's vision, they were eager to promote the *auteur* as a genius rather than a selfless and sacrificial messiah devoted to the spectators' liberation. To the director's question about his own point of departure ("But from what point had we set out?"), Delahaye responded: "From the vision that you had of things, from the direction that you had imprinted on your vision."[91] Because this remark was more reflective of the *politique* credo than Bresson's own idea, the director tried to protest against this ocularcentrist notion, but to little avail: "Good. But then, there, we enter…" he countered, without finishing his sentence. Bresson's almost mystical account of the cinematograph was at odds with the more mechanical vision of the *Cahiers*. At a subsequent moment in the interview, another discrepancy between the two perspectives became manifest. Delahaye pointed to the "disparity between the things that you show and the real elements," which he saw as a tension between a "sociological documentary" and a "timeless fable." When the young journalist stubbornly sought to bring the conversation around to the significance of *mise-en-scène*, Bresson would have none of it. For him any disparity came from the fact that "cinema copies life, or photographs it, while as for me, I recreate life starting from elements in as natural, as crude a state as possible."

Au hasard Balthazar, an exemplary enactment of Bresson's mania of precision and cinematic purity, took on a different aspect when filtered through the prism of auteurist orthodoxy. If the interview was the *politique des auteurs*'s privileged tool, its pertinence, outside of its polemical merit, did not grant the film "its value as an *œuvre*."⁹² This point echoed Bazin's 1957 critique of the *politique*, particularly concerning the problematic cult of the personality and the spurious opposition between *véritables auteurs* and *metteurs-en-scène*. This critique, which in Bazin's words was above all the function of a "family quarrel," partook of the vaunted critical notion through a deformed mirror: "This notion of auteur is subsequently opposed to the distinction author-subject because the dignity of being included in the cenacle of authors involves more than the valorization of the working material. At least to a certain extent, the auteur is always concerned with himself. No matter what the script is, he's always telling the same story."⁹³

The *politique* method was controversial and came under criticism for its lack of socio-historical dimensions, as well as for the blatant way in which the critics instrumentally used the authors' status to serve their own image. Barthélémy Amengual publicly indicted the critics for using selected films as "perfect monads" that would enable them to "define their own allegiance, certitudes, illusions, resemblances, values. Melting pots, or rather pieces of the world, picnic spots, the films only reflect the preoccupations and aspects that the critics ascribe to them."⁹⁴ Amengual went even further, rejecting the idealized vision of the *auteur* as the sole creator, and castigating the fight for authorship as a purposeless battle:

> It is obvious that there are film authors. But to these real authors and often, alas!, more numerous than they [the critics] would need for the production of one film, the Cahiers prefer this ideal auteur, with capital A, that they invent with shameless liberty from reels signed by the same hand. And so it becomes an idealistic full circle. Real films and authors (of all sorts) are forgotten by the world and history to enter the museums of imagination and monetize the absolute in their new quality of pure cinema.⁹⁵

Responding to Amengual, Eric Rohmer defended the position of *Cahiers* and his fellow critics:

> Today, in every domain—painting, music, literature—the politics of select fragments gives way to that of complete works. What remains are not works, but authors. Rightly or wrongly, given what we can read in club and library film programs, I bet it will not be otherwise for cinema. Film posters highlight the director's name; rightly so. I understand he is not given "absolute paternity over every little detail" along with his professional ID. It's up to him to conquer this

paternity, and we see that he can, if he has a minimum of character, authority, and genius.[96]

Rohmer's distinction between "the absolute paternity of every detail" and "the professional ID" was essential to the *politique des auteurs*: it articulated a notion of film authorship that, even if it never attained the status of theory in the pages of *Cahiers*, was worthy of the critical French tradition from Diderot to Baudelaire, and was highly influential in the subsequent theory as well as practice of cinema. For all its influence, however, it ignored or overlooked many other aspects of film authorship, concerns such as copyright and ownership laws as well as other legislative and economic determinations that are essential to the world of cinema.

Bresson's Campaign for Film Authorship

As has become apparent, Bresson's notion of authorship diverged in key regards from that of his Nouvelle Vague contemporaries, especially in its emphasis on the role of labor within the work of film artists. To grasp the importance of Bresson's different understanding about the production of art, it is essential that it be considered within the larger context of French debates about film authorship during the 1950s. During this decade in France, cinema found recognition as a legitimate cultural praxis; in this endeavor, the campaign for the filmmaker's status as *auteur* played a particularly prominent role. Bresson was active as a lobbyist and a spokesman in the movements which sought to secure *the auteur*'s status. The *politique des auteurs* was passionate and influential; nonetheless, in postwar exchanges about French film authorship, it was not the sole voice, much less the dominant one.

An initiative to modify and update the legislation on copyright and distribution had received strong support, but in spite of the pressure applied by professional organizations, the resolution did not reach the floor of the Assemblée Nationale. The last months of peace before the onset of German occupation in the late spring of 1940 had seen a dynamic and conjoint mobilization of a large number of organizations eager to centralize their efforts under the rubric "Société du droit d'auteur cinématographique."[97] In October 1939, an interministerial committee had been formed, including representatives from the Ministries of Commerce, Finances, Fine Arts and the General Commissionership (directed since August

1939 by Jean Giraudoux), and charged with solving the issues of the "entire French film production."[98] However, the enthusiasm generated by this initiative was short-lived; by March 1940 the government took exception to the original propositions of *auteur* societies. The numerous initiatives during the last decade of the Third Republic to recognize French cinema as "œuvre de l'esprit" would come to naught. After Philippe Pétain assumed power, cinema, now reduced to a corporatist industry under a collaborationist government, fell under the laws of "industrial activities."[99]

After the Liberation, the status of authors and copyright issues would assume renewed importance within a larger process of professional restructuring. Discovering the films of Orson Welles, forbidden during the Occupation, or those of Roberto Rossellini, spectators sought to ascribe authorship to whom they believed it was due. Within the film world there was intense confusion, reinforced by fierce exchanges between the SACD (Société des Auteurs et Compositeurs Dramatiques) and the AAF (Association des Auteurs de Films). The filmmaker Marcel Pagnol, the SACD director since 1944, associated the film author with the scriptwriter, and argued that a film director did not deserve to be considered the author of a film unless he at least co-wrote it. The AAF pondered the different needs and profiles of scriptwriters, filmmakers, and technicians, many of whom were unionized and largely opposed to the notion that the filmmaker might be a film's sole author. To Pagnol's virulent insistence that the writer be considered the legitimate author of the movie, the majority of the AAF members responded by emphasizing the collective dimension of film production and eschewed any attempt to grant responsibility to an individual creator.

Amidst these legal and professional battles, the cinephilic movements pursued action on a variety of fronts. André Bazin had founded the first ciné-club in 1943, and in 1945 had established the French Federation of Ciné-Clubs (FFCC—Fédération Française des Ciné-Clubs). In October 1946 the CNC (Centre National de la Cinématographie) was created.[100] Alexandre Astruc's seminal article on the *caméra-stylo* appeared in 1948 and important film journals (chronologically *Téléciné, Image et Son, Cahiers du cinéma, Positif, Cinéma*) published their first issues between 1946 and 1953. The Cannes Film Festival opened in 1946 and its grand prize, the Palme d'Or, would be awarded to the director. This critical and professional effervescence found its most visible extension in the 1958 explosion of the Nouvelle Vague. A decisive moment also came with the 1949 Biarritz Film Festival;[101] here the public image of the filmmaker enshrined as the absolute author of a film or a body of films assumed clearer shape, fueled by examples from abroad (the Russians, the neo-realists, Orson Welles, and William Wyler) and culled from the history of French cinema (René Clair, Jean Vigo, and Jean Renoir). In the company of Bazin and Cocteau, we find Bresson, who ardently spoke in favor of the distribution of less known films "to whom cinema owes a lot, I would even say everything, and that Cocteau named, by analogy with what we call the 'damned poets,' 'damned films.'"[102]

Of key importance for contemporary understandings of film authorship was the promulgation of the 1957 law regarding artistic property.[103] This legislation legally confirmed what cinephiles had endorsed, namely the filmmaker's authorship. It recognized cinema as an "œuvre de l'esprit" as opposed to "œuvre de collaboration." The law, passed in March of that year, was the first modern piece of legislation to regulate the creative rights of filmmakers. The legislation that had previously applied to cinema, with some minor alterations, in fact dated back to 1791 and 1794.[104] Discussions about the status of cinema as a prominent postwar cultural practice had already animated the professional organization two weeks after Liberation (and to a large extent revolved around the role of the film author); the juridical and political factors that intervened in the process were slow to catch up. A parliamentary commission had been charged in 1946 to work on a new law that would not be passed until more than a decade later.

During the ten years after the law's implementation in 1958 and up to the creation of the SRF (La Société des Réalisateurs de Films), French cinema faced a tenuous situation, both in regard to the legal interpretation of the law as well as artistic freedom of expression. The Nouvelle Vague filmmakers did not figure within these prominent and extensive negotiations and altercations. Truffaut, Rohmer, and Godard dealt directly with producers or functioned as their own producers; they did not concern themselves with the mundane details and legislative particulars of authorship. Only when opposing acts of censorship to their films would they participate in legal debates.[105]

As the application of the 1957 law demonstrated, matters were anything but clear. For example, film distribution was considered to be subject to the same guidelines as the creative activity of filmmaking. But it soon became obvious that the producer, holder of the economic power, was often in a position to constrain the filmmaker, to impose cuts and modifications that would yield more "marketable" films. In theory, the law of March 1957 recognized the equal rights of filmmakers and producers; it was not before 1968, however, that filmmakers put in place structures that regulated potential conflicts with producers. In June 1968, in his capacity as honorary president of the SRF, Robert Bresson presented the inaugural address: "We have gained a big victory," he rejoiced. "We are in the possession of a very powerful weapon, for the others need us, while we don't need them. Something is about to start!"[106]

It is surprising, even startling, to realize that Bresson played such an active role in these discussions. His presence surely is at odds with his reputation as a reclusive filmmaker and an adept of creative solitude who, so it is claimed, had no interest in current events and political problems. But here he was, making common cause with other representatives of the profession. Apart from his public intervention at the Biarritz Festival, Bresson's presence in the debates concerning the profession has remained virtually overlooked and forgotten. Nonetheless, his comments and declarations confirm that he figured actively and seminally within the debates and conflicts that animated organizations, unions, and other groups between 1943 and 1968.

The impetus behind Bresson's inaugural speech goes back to the Liberation. That became particularly visible in December 1944, when Marcel L'Herbier resigned from the presidency of the AAF (L'Association des Auteurs de Films). Marcel Pagnol, author of plays and novellas, and held in contempt by Bresson, compromised the identity and autonomy of the AAF and sought to merge the AAF with the SACD. Pagnol was adamant in his belief that the film author was either "1) the author of the original work that provided the plot; 2) the screen writer and the dialogue writer who gave the written form; 3) the musician who composed the music for the film."[107] In contemporaneous debates about the paternity of *Les Anges du péché* (1943), written by Jean Giraudoux, from a story by Raymond Bruckberger, Bresson defended the film as his own work: "Il faut un auteur!" As challenging as it was to deny that "Bresson dominates all the elements of the film,"[108] in Pagnol's eyes he had no right to call himself the author. Bresson's public altercation with Pagnol explains the latter's cold reception of *Les Dames du bois de Boulogne*, an adaptation of Diderot's novella; Pagnol deemed the film to be an unrecognizable Diderot, solely focusing on the drama of the soul and as such stripped of any social inscription.

Bresson defended the filmmaker's absolute paternity in a number of public appearances. Asked if *Pickpocket* is the work of one person, his answer was apodictic: "It must be."[109] The film must have one master and only one, and the master's vision must impregnate the entire work. His *Notes* reiterate this emphasis:

"From Madame de Sévigné: When I listen to myself only, I do wonders."[110] Or "Not have the soul of an *exécutant* (of my own projects). Find, for each shot, a new pungency over and above what I had imagined. Invention (re-invention) on the spot."[111] Elsewhere, in an interview, he declared that "the author of the film must not be a subordinate (*exécutant*). He must be the creator from the very beginning."[112] Bresson thinks of himself as a creator insofar as he executes his own vision which gives rise to the autonomous film. Such an uncompromising emphasis on creative integrity nonetheless does not prevent Bresson from advocating for a community of *auteurs* and insisting that

> the belief that there is only one and unique vision of the world is absurd. There should be fewer and fewer metteurs-en-scène and more and more auteurs. There are among the young ones. One should count on them. I do believe in the future of films made far from the official production, with affordable machines (the camera and the sound-recorder), far from the terribly contagious studios.[113]

Such concerns about authorship echoed and figured within debates going on throughout the film community. His radio interventions highlighted the ongoing discussion in the profession and attested to Bresson's lively commitment to these pressing issues. Once the law of 11 March 1957 finally recognized the filmmaker's intellectual property, and especially after the vocal success of the *politique des auteurs*, the topic would become less prominent in his interviews. His job in this regard seemed to have been completed. The persistent problem subsequently invoked by Bresson was the difficulty to secure funding for his films, a difficulty that in his mind derived from the refusal to work with acclaimed stars and was connected with the pressures of the film industry.

Robert Bresson's role in the authorship debate continued in his endeavors for the SRF, whose honorary president he became when the organization was founded in 1968. The organization offered support to film authors struggling with their "freedom of expression during the 1960s,"[114] but also served to solve the confusion regarding how the 1957 law should be put into practice. Conceived during the chaos and enthusiasm of May 1968, this institution addressed perennial problems in French cinema and is still in place today. Bresson's poignant words from the SRF's manifesto have lost none of their relevance and resonance: "The SRF, which is not a unionized group, nor a fee collection society, stands in every place where the moral rights and the freedom of creation are in danger."[115]

Vocation and Profession

The "maniac of truth" is not simply a solipsist or a fanatic; as a creator, he confronts the evolving socio-political constraints of the professional community to which he belonged, and chose to respond to them. Looking closely at the evolution of Bresson's profile over half a century of cinema, one notices that however uncompromising and self-assured his posture might have seemed, he remained mindful that he worked within a community of filmmakers and that his endeavors figured within a collective context. Bresson might have vociferously affirmed the autonomy and singularity of the film *auteur*, and especially his own.[116] Nonetheless, his career demonstrates, in a richly layered and complex way, how the notion of film authorship took root and evolved within the historical context of twentieth-century France. The romanticized figure of the solitary genius, the emergence of the new artist from the tension between the noble world of the "liberal" arts and the amateur sphere of "mechanical" techniques, or the legitimation of select groups and organizations for the protection of the artistic practices, are the most emphatic lines in the story of film authorship.

Authorship in fact has long been linked to vocational singularity. Paul Bénichou describes how French commentators during the eighteenth century begin to oppose the artist to the artisan, to accentuate the importance of artistic vocation over professional endeavor. This led to a "sacralization of the writer"[117] and to a "charismatic" definition of literary activity as fundamentally distinct from any professional constraints. Starting with the Enlightenment and spanning the age of Romanticism, literary pursuit underwent an "anthropological mutation":[118] the poet or the philosopher became agents of a "sacerdotal laity," "modern masters," both chosen prophets and damned souls, providential beings of a superior nature.[119] Within the world of cinema, Bresson's example brilliantly reiterates a persuasion at work throughout the history of authorship in France, starting with Montaigne, accelerating during the eighteenth century, and culminating in the nineteenth-century romantic celebration of the artist.

Parallel to the romantic aggrandizement of artistic vocation, a seemingly opposite tendency had also gained momentum, namely the intense professionalization of artistic activity, particularly in the setting up of societies of authors and the development of legal protections. Originating during the Renaissance and cultivated during the classical age, this tendency stood in opposition both to amateurism (typical of the Ancien Régime) and to pure art trends, which abounded during the nineteenth century.[120] As in the other arts, the configuration and crystallization of the author in French cinema brought together professionalization and an emphasis on vocation. Although this blend of vocation and profession, particularly characteristic of the romantic age of literature, abides in the institution of film authorship, one should not be too hasty to promote cinema to the rank of the arts and neglect its technological status. This is where Bresson's case offers a variation. The institutional autonomy constitutive of literary practices, an inheritance of the "amateur" (rather than lucrative) aura of "liberal arts," did not apply to cinema, which was held up as a visual art by Bresson and his defenders. Bresson's idea of cinema as a "framed vision" rendered it more akin to painting or photography (and he practiced as well as professed both) and, for that reason, more appositely placed within the institution of the "mechanical arts."

Although a fierce advocate of auteurism, Bresson did not believe that the work of the artist lay in rendering conceptual ideas in filmic forms. He praised the Nouvelle Vague filmmakers, but warned against intellectualism.[121] He wanted to work with his hands and considered his films to be objects.[122] In his *Notes*, he paid particular attention to the special type of spectatorial engagement he sought to generate and insisted on the importance of film's material presence. "Your film—let people feel the heart and the soul there, but let it be made like the work of hands."[123] Or elsewhere: "Your film is not made for a stroll with the eyes, but for going right into, for being totally absorbed in."[124] Asked about his place in the community of filmmakers, Bresson used Cocteau's words and spoke of feeling "apart in this terrible trade," relying on the cinematograph as the only available means to fill in the emptiness that comes from not being able to paint. Perhaps, he quipped, "I'd do it better with manual labor." Defending his films as crafted objects rather than conceptual projects did not mean that Bresson thought of himself as an artisan. On the contrary, he had nothing but contempt for "les gens du métier," pedantic individuals studying and making films within the limits of an entertainment industry to which they remained uncritically and blindly beholden. Bresson provides a prime example of the conflation of the man and the œuvre; he was an author who consciously lived at a distance and relished his inner exile, viewing it indeed as a catalyst for his continuing creativity and the signature of his elusive artistry. At the same time, his practice and work offered living proof that without the professional dimension, the film landscape, at least in France, would be shaped by a few privileged artists who idealized the creative process while working under the protection of rich patrons; without the vocational dimension, the film industry would operate as any other lucrative industry.

Often overlooked in philosophical approaches to film, invoked as a defensive strategy by film sociologists,[125] the dynamic generated by the place of artistic vocation amidst the constraints of the profession is essential for any full understanding of film authorship. Although it is an undeniable fact that filmmaking spans the regimes of profession and vocation alike, it is the vocational dimension that, with its blend of "religious sacralization" and artistic inspiration, drives the valorization of work.[126] Film criticism has not been unduly burdened by sensitivity toward the financial difficulties of artistic endeavors, and has relegated the professional dimension of authorship to an issue of secondary importance, if it is considered at all. This dichotomy is spurious, for artistic vocation can only thrive in artistic communities.

Even if Bresson has come to be thought of as a singular and solitary creator, we should not forget that his strategic self-promotion as a film *auteur* emphasized an artistic evolution that started with Les Anges du péché and often made reference to his experience as a prisoner of war. His first feature, *Affaires publiques*, was severely repudiated by Bresson himself, and various accounts (albeit in some cases anecdotal) insist that he fabricated an implacable public image that forbade any return to his activities before his wartime incarceration. But even the somewhat vague reconstitution of his activities during the 1930s at least intimate that he circulated in a variety of artistic circles. In Antony Penrose's memoir about his father, the English Surrealist painter Roland Penrose who collaborated with Bresson on *Affaires publiques*, we find mention of the friendship between the two men, as well as of the close connection between Bresson and Max Ernst.[127] Involved in different artistic pursuits, he also embraced commercial projects such as the fashion photographs of Coco Chanel. Bresson cultivated an eclectic style. Nonetheless, his perfectionism and manic precision were already apparent in these earliest stages of his career.

In his descriptive account of Bresson's activities in the 1930s, Colin Burnett characterizes the director as a "surrealist,"[128] highlighting his penchant for "straddling the disparate milieus of avant-garde and commercial art. In an analysis of his photographs, the pattern of his activities can justifiably be labeled Surrealist, even if his art was not always in that style."[129] Bresson's connection to the Surrealist milieu was in keeping with his exposure to a diverse, multi-modal artistic field, and makes it clear how the access to the status of artist (and author) was in his case mediated by the Surrealist institution. In crucial regards, avant-garde movements of the early twentieth century modeled themselves after the literary and artistic fraternities of Romanticism. The effect was generational; it offered a collective re-enactment of an experience that, at a personal level, might well seem subjective and inconclusive. The community provided by these circles and milieus no doubt contributed to a collective understanding of the artistic endeavor.

These first incidences demonstrated that from its inception Bresson's career spanned both regimes of community and singularity. The organization of the first cine-clubs and the professionalization of film criticism strongly inflected the evolution of film authorship, enabling the emergence of a "modern system" that little by little helped to foster the informal "vocational regime" of "practices abandoned to institutional anomie, marginalized, even eccentric."[130] At the same time, these very practices were valued, emphasized, and exploited by the critics who favored a new embodiment and representation of artistic excellence, an impetus that would push the entire function of film authorship towards something that resembled the romantic conception of the inspired creator. The *politique des auteurs* started as an attempt to emancipate the artist, and eventually succumbed to the very rhetoric that it sought to overcome.

The coexistence of these two regimes was already consolidated in the late 1950s and early 1960s. For the film profession, as noted, a key enabling act of legislation came with the law of 1957. But the generation effect that brought together cinephiles, film critics, and aspiring filmmakers was essential in the constitution of the *auteur* figure and its critical recognition. It provided a most efficient way to live collectively an experience that, at an individual level, could seem purely personal, even more so when the aspiration to singularity tends to become the norm. Members of a generation not only distance themselves from certain traditions in the past; they also share a common experience that is projected onto the canvas of history and forge a "common" identity based on the same references, the same expectations, and the same sensitivities.

As a driving force behind his generation,[131] Godard, it has been suggested, not only became an undisputable *auteur*, but the creator of the *auteur* status. In an article titled "Godard, créateur de statut," the sociologist Nathalie Heinich extends her richly layered explorations of the artist community in nineteenth-century France to the realm of cinema.[132] She argues that the Nouvelle Vague brought a comparable intensity and emphasis to the cinema, fulfilling a quest that had been underway for a long while. According to the French sociologist, only the cinephilic movements of the 1950s and 1960s could sustain the figure of the autonomous artist. In this light, Heinich argues, Godard would inaugurate for the cinema what Foucault spoke of as the "modern age,"[133] confirming thus that in the early 1960s, France would be the only country to truly recognize and promote the status of film *auteur*.

Foregoing the cliquishness and connoisseurship of the cinephilic movements in the 1950s, Bresson's example suggests that what has been deemed the creation of the *Cahiers* critics and their *politique des auteurs* was in fact part of a larger and more complex nexus of forces within French intellectual, artistic, and legal history. We need to consider this wider context if we are to understand fully how filmmakers became raised to the rank of *auteurs* and how film gained the status of a modern art. And it is in this regard that we need to consider Bresson and his work. As the embodiment of artistic originality and uncompromising commitment to "true art," Bresson becomes the guardian of an aristocratic ideal well known within French culture. Cast in a romantic mold, Bresson's figure is coupled with what Heinich identifies as the foremost factor in the legitimation of the artist, namely "the bereavement of the aristocratic ideal."[134]

Bresson admitted to being moved by the "fervor he awakened in the young filmmakers." "I would love to work with young people and have them work, for certain parts, in my place. It would resemble the Renaissance painting studios. I would also feel a continuity, I would have the impression of living on through the others."[135] He might never have had a school, but his influence on the history of French cinema is persistent. Jacques Aumont went as far as to claim that "any French filmmaker whose work is in the least interesting in France owes something to Bresson."[136] In an ironic twist, the problem here was not so much providing a heritage for the heir, but rather finding a suitable filmmaker heir for the great heritage of French culture.

Notes

1. Kent Jones, "Adieu," *Cahiers du cinéma* 543 (February 2000): 32: "Ainsi, le fait que Bresson soit pratiquement né avec le 'siècle du cinéma' et ne lui ait pas survécu, paraît dans l'ordre des choses, comme le coucher du soleil et le lever de la lune."
2. Jean-Michel Frodon, "Bresson et la beauté du monde: un des plus grands artistes de ce siècle est mort," *Le Monde* (18 December 1999) :1.
3. Seán Burke, *The Death and Return of the Author: Criticism and Subjectivity in Barthes, Foucault and Derrida* (Edinburgh: Edinburgh University Press, 1998), xiii.

4. Frodon, "Bresson et la beauté du monde."
5. (No author) *Australian* (3 January 2000): 16.
6. Amy Taubin, "Remembering a Master of Precise Gesture and Cinematic Emotion," *The Village Voice* (4 January 2000):103.
7. Brian Baxter, "Cinematic Genius in Search of Inner Passion and Complexity," *The Guardian* (22 December 1999).
8. Jim Hoberman, "Saints and Sinners," *The Village Voice* (26 December 1999): 59.
9. Roland Barthes, "On est entré avec lui dans le cinéma pur," *Le Monde* (23 December 1999): 31.
10. Luigi Paini, "E morto Robert Bresson: il cinema come continua ricerca della perfezione," *Sole 24 Ore* (22 December 1999): 7.
11. Louis Skorecki, "Prophète à son insu," *Libération* (22 December 1999): 3.
12. Paul Schrader, "Robert Bresson: In Memoriam," *The Village Voice* (11 January 2000): 103.
13. Paul Schrader, *Transcendental Style in Film: Ozu, Bresson, Dreyer* (Berkeley: University of California Press, 1972), 82–86.
14. Ibid., 83.
15. Ibid., 83, my emphasis.
16. Nicole Brenez et al., "Robert Bresson—A Symposium," in *Robert Bresson (Revised)*, ed. James Quandt (Toronto: TIFF Cinémathèque, 2011), 624–25.
17. Nathalie Heinich's sociological study on the formation of artist communities and the construction of the notion of "artist" after the French Revolution identifies three central models: the saint, the genius, and the hero. See *L'Élite artiste: excellence et singularité en régime démocratique* (Paris: Gallimard, 2005).
18. Schrader, *Transcendental Style in Film*, 87.
19. In addition to Schrader's well-known study, see Susan Sontag, "Spiritual Style in the Work of Robert Bresson," in *Against Interpretation* (New York: Farrar, Straus & Giroux, 1966), 177–84. See also Amédée Ayfre, *Conversion aux images? Les Images et Dieu, les images et l'homme* (Paris: Editions du Cerf, 1964). See the more recent Joseph Cunneen, *Robert Bresson: A Spiritual Style in Film* (New York, London: Continuum, 2003).
20. René Prédal, *Robert Bresson: L'Aventure intérieure* (Paris: L'avant-scène cinéma, 1992), translated in *Robert Bresson (Revised)*, 77.
21. Ibid., 77.
22. Brenez, "Robert Bresson—A Symposium," 626.
23. Schrader, *Transcendental Style in Film*, 87.
24. Brenez, "Robert Bresson—A Symposium," 626.
25. See Brian Price, *Neither God Nor Master: Robert Bresson & Radical Politics* (Minneapolis: University of Minnesota Press, 2011).
26. See Sontag, "Spiritual Style in the Work of Robert Bresson." See also Ayfre, *Conversion aux images?*.
27. Agnès's words in *Les Dames du Bois de Boulogne*, "Je lutte," are often quoted, including by Godard in his *Histoire(s) du cinéma*.
28. Schrader, "Robert Bresson: In Memoriam," 103.
29. Ibid., 100: "In 1972 Robert Bresson, responding to my recently published book, *Transcendental Style in Film: Ozu, Bresson, Dreyer*, wrote me, 'I have always been surprised not to recognize myself in the image formed by those who are really interested in me'."
30. Brenez, "Robert Bresson—A Symposium," 627.

31. See the collection of interviews, *Robert Bresson par Robert Bresson: Entretiens (1943-1983)*, ed. Mylène Bresson (Paris: Flammarion, 2013).
32. Robert Bresson, *Notes on the Cinematograph*, trans. Jonathan Griffin (London: Quartet Books, 1986), 1.
33. Ibid., 1.
34. Ibid, 9.
35. Ibid., 55 and also 10: "No part of the unexpected which is not secretly expected by you."
36. Ibid., 17.
37. Jacques Aumont, *Les Théories des cinéastes* (Paris: Nathan Cinéma, 1999), 12: "Bresson et la rencontre."
38. Ibid., 13: "Un éclair de vérité sur le réel."
39. Bresson, *Notes*, 20.
40. Ibid., 18.
41. Ibid., 33, in capitals in the original.
42. Michel Delahaye and Jean-Luc Godard, "La Question: Entretien avec Robert Bresson," *Cahiers du cinéma* 178 (May 1966): 26–35.
43. Bresson, *Notes*, 48.
44. Ibid., 13, in italics in the original.
45. Ibid., 38. Cf. the French edition, *Notes sur le cinématographe* (Paris: Gallimard, 1975), 81.
46. Ibid., 42.
47. See, for instance, Balzac's *The Unknown Masterpiece* or Borges's *The Yellow Rose*.
48. "Une mise en scène n'est pas un art," *Cahiers du cinéma* (February 2000). See also Robert Bresson, "L'art n'est pas un luxe, mais un besoin vital," *Le Monde* (11 November 1971).
49. Bresson, *Notes*, 54.
50. Ibid., 39. See the French version, 82: "Faire apparaître ce qui sans toi ne serait jamais vu."
51. Ibid., 61.
52. See the interview broadcast on the TV show *Le Masque et la plume*, France Inter (9 January 1960), transcription in *Bresson par Bresson*, 94: "Je voudrais que le spectateur assiste à une vraie naissance et non pas à quelque chose qui a déjà eu lieu, une naissance qui a déjà eu lieu."
53. Jacques Doniol-Valcroze and Jean-Luc Godard, "Entretien avec Robert Bresson," *Cahiers du cinéma* 104 (February 1960), reprinted in *Bresson par Bresson*, 86.
54. François-Régis Bastide, "Interview avec Robert Bresson," *Le Masque et la plume*, France Inter (30 April 1966) in *Bresson par Bresson*, 163.
55. Georges Sadoul, "Conversation plutôt qu'interview avec Robert Bresson sur *Mouchette*," *Les Lettres françaises* (6 March 1967), reprinted in *Bresson par Bresson*, 236: "On cueille le rare, ce qui se produit à la seconde même et ne se reproduira plus."
56. "Propos recueillis par Pierre Montaigne," *Le Figaro* (24 September 1974), reprinted in *Bresson par Bresson*, 288: "Je ne me prends pas pour Dieu, mais il est vrai qu'il me faut dominer une création comportant bien des choses visibles et invisibles. Cela avec une certaine tendresse pour mes personnages et ce qu'ils incarnent."
57. *Le Masque et la plume*, France Inter (22 March 1975), transcribed in *Bresson par Bresson*, 305: "et que cette caméra, qui est une loupe, traverse les visages et arrive, si on fait très attention, à vraiment pénétrer au fond des gens, à arriver à ce cœur du cœur dont parle Proust et qu'il faut essayer d'atteindre. ... Quand on me juge, on me juge exactement sur le même plan que si j'étais metteur en scène. Je ne suis pas metteur en scène, je ne fais pas de scène. Je suis cinéaste, si vous voulez, mais je ne dirige pas les acteurs, c'est moi que je dirige et mes

contacts avec mes modèles sont des contacts télépathiques. C'est une espèce de divination. Divination à laquelle j'arrive grâce à ces deux appareils que sont la caméra et le magnétophone."

58. Michael Haneke, "Terror and Utopia of Form Addicted to Truth: A Film Story about Robert Bresson's *Au hasard Balthazar*," in *Robert Bresson (Revised)*, 389. Cf. Haneke's comments about Bresson's use of models: "That notwithstanding, the 'non-acting' of his always painstakingly, even lovingly chosen amateurs, the monotony of their manner of talking and moving, their presence—reduced to mere existence—was and is a liberating experience (far more than the casual 'naturalness' of the young actors in the cerebral fireworks and more intellectual jokes of his younger colleague Godard). It gave back to the people in front of the camera their dignity: no one had to pretend any more to make visible emotions that, because acted—could only be a lie anyway. It had struck me as obscene to watch an actor portray, with dramatic fury, someone suffering or dying—it robbed those who were truly suffering and dying of their last possession: the truth. And it robbed the viewers of this professional reproduction of their most precious possession as viewer: their imagination. They were forced into the humiliating perspective of a voyeur at the keyhole who has no choice but to feel what is being felt for him and think what is being thought… The lie that pretense is reality has become the trademark of cinema—one of the most profitable in the annals of business."
59. Roland Monod, "En travaillant avec Robert Bresson," *Cahiers du cinéma* 64 (November 1956): 16–20.
60. "Quand je me trouve devant un interprète, plus sa puissance d'expression augmente, plus la mienne diminue. Or ce qui m'importe, c'est de m'exprimer, et non pas que lui s'exprime." See "Une mise en scène n'est pas un art," 5.
61. Michel Maingois, "Le Graal, le moteur, par en dessous de l'action," *Zoom* (November 1974), reprinted in *Bresson par Bresson*, 296: "Une espèce de théâtre photographié, où il est difficile pour le metteur en scène d'imposer sa volonté."
62. Delahaye and Godard, "La Question": "Pour moi l'improvisation est à la base de la création au cinéma." See also the interview on *The Trial of Joan of Arc*, in *Le Masque et la plume*, France Inter (2 June 1962), reprinted in *Bresson par Bresson*, 117: "Je crois beaucoup à l'improvisation, mais dans un cadre très prémédité, très strict."
63. Bresson, *Notes*, 4.
64. Q&A with Bresson in 1974 at a screening of *Lancelot du Lac*, reprinted in *Bresson par Bresson*, 282.
65. Bresson, *Notes*, 27.
66. Roger Stéphane, Louis Malle, Marguerite Duras, Jean-Luc Godard, and François Reichenbach, "Pour le plaisir: table ronde autour de *Au hasard Balthazar*," *Cinéma*, ORTF (11 May 1966), reprinted in *Bresson par Bresson*, 202: "C'est un curieux mélange, c'est un mélange d'eux et de moi, une espèce de lumière venant d'eux sur moi et de moi allant à eux, c'est une espèce d'amalgame obtenu non pas par une direction d'acteur ou par une mise en scène, mais par une sorte de divination, d'accord réciproque, une espèce d'amitié sur toutes choses, mais absolument pas, je le répète, de direction d'acteur, pas de mise en scène."
67. Thomas Hobbes, *Leviathan* (London: Penguin, 1995), 218.
68. Two major reasons stand behind Bresson's comparison of himself to the painter: 1) he is acting out against the dominant attitude that considered the scriptwriter as the legal and publicly recognized author; and 2) he takes recourse to a classical model, at work in the 1920 and 1930s, now obscured, but whose legacy he embraces. This alignment also provides a way

of separating himself from the Nouvelle Vague generation; secretly he aspires to be a leader and not one of them.
69. Delahaye and Godard, "La Question," translated as "The Question", reprinted in *Robert Bresson (Revised)*, 635. For the original French text, see *Bresson par Bresson*, 174: "L'image que vous avez en vue, il faut la prévoir, c'est-à-dire la voir à l'avance, la voir littéralement sur l'écran (en tenant compte du fait qu'il risque d'y avoir un décalage, et même une différence totale, entre ce que vous voyez et ce que vous aurez) et cette image, il faut la faire exactement comme vous désirez la voir, comme vous la voyez en fermant les yeux."
70. Michel Ciment, "I Seek Not Description But Vision: Robert Bresson on *L'Argent*," in *Robert Bresson (Revised)*, 509.
71. Bresson, *Notes*, 70: "Talking of automatism, this also from Montaigne: We cannot command our haire to stand on end; nor our skinne to startle for desire or feare. Our hands are often carried where we direct them not."
72. More than forty years earlier, Maurice Tourneur had invoked the figure of the painter to illustrate the complexities of the relationship between filmmakers and producers. See "Tourneur defends director control," a letter addressed to American producers, published in *Variety* on 28 June 1923: "The director is to the motion picture what the artist is to the painting."
73. Jean-Pierre Jeancolas, Jean-Jacques Meusy, and Vincent Pinel, *L'Auteur du film: description d'un combat* (Paris: SACD; Arles: Actes Sud, 1996), 119: "L'histoire du cinéma moderne, qu'on la fasse commencer à 1940 ou à la fin de la guerre, est, entre autres, celle où se précise, particulièrement en France, une figure de l'auteur responsable et reconnu comme tel par la loi. Cet auteur se définit d'une manière objective dans sa relation à l'œuvre (ou au film) et de manière conflictuelle souvent, dans sa relation au producteur."
74. *Robert Bresson: Éloge*, ed. Philippe Arnaud (Milan/ Paris: Cinémathèque Française/Mazzotta, 1997), 35. The sentence has a double meaning in French: "Bresson is apart in this terrible trade" as well as "Bresson is on his own in this terrible profession."
75. "Framed: James Quandt on Robert Bresson's *L'Argent*," *Artforum* 51.3 (November 2012).
76. "Entretien avec Robert Bresson, par Serge Daney et Serge Toubiana," *Cahiers du cinéma* 348–349 (June–July 1983), reprinted in *Bresson par Bresson*, 334.
77. Bresson's *Genesis*, a film to be produced by Dino De Laurentiis, would become John Huston's *The Bible*.
78. Michel Ciment, "The Poetry of Precision," *American Film* (October 1983), reprinted in *Bresson par Bresson*, 328.
79. "Entretien avec Robert Bresson, par Serge Daney et Serge Toubiana," In *Bresson par Bresson*, 334.
80. Yvonne Baby, "Entretien avec Robert Bresson," *Le Monde* (11 November 1971), reprinted in *Bresson par Bresson*, 263.
81. Robert Bresson, "'Il faut un auteur!' Enquête sur le cinéma français," *Je suis partout* (10 September 1943): "Nous poussons l'amour du style jusqu'à la manie: le film est le type même de l'œuvre qui réclame un style, il faut un auteur, une écriture. L'auteur écrit sur l'écran, s'exprime au moyen de plans photographiques de durées variables, d'angles de prises de vues variables. Pour un auteur digne de ce nom, un choix s'impose, dicté par ses calculs ou son instinct, et non par le hasard."
82. "Entretien avec Robert Bresson," *Unifrance Film* 45 (December 1957), reprinted in *Bresson par Bresson*, 70: "Pourtant, il faudra bien un jour arriver à s'exprimer par le cinématographe

comme on s'exprime par le pinceau ou par la plume. Un film doit être l'œuvre d'un seul et faire entrer le public dans le monde de ce seul, je veux dire dans un monde qui lui est propre."
83. Marc Cérisuelo, "Cinéphilie," in *Fondus enchaînés: Essais de poétique du cinéma* (Paris: Seuil, 2012), 135–45.
84. Cf. Colin Burnett, "Bresson in the 1930s: Photography, Cinema, Milieu," in *Robert Bresson (Revised)*, ed. James Quandt (Toronto: TIFF Cinémathèque, 2011).
85. Delahaye and Godard, "The Question," in *Robert Bresson (Revised)*, 635–36.
86. See Anne Wiazemsky, *Jeune fille* (Paris: Gallimard, 2007).
87. Delahaye and Godard, "The Question," 636.
88. Ibid., 636.
89. Ibid., 644: "So, in the composition of a shot, of a sequence, at first there is the rhythm. But the composition ought not be premeditated, it ought to be purely intuitive. For example, it arises especially when we shoot out of doors, and when we approach a setting absolutely unknown the day before. In the face of novelty, we must improvise. That is what is very good: the necessity to find, and quickly, a new equilibrium for the shot that we are making. To sum up: I do not believe in too long reflection there either. Reflection reduces things to being no longer anything but the execution of a shot. Things must happen impulsively."
90. Ibid., 640.
91. Ibid., 641.
92. André Bazin, "De la politique des auteurs," in *La Politique des auteurs: Les Textes*, ed. Antoine De Baecque and Gabrielle Lucantonio (Paris: Cahiers du cinéma, 2001), 116.
93. Ibid., 112: "Ce concept d'auteur s'oppose donc par conséquent à la distinction auteur-sujet parce qu'être digne d'entrer dans le cénacle des auteurs implique davantage que la mise en valeur d'une matière première. Dans une certaine mesure au moins, l'auteur est toujours à lui-même son sujet. Quel que soit le scénario, c'est toujours la même histoire qu'il nous conte."
94. Barthélémy Amengual in "Eric Rohmer répond à Barthélémy Amengual," in *La Politique des auteurs: Les Textes*, ed. Antoine De Baecque and Gabrielle Lucantonio (Paris: Cahiers du cinéma, 2001), 118.
95. Ibid., 120.
96. Eric Rohmer's response to Amengual in *La Politique des auteurs: Les Textes*, 121: "Dans tous les domaines, aujourd'hui, peinture, musique, littérature, la politique des morceaux choisis cède le pas à celle des œuvres complètes. Ce qui reste, ce ne sont pas des œuvres, mais des auteurs, et, au cinéma, à lire les programmes des ciné-clubs et des cinémathèques, je gage qu'il n'en sera, à tort ou à raison, pas autrement. Le nom de metteur en scène prend, sur les affiches, la place d'honneur, et c'est justice. Je sais que 'l'absolue paternité du moindre détail' ne lui est pas accordée en même temps que sa carte professionnelle. A lui de la conquérir et nous constatons qu'il y parvient, s'il a un minimum de caractère, d'autorité, de génie."
97. Cf. the minutes of the meeting of the SACD commission, 3 May 1939.
98. Cf. minutes of the meeting of the SACD commission, 11 October 1939.
99. See Robert Paxton, *La France de Vichy* (Paris: Seuil, 1973), 204–10: the reorganization of cinema by the laws of Vichy found a legal basis in the law of 16 August 1940 concerning the "provisory organization of industrial production." The COIC (Comité d'organisation de l'industrie cinématographique), was established by the law of 26 October 1940, and under the directorship of Raoul Ploquin.
100. As early as 1946, the CNC enjoyed a non-commercial status.

101. See Frédéric Gimello-Mesplomb, "Objectif 49 et le Festival du film maudit au-delà de la légende," in *Objectif 49: Cocteau et la nouvelle avant-garde* (Paris: Séguier, 2013), 11–19.
102. Robert Bresson, "Le Festival du film maudit," in *Bresson par Bresson*, 43: "Auxquels le cinéma doit beaucoup, je dirai même tout, et que Cocteau, par analogie avec ce qu'on appelle les 'poètes maudits,' a appelés les *films maudits*."
103. See *Revue Internationale du Droit d'Auteur* 19 (April 1958), a special issue devoted to the law of 1957.
104. The case of Beaumarchais's disagreement with the actors' interpretation of his plays at the Comédie Française led to his defense at the Assembly (L'Assemblée Constituante) by the deputy Le Chapelier who emphatically declared on 19 July 1791 that "La plus sacrée, la plus inattaquable et la plus personnelle des propriétés est l'ouvrage de la pensée de l'écrivain."
105. Cf. the cases of Godard's *Le Petit soldat* or Rivette's *La Religieuse*.
106. Quoted in *Le Film Français* (5 July 1968), referred to in Jeancolas, Meusy, and Pinel, *L'Auteur du film*, 155: "Nous avons remporté une grande victoire: nous sommes plus de cent. Nous disposons d'une arme très forte, car les autres ont besoin de nous alors que nous n'avons pas besoin d'eux. Quelque chose commence!"
107. Marcel Pagnol, Letter to Raymond Bernard (AAF). Quoted in Jeancolas, Meusy, and Pinel, *L'Auteur du film*, 131. In a private letter to Prévert, Pagnol writes: "Lorsque nous dénions au metteur en scène la qualité d'auteur, ce n'est pas à l'homme que nous refusons cette qualité, c'est à sa fonction. Il est bien évident que Marcel Carné ou Jean Renoir, s'ils écrivent le manuscrit d'un film, seront des auteurs, et nous les recevrons avec tous les honneurs dus à leur talent… S'ils réalisent le manuscrit d'un autre, ils ne sont que des exécutants, comparables aux chefs d'orchestre. Nous n'avons aucun mépris pour les metteurs en scène, bien au contraire. Jean Renoir, René Clair, Duvivier, Carné ont fait beaucoup pour l'art français. Mais s'ils ont besoin du manuscrit d'un autre, ils ne sont que des réalisateurs, et non pas des auteurs. Leur création est secondaire, ils ne peuvent la commencer avant que l'auteur n'ait fini la sienne. L'auteur est donc la source et l'origine de l'œuvre commune. Le metteur en scène est le chef inspiré des exécutants. Ils sont d'ailleurs inscrits au Syndicat des techniciens, ce qui me paraît, en somme, légitime. Nous devons vivre avec eux en bonne intelligence, et même en parfaite amitié. Mais songez à ceci: sans eux, nos films seraient moins bons. Sans nous, leurs films ne seraient pas. Or ils prétendent prendre notre place, ce n'est pas juste."
108. Lo Duca, "Un acte de foi," *Cahiers du cinéma* 1 (April 1951): 47: "Bresson domine toutes les composantes du film."
109. "Les Rythmes d'un film doivent être comme les battements d'un cœur," interview in *L'Express* (23 December 1959), reprinted in *Bresson par Bresson*, 79.
110. Bresson, *Notes*, 72.
111. Ibid., 1.
112. Pierre Ajamé, "Le Cinéma selon Bresson," *Les Nouvelles littéraires* (26 May 1966), reprinted in *Bresson par Bresson*, 216: "Il faut laisser le film prendre son visage et regarder ce visage dans tous les sens, et essayer de suivre ce qu'il devient quand il se forme. Tandis que les films qui sont des exécutions de plans préconçus ne sont au fond et ne seront jamais que de l'artisanat."
113. Yves Kovacs, "Entretien avec Robert Bresson," *Cahiers du cinéma* 140 (May 1963), reprinted in *Bresson par Bresson*, 126: "La croyance qu'il n'existe qu'une seule et unique vision des choses est absurde. Les méthodes actuelles de films à la chaîne encouragent cette absurdité. Il faudrait qu'il y ait de moins en moins de metteurs en scène et de plus en plus d'auteurs de

films. Il y en a parmi les jeunes. C'est sur eux qu'il faut miser. Je crois à l'avenir des films faits en dehors de la production officielle, avec des appareils (caméra et magnétophone) peu coûteux, loin des studios terriblement contagieux."

114. In addition to the return of "la censure des maires," the "scandals" animated debates, for example the one around Rivette's *La Religieuse*, forbidden by the minister Yvon Bourges in 1966, and the response formulated by the "Manifeste des 1789" signed by the majority of active filmmakers. The same treatment is reserved for many of the so-called "political" films, like Godard's *Le Petit soldat* or Chris Marker's *iCuba Si!*.
115. My translation: "La SRF, qui n'est ni un syndicat ni une société de perception, est partout où le droit moral et la liberté de création sont en danger."
116. In an interview, Bresson quotes Cocteau and claims that he feels "apart" in the world of cinema.
117. Paul Bénichou, *Le Sacre de l'écrivain. 1750-1830. Essai sur l'avènement d'un pouvoir spirituel laïc dans la France moderne* (Paris: José Corti, 1996).
118. Daniel Fabre, "Le Corps pathétique de l'écrivain," *Gradhiva* 25 (1999): 2, quoted in Heinich, *L'Élite artiste*, 76.
119. The ultimate figure would be Nietzsche's Zarathustra. See Heinich, *L'Élite artiste*, 75–77.
120. This tendency in the literary arts culminated with the refinement of copyrights and the creation in 1838 of the Société des Gens de Lettres (SGL), which was open to all authors.
121. François-Régis Bastide, Interview with Robert Bresson, in *Le Masque et la plume*, France Inter (2 June 1962), transcribed in *Bresson par Bresson*, 118: "Je pense qu'il faut d'abord travailler et ensuite réfléchir. Il ne faut pas faire l'inverse."
122. Yvonne Baby, "Entretien avec Robert Bresson," *Le Monde* (11 November 1971), reprinted in *Bresson par Bresson*, 265: "Je souffre de ne pas travailler avec mes mains. J'aime regarder mes films comme des objets."
123. Bresson, *Notes*, 15.
124. Ibid., 47.
125. See, for example, the sociological perspectives of film theorists such as Laurent Jullier or Jean-Pierre Esquénazi.
126. Heinich, *L'Élite artiste*, 79.
127. Antony Penrose, *Roland Penrose, the Friendly Surrealist* (Munich, New York: Prestel, 2001).
128. See Burnett, "Bresson in the 1930s," 212.
129. Ibid., 215. Of course, Burnett's notions of "low" and "high" culture are categories of more recent vintage; Burnett applies them retrospectively and, in so doing, accounts for the formal qualities of an individual case, but ignores the sociological context.
130. Heinich, *L'Élite artiste*, 66.
131. See for example Godard's statements in *Jean-Luc Godard par Jean-Luc Godard*, ed. Alain Bergala, rev. edn (Paris: Editions de l'étoile, 1998), 124: "Hé bien, non! Le cinéma n'est pas un métier. C'est un art. Ce n'est pas une équipe. On est toujours seul; sur le plateau comme devant la page blanche."
132. A sociological study of the aesthetic, economical, and political forces that led to the formation and legitimation of the artist-function after the French Revolution, *L'Élite artiste* investigated the changes brought about in the domain of the arts during the nineteenth-century French birth of the democratic Republic.
133. Nathalie Heinich, "Godard, créateur de statut," in *Godard et le métier d'artiste*, ed. Gilles Delavaud and Jean-Pierre Esquénazi (Paris: L'Harmattan, 2001), 307: "Une fonction,

autrement dit la résultante d'un certain nombre d'opérations permettant d'affecter à un être la qualité d'auteur: opérations qu'il revient aux sciences sociales de décrire, de façon à déterminer ce qu'est, pour une culture donnée, un auteur, dans toute la variabilité de cette notion. ... le cinéma, ayant dû attendre au moins une génération pour attirer un public autre que populaire, dut attendre encore plus longtemps pour que la notion d'auteur y trouve véritablement sa place. Ce cadre n'a rien de mystérieux, et nous le connaissons tous: il s'agit de la conjonction de la position de critique et de la position de réalisateur, ou encore, plus généralement, du rôle de l'intellectuel et du rôle du créateur."

134. Heinich, *L'Élite artiste*, 139: "Le deuil de l'idéal aristocratique."
135. Ajame, "Le cinéma selon Bresson".
136. Aumont, *Les Théories des cinéastes*, 46.

CHAPTER TWO
An Elusive Style

> Bresson is a dangerous master for his imitators.
> — Luc Moullet, "Blue Collar Dandy"

A Singular Community

With a discourse inflected by mourning, the obituaries written for Bresson emphasized the importance of his legacy and positioned the filmmaker as the father of a province called *The Cinematograph*. According to Thierry Jousse, Bresson and Hitchcock are the two filmmakers who have had the most profound influence on modern film and contemporary cinema. Despite their different resolves and approaches, they both "*invented* a communication form, abstract and subtle."[1] Bresson's importance for the history of cinema, cautions Kent Jones in his homage to the late film director, "cannot be underestimated, but it can be mischaracterized." In fact, he continues, "I think that Bresson imbued filmmakers like Assayas, Denis, and the Dardenne Brothers with a faith in the material world to reveal itself through juxtapositions rather than rhetorical enhancements."[2]

In the same vein, Thierry Jousse[3] suggests that Bresson's formal influence, manifest in his inimitable deployment of ellipsis and fragmentation as well as the subtle use of sound and a fundamentally minimalist approach to *mise-en-scène*, is less significant than the "moral" impact he had on generations of directors. The testaments gathered in the special issue of *Cahiers du cinéma* to celebrate Bresson's career draw the portrait of an artist who enticed and taught filmmakers to have the courage of their aesthetic convictions, to develop a responsible attitude toward the image and a style of their own.[4] "Bresson's posterity is vast and complex," estimates Jousse:

> In French cinema, his influence is felt very early on, in filmmakers like Melville, though one might also argue the opposite. But it is undoubtedly during the Nouvelle Vague that Bresson's shadow started to haunt French cinema. Bresson's influence on the Nouvelle Vague is not only formal, but also, and especially, moral. In a certain sense, Bresson demands that his disciples create their own form.[5]

Reevaluating the history of French cinema, Jousse concludes that in the evolution of *auteur* cinema, "along with Renoir, Bresson is, for the French filmmakers at least, the most essential link in the chain."

Echoing his *Cahiers* colleague, *Positif*'s Michel Ciment believes that "there have always been in the French cinema two great movements, the source Renoir, and the source Bresson. Whatever one might think or say, there are none else."[6] The formal Bressonian thread woven into the texture of French film history stipulated cinema as writing.[7] Ciment goes even further in his homage, arguing that Bresson appends his signature on his œuvre by declaring his auctorial intentions: "The entire notion of *auteur cinema* ensues from here, to Antonioni, to Godard, to Wenders. Not that there weren't auteurs before, but they would be so without premeditation, proving the concept as it was taking place."[8] The implication is not just that Bresson founded a Bressonian model of filmmaking, but that he provided the defining embodiment of auteurism in cinema. This extreme interpretation points to Bresson's example as the prototype for an *auteur*. Bresson occupies the "transdiscursive" position of an author of "a tradition or a discipline within which new books [in this case, films] and authors can proliferate,"[9] as demonstrated by Foucault's conceptual framework evoked in the introduction, a framework that positions Marx and Freud as the transdiscursive authors in the realm of theory. Although the eulogistic tone of tributes like those by Michel Ciment, Thierry Jousse, or Kent Jones are functions of a solemn occasion, it is nonetheless tempting to examine more closely both the question of legacy and its rhetoric.

Indebted to Bresson and openly acknowledging his influence, filmmakers as diverse as Jean Eustache, Bruno Dumont, Monte Hellman, Andrei Tarkovski, Louis Malle, R.W. Fassbinder, Béla Tarr, Maurice Pialat, Jean-Marie Straub, Chantal Akerman, Philippe Garrel, and Lucrecia Martel, to name just a few, have nonetheless fashioned their own singular cinemas and gained recognition as *auteurs*. Bresson's idiosyncratic approach has been conducive to emulation and at the same time has enabled and encouraged others to develop a personal and authentic cinema. How does such an intransigent and imposing style impress itself on formed personalities and independent minds, even on baroque and histrionic sensibilities? How might these different forms of deference help us to better understand Bresson's own cinema and the place it has come to occupy in the medium's history? These kinds of questions might assist us in comprehending how the reverence for an *auteur* role model also serves to legitimate new creators as they seek to join the community of film professionals. The resonance of Bresson is undeniable; nonetheless, the terms of his impact on other artists deserve more careful scrutiny and qualification.

With its focus on *mise-en-scène* that both exposes and fosters an *auteur*'s vision of the world, classical auteurism emphasizes the artist's individuality and ambition to negotiate and overcome industrial and technological challenges. The *auteur* manages to affirm a distinct view of the world in spite of, even in opposition to, the collective nature of film production; it is the individual and individualized quality of the director that defines his very humanity and style and differentiates him from his peers. The campaign for the aesthetic legitimation of cinema relied heavily on each individual author's immanence, and on the emancipatory potential of this individuality. The French philosopher Jean-Luc Nancy reminds us how "some see in [the individual's] invention Europe's incontrovertible merit of having shown the world the sole path to emancipation from tyranny and the norm by which to measure all our collective or communitarian undertakings."[10] But just as we conceive of the individual as a foundation for emancipation, we run the risk of overlooking that he is "the stumbling block to a thinking of a community." Moreover, the individual "is merely the residue of the experience of the dissolution of community. By its nature the individual reveals that it is the abstract result of a decomposition."[11] How can this very individual provide the foundation for the formation of a community, even if it is a community of singularities?

The discourse of film authorship is mined with unresolved contradictions that inform and complicate our understanding of communities. That the concepts of individual and individuality have had such a strong influence on our understanding of film history becomes especially clear when one sets out to disentangle the complexities intrinsic to the culture of authorship. The previous chapter examined the role of an individual's authority in establishing cinema as a legitimate art form, focusing on constellations of layers that made Bresson an author figure. The chapter attempted to elucidate the operations that led to Bresson's canonization as an entity comparable to what Nancy calls a "figure of immanence, the absolutely detached for-itself, taken as origin and as certainty."[12] Despite the widespread persuasion that the "real" person of an artist is of little interest in any understanding of his or her work, discourses of authorship (including obituaries and biographies) have a propensity to replace disappeared individuals with an "*operative immortality*"[13] that passes into their works. In this sense, whenever the question of legacy comes into play in the formation of authorship, it mainly serves to reinforce the status of the individual-subject. The author gets separated from the community and at the same time becomes the standard for the constitution of that very same community. Bresson's case is particularly poignant because his status as an *auteur* crosses the temporal and national borders of film production, complicating our understanding of how influence and legacy function within the culture of authorship.

Film criticism operates on the basis of the singularity of film *auteurs*. Speaking about Bresson, Eric Rohmer once said that he "eludes all classification" ("Bresson se dérobe à tout classement"). In his glowing review of *A Man Escaped* from 1956, he went on to extol the French director's individuality. "Robert Bresson is not a master, but an example," insisted Rohmer:

> It is not that he holds off theories, quite the contrary: his intentions are clear and come across so sharply in his work that one does not need any further commentary. The first of these ideas is that cinema is a difficult, rigorous art, fervent about perfection. Bresson shows no disdain for the audience, who should simply be as demanding as the filmmaker. It is essential to rid oneself of the many unfortunate habits, sequels of the theater whose scales smear the screen. The cinematographic art has not yet found its own (vrai) voice, its true nature.[14]

Not only was Bresson praised for distilling a pure, individual style of his own, rigorous and uncompromising, but for individualizing the art of cinema and keeping it from the influence of other arts. Like Bazin, whose essay "*Le Journal d'un curé de campagne* and the Stylistics of Robert Bresson" relied on Bresson's work in order to make an assessment of cinema's relationship to the other arts, Rohmer praised the individualized aesthetics for its "irrefutable purity," its ability to instill in viewers a love for the medium and to reveal a cinematic beauty that had previously not seemed visible.[15] We have grown accustomed to the markedly hagiographic tone of Bresson criticism. Rohmer's praise only differs from that of others insofar as it already extended Bresson's importance beyond his body of work. More precisely, it identifies the presence of this elusive Bressonian *je-ne-sais-quoi* "in that or other film that we love, coming from Europe or Hollywood," which prompts the critic to exclaim "*C'est du Bresson*, which is to say that the author broke with a certain flashiness, resolutely rejected an indulgence from which we would wish to abstain."[16]

As much as Rohmer's panegyric employs the rhetoric of the *politique des auteurs*, hallowing the singularity of the director's vision of the world and the rigor of his approach, it also suggests that Bressonianism provides a moral attitude towards the image. Despite the fulsome praise of a "mythical Bresson," Rohmer's tribute grants a sense of how individual style becomes operative within the ethics of the image. In Rohmer's analysis, formal and rhetorical enhancements only prompt a "Bressonian" style when they are part of a singular vision (meaning both individual and original). As it gathers shape and assumes substance, such a vision furthers the emancipation of the art of a cinema not yet mature and autonomous, at the same time shaping the viewer's attitude towards the medium. It is within this larger dynamic of revealing cinema's artistic possibilities that we are to understand Bresson's systematic avoidance of commonplaces, the gravity of the "brief tone, without the awkwardness and the guttural pronunciation of the professional speaker," the "melody of familiar sounds, this whisper of silence," as well as the way in which the director painstakingly fills "time that others can only inflate with waiting." The author's singular earmarks, however, cannot be simply isolated and replicated. In the case of the Bressonians, how are we to account for the ways in which their deference to Bresson's example prompted them to locate and promote their own singularity? How might a particular style transcend the limits of its indivisibility, its individuality, and bring together a community?

"Style: Whatever Is Not Technique"

Since Bresson's work is deemed to be so exemplary, reducing its singular quality to a reusable signature or a simple formula would invalidate the earnestness of his status. For his example to be so striking, Bresson's importance would have to transcend the limits and limitations of his style, providing a model of creative rigor and aesthetic purity, revealing new possibilities for an art still in search of its own place in the realm of aesthetics. More than the cultivation of a personal style, it is Bresson's agenda to free the cinematograph from the influence of other arts that earned him the reputation of an intransigent author. Bresson developed a strict attitude towards the medium and affirmed his own style, manifesting a "faith in the material world" and a desire to redeem it, attributes that Kent Jones later considered to be essential to any full understanding of Bresson's legacy.

In Bresson's inimitable and idiosyncratic formulation, the cinematograph is "a new way of writing, therefore of feeling," "a writing with images in movement and with sounds."[17] Seemingly straightforward, these sentences assume enhanced significance in the epigraph of *Pickpocket* (1959): "The style of this film is not that of a thriller. *Using images and sounds,* the *author* of this film strives to express the nightmare of a young man" (my emphasis). The painstaking choreography of the following sequence constitutes one of the most impressive *tours de force* in the history of cinema. "Dig into your sensation. Look at what there is within," urges Bresson in his *Notes*. "Don't analyze it with words. *Translate* it into sister images, into equivalent sounds. The clearer it is, the more your style affirms itself. (Style: whatever is not technique.)"[18] With their light phenomenological flavoring,[19] these lines bear out the elusive distinction between "style" and "technique." Slippery and difficult to grasp, it is invoked by the filmmaker in order to individualize his own method. This form of self-commentary serves Bresson's purpose to affirm his *autoritas*, and should also be considered as part of a deliberate process of self-exegesis and self-promotion that goes back to the Renaissance.[20] In Bresson's circumscribed case, such guides could be seen to function as a scaffold for the monument he intended to build; once he "finds" his own style, to repeat Louis Malle's words,[21] he will be less adamant about his principles and will allow for spontaneous explorations and even detours.

To be sure, the conceptual demarcation between style and technique is anything but straightforward. How, indeed, are we to explain the relation between style and technique? In David Bordwell's definition, for example, the two concepts are inextricably bound. For him style is the "film's systematic and significant use of techniques of the medium," a modality that encompasses "the history of film forms, of genres, and modes."[22] In this understanding, style shapes the viewer's experience. It "is not simply window-dressing draped over a script; it is the very flesh of the work," "the texture of the film's images and sounds, the result of choices made by the filmmaker(s) in particular historical circumstances."[23] No matter how strongly the spectator may be invested on a variety of levels (be it on that of "plot or genre, subject matter or thematic implication"), it is the shaping of materials by the tools of the medium that creates "the texture of the film experience." Indeed, "the audience gains access to story or theme only through that tissue of sensory materials." For this reason, claims Bordwell, the actual organization of these materials, the staging and composition of a shot, the editing, the relationship between music and the film's action "can hardly be a matter of indifference."[24]

Bordwell's definition, with its particular attention to the dynamic workings of style, might at first glance seem alluring in fathoming Bresson's project. Could it be that the French film director simply insists on a specific choice of words in order to distinguish his cinematograph from "conventional" cinema, or is there more at work in this distinction? To probe the complexity of this issue, much of this chapter will be devoted to Bresson's *Mouchette*, his last black-and-white feature, made shortly after *Au hasard Balthazar*, a rare instance of productivity for the elusive film director. My account of Bresson's negotiation of style will start from the rich sample and challenging material provided by the opening shots of *Mouchette*.

The beginning of *Mouchette* (which follows a short prologue) provides an intriguing display of how Bresson constructs cinematic time and space, even more so since the episode is not to be found in the film's source, Georges Bernanos's novella *Nouvelle histoire de Mouchette*.[25] The filmmaker invents a different narrative frame, recoding the story, and allowing a unique approach to his materials. The sequence alternates between shots of a gamekeeper spying, a poacher setting snares, and trapped quails struggling to get free. The logic that links the gaze to its object, to what is seen,[26] turns this confrontation between the gamekeeper Mathieu and the poacher Arsène into a gripping action scene that anticipates the dynamic of the film as a whole. These are scenes from a hunt, in fact a triple hunt, that of the film action, that of the film's camera—and that of the film to come. A gamekeeper tracks a poacher just as the camera tracks its next visual object. In this way the opening points ahead to a film in which the young protagonist Mouchette will be an object of prey, pursued and tormented by an entire community, hounded to her death by suicide. Scene after scene, not all of which are to be found in the novella, sustain this inexorable rhythm and drive the narrative to its lethal outcome.

As the gamekeeper frees a quail and leaves the forest, the camera follows him, capturing his subsequent encounter with schoolgirls noisily entering the schoolyard. One of the pupils stands out and stands apart, both by dint of her strange appearance and her awkward behavior. Unlike her classmates who hurry to morning classes, she stares at the forest, as if attracted by an unknown force. She emerges from her daydream only after a fellow student calls her to order by speaking her name: "Mouchette." The camera cuts and draws close to the gamekeeper, fixing on a terse encounter with his wife. He shows her Arsène's snares and identifies the guilty party: "It is him again." As we hear these words ("C'est encore lui"), the camera cuts to the poacher at the village café counter; we see him exchanging seductive glances with the waitress Louisa. Urging him to leave ("Arsène, pars!"), she directs our gaze towards the door in a classical shot-reverse shot. "Pars. Et reviens!" she insists, in a view that extends her gaze and gives way to a reverse shot of a man entering the café. It is, we realize, the gamekeeper, who is identified as Mathieu. A short verbal exchange between the two grants a very brief intermission to Bresson's tightly sutured exposition. A silent scene follows Mathieu's departure. Two other men enter the café and it quickly becomes apparent that they are smuggling alcohol. Their arrival coincides with a police raid, which increases the tension and delays the delivery of the forbidden liquor. The two men return to what appears to be their home where, once again, we see Mouchette.

An emphasis on tracking and the theme of the hunt is of course to be found throughout Bresson's cinema. Such an approach informs the stories of the pickpocket, the war prisoner who escapes, and even the recast Jeanne d'Arc. The formal and narrative logic of the hunt, however, could be seen as a strange (even bizarre) imposition on Bernanos's material, given the novella's supernatural drama of a girl driven to death by the temptation of evil. Georges Sadoul expressed surprise at feeling so enthralled by Bresson's "drama of the soul," a fascination that made him oblivious to everything else: "More often than not I was so caught in the action that I felt deprived of any analytical or critical sense."[27] Such a response was surely out of keeping with what Bresson had in mind. He was altogether opposed to anything reminiscent of literary or theatrical conventions. "If there is action, it is internal," he maintained in his characteristic style, reiterating the specificity of his "models" who allegedly "react" instead of "acting." Insisting once again on the importance of his models' blankness, Bresson reminded Sadoul that for him "editing a film means to connect beings through gazes," emphasizing that montage is the very principle of representation, and not a simple grammatical tool.

The initial sequence of *Mouchette* is formally arresting and, yet, in its seemingly classical deployment of shot-reverse shot, is very much in keeping with the conventions of the commercial cinema that Bresson abhorred. In creating this scene, Bresson augmented Bernanos's novella and in the process rewrote its narrative. What might appear at first glance to be a conventional approach in fact provided the means for a radical reinterpretation of the source material and a striking intervention in the rules of literary adaptation. In this way, Bresson desisted from any blind deference to Bernanos. His approach bears similarity to what Rainer Werner Fassbinder once described as the eschewing of any misguided desire to let oneself be blindly guided by the author's designs. "A film that comes to grip with literature and language," observed Fassbinder, "has to make of this confrontation something absolutely intelligible, clear and transparent."[28] Bresson would argue that his strategy was a function of intuition, of knowing what formal choice was appropriate to the overall mood and ambience of a given moment. This is in keeping with Béla Balázs's notion of the *Einstellung*, which translates as shot or set-up, but also connotes both a world view and a moral attitude.[29] For any single scene or shot, according to Balázs, there is one particularly appropriate *Einstellung*; and for him, this is both a matter of formal choice as well as moral perspective.

In his reflections about the ideological challenges of cinematic adaptation, Theodor W. Adorno observes that the distance between the empirical world and language is "abolished in film," and that "the semblance of immediacy cannot be avoided." Nonetheless, "film must search for other means of conveying immediacy" beyond the mimetic reproduction of the world. Writing in 1966, he concludes that "the obvious answer today as forty years ago, is that of montage which does not interfere with things, but rather arranges them in a constellation akin to that of writing."[30] Unlike conventional cinema, which provides entertainment and distraction and "artificially" reproduces the world, Bresson's cinematograph is intended to be a form of writing (écriture), and not a mirror-like representation nor a mimetic form of drawing. The cinematograph does not seek an immediate expression of the world, but rather a mediated one, and the means (tools) of this mediation assume a conspicuous presence. The cinematograph does not pursue a definitive representation, but rather one that, in the words of Jacques Aumont, is "constantly deferred, reprised, contradicted."[31]

Bresson's own écriture does more than rethink the dialectic between framing and montage. Its basic principle involves the use of images emptied of any predetermined value, whose meaning, power, and efficiency derive from their capacity to connect with one another. Bresson's singular montage and fragmentation, his usage of the models and ellipsis are in keeping with the deferral and contradiction that intervene in the representation of the real. Nowhere are these dynamics more salient than in Bresson's grappling with Bernanos's novels. The relationship between these two forms of "writing" is not unproblematic, especially when the novelist's exact sentences are delivered on screen. How can Bresson's art of the cinematograph render the work of Bernanos and still maintain its own artistic autonomy? How might we characterize the relationship between Bresson's "writing with moving images and sounds" and the literary art?[32]

Cinematographic Writing

When asked to sum up *Mouchette*'s story, Bresson reacted with displeasure, the very possibility that one could do this seeming to him simply "awful" (*affreux*). Even though Bresson was altogether loath to undertake such an enterprise, summarizing the plot would be the first step towards an analysis of the relationship between the film and the novella. Halfway through the narrative, Bernanos actually provides an overview of Mouchette's meanderings: "Running away from school, waiting at the roadside, wandering through the woods lashed by the wind and the rain, meeting Arsène—none of this added up to a real story. It had no beginning and no end, it was more like a confused noise in her head, a kind of a funeral hymn."[33] While Bresson transposed the written text into cinematographic writing, he enacted the rift between text and film by proceeding to the most literal, the most physical depiction in order to respond to the writer's imagery of the "woods lashed by the wind" and their sensuous associations:

> *And when the noise disappeared there was a fathomless dark silence, a silence of all her senses, and a certain voice, almost unintelligible, calling her name, so low that she could scarcely hear it, so familiar, so unique that even before she heard it she could almost feel two syllables inside her... Mouchette... Arsène had only said her name once, just as... She did not even know for sure if it was her name. There was something in it of a man's sob, and of fear and anger mixed, and of an animal threatened in his lair. However well Mouchette might stand up to pain, she had her fill. When her father beat her, she bowed beneath the blows without shame and wanted to die, incapable of feeling any rancor towards her torturer, and bound to him by a strange feeling of complicity in his fury and his hatred. Such things she could only think of with bitterness, but at*

least once the humiliation had passed she began to consider ways of getting her revenge and to regain the pride which, it seemed, nothing could destroy without destroying her too. And now that pride had died, was dead... Why?[34]

Ending the passage with the question "Why?", Bernanos lets the query drive the remaining pages. As Mouchette is subject to further atrocity and humiliation, Satan's machinations will make the seduction of death grow more alluring; suicide will assume the tempting prospect of redemption.

Indeed, such is the cinematographic project of *Mouchette* that any attempt to provide a plot summary tells us little about the film. More than any of Bresson's previous features, with the possible exception of *Au hasard Balthazar*, *Mouchette* is defined by its tight composition. Although the lines delivered by Bresson's actors come from the novella, the adaptation reflects the filmmaker's acute mindfulness of the relation between the literary text and the filmic extension. In its treatment of temporality Bernanos's novella demonstrates numerous signs of what we might call literary cinematographism, parceling out the twenty-four-hour story in uneven and discontinuous episodes. One might well expect Bresson to respect this fragmentation, even to accentuate the rhythmic disposition of episodes. Instead, he incorporates the scenes into a linear plot and uses dissolves and sonic bridges to connect them. In this regard, Bresson's framing and editing follow rather than oppose Bernanos's sequential treatment of time and space. Bernanos's less than twenty-four-hour narrative starts with Mouchette's departure from school and ends with her suicide the next morning. Mouchette's sensations and perceptions interrupt the eventful night, and incidents from the past are recalled to flavor the story and assure its development. Though faithful to the third-person narrative, Bresson avoids flashbacks or any form of temporal rupture, and instead reconstitutes the events over several days, with a painstaking straightforwardness.

The distance between a literary text and its cinematographic counterpart is a significant factor in any attempt to apprehend cinema's place within the arts. In this case, commentators paid less attention to the formal discrepancy between Bernanos's novella and Bresson's adaptation, focusing instead on the filmmaker's thematic fidelity even as he remains faithful to his own cinematographic aesthetics. Tony Pipolo, for example, believes that "the cumulative structure of the novella, building in intensity without unbalancing the weight of each experience, is not unlike Bresson's approach."[35] To be sure, he notes that Bresson "expands the duration of the story from twenty-four hours to nearly five days and frames the narrative between two hunting scenes in the woods, neither of which is in the original."[36] Bresson himself admitted that he invented these hunting scenes to foreground animal imagery, not unlike his strategy in *Balthazar*. The formal consequences of this addition, however, made for a decisive variance between his cinematograph and the literary source.

Examining cinema's place in what he calls the "aesthetic regime of the Art," Jacques Rancière uses Bresson's adaptation of *Mouchette* in a discussion about the principles of correspondence between the arts. Rancière believes that "it is quite *simple* to formulate the problem of such an 'adaptation'," for "literature is not simply the art of language that needs to be transposed in plastic images and cinematic movement. It is a practice of language that also involves a particular idea of imagery and mobility. It invented for itself a certain cinematographism."[37] Such "cinematographism" abounds in Bernanos's prose, as Bresson himself was well aware. In Bernanos, claimed the director, "there is no analysis and psychology, but painting. What suits me well in Bernanos (and has a direct link to his characters) is that he produces surreal with real."[38] Bresson found this aspect of the prose convenient as he was proceeding to "consolidate [his] system (which would be more appropriate to call an antisystem): no actors, no acting, no *mise-en-scène*, dissemblance of the interpreters with the invented characters, surprises instead of takes."[39] In his work on *Diary of a Country Priest*, Bresson found his bearings in the "incommensurable and tenebrous field of the cinematograph, like a one-eyed person in the realm of the blind." Building on this discovery, he deemed it "resolutely unreasonable" to use the camera only "to reproduce the mimicry of actors, even the very talented ones."[40]

Bresson's singular approach to adaptation catalyzed extensive commentary in the writings of André Bazin.[41] Considering the film version of Bernanos's novel to be a stunning work, Bazin went on to ponder the consequences of such literary cinematographism for contemporary cinema. Bresson, he claimed, had successfully managed to negotiate not only the novel's most "literary" dimensions, but also its "visual" aspects. In most adaptations the "filmmaker, having transformed the narrative into visuals, must put the rest into dialogue, including the existing dialogue of the novel, although we expect some modification of the latter, since spoken as written, its effectiveness and even its meaning will normally evaporate."[42] But the "high relief" of the novel's characters is not to be found in Bresson's cinematographic transposition. "In the process of showing them [the characters] to us," continues Bazin, "Bresson is hurrying them out of sight. In place of the powerfully concrete evocations of the novelist, the film offers us an increasingly impoverished image which escapes us because it is hidden from us."[43] It is the film that becomes literary, Bazin concludes, "while the novel teems with visual material."[44] Indeed, "if there is painting in the novel, instead of analysis and psychology, it is done with words," as Bresson himself stressed years later when he made *Mouchette*. "I escape to words. If there is analysis and psychology in my films, it is done with images, in the style of portrait painters."[45] As an art that is essentially visual, Bresson's cinematograph aims to purge itself of the visual excess which literature has employed in the attempt to sustain an imaginary world beyond the printed page. The film counterpart proceeds conversely by raising the written word to a higher level of abstraction.

Instead of taking their cue from Bernanos's cinematic novels, which seem to be organized like shooting scripts, Bresson's scenarios respond with a formal retrenchment that in a most unexpected way brings cinema back to literature. Bazin and Rancière concur on this point. What might appear to be a gesture of artistic regression in fact allows the adaptation to assume expressive powers. In going back to literature, Bresson confers upon his cinematographic art an enhanced autonomy. Nonetheless, both critics insist that the relationship should not be isolated from the larger narrative dynamic. Alluding to the suspenseful role of the intense cinematographism, Bazin analyzes the example of the rabbit's eye in Bernanos's text, where it mainly serves to release the narrative tension by offering a moment of respite in the continuum of facts, events, and emotions. If the prose of *Diary of a Country Priest* is punctuated by such suspenseful moments, for instance when Bernanos describes "the rabbit's still limpid and gentle eye" in the Count's game-bag, this visual emphasis does not figure in Bresson's impoverished image of the rabbits delivered to the presbytery. The same mechanism (and the same image) appears in *Mouchette* when Arsène takes the girl to his hut during the storm after finding her in the woods. Prolonging the suspense of what is to happen after Mouchette enters the hut,[46] Bernanos lingers on Arsène's bag "full of rabbits, not quite stiff yet, sticky and glistening with blood and water."[47]

Rancière takes Bazin's analysis a step further. "By dropping the over-sensual image," argues the French philosopher, "Bresson also removes the suspenseful power inherent in the hyper-sensorial description."[48] Central to Bresson's adaptation, this reversal reflects a critical transformation of the relationship between literature and cinema. In Rancière's assessment, during the twentieth century literature overturned the hierarchal order of the classical "representational regime," that is, both the preeminence of the storyline and of causal necessity as well as the insistence on mimeticism as the standard for veridical art. Bresson's work continues this project by granting an evocative power to flat images that have been emptied both of their photographic and of their dramatic content, images that bear out a variance between "showing" and "signifying."[49] Text and film become connected in an unexpected way, since between the literary material and its cinematographic treatment there is "not just a gap, but a counter-movement."[50]

For Rancière, this shift is critical: just as modernist literature learned how to incorporate visual imagery, Bresson demonstrates the autonomy of the cinematograph by liberating the literary word in the filmic extension. In this sense, the close formal analysis of *Mouchette* goes beyond the critical tendency to read Bresson's films as enactments of Astruc's theory of the *caméra-stylo* while nonetheless revealing the director's manic negotiation of *mise-en-scène*.[51] Bresson's adaptation project seeks to grant cinema its autonomy vis-à-vis the other arts, and especially with regard to literature. It also makes clear that the well-known signatures of his style can be misleading and that such a formalistic approach, when applied formulaically, cannot account for the complexities at the heart of Bresson's work and of his understanding of authorship.

"Model. All Face"

When the heirs of Bernanos insisted that *Mouchette* be adapted by the director of *Diary of a Country Priest*, the project fell into place with dispatch. *Mouchette* would come out only one year after *Au hasard Balthazar*, a rare instance of a quick turnover in the career of the rigorous filmmaker. "I was burning with desire to make a new movie," confessed Bresson, explaining that he was eager to explore in more depth his theory of the model.[52] A thematic continuity between Bresson's last two black-and-white films is readily apparent and it comes as no surprise that scholars view *Mouchette* and *Balthazar* as being of a piece. Often compared to animals in the novel (the quails and wild hare hunted by Arsène and Mathieu), Mouchette is, in Bresson's own words, a "tracked down half-animal," just like Balthazar. Snubbed by her classmates, singled out by the school mistress, scolded and scorned by her father, raped by Arsène, Mouchette suffers in silence the violence of her impoverished life. Overcome by shame, plagued by a vehement contempt that she does not know how to articulate, she turns against the people around her, disappearing in the clear water of a pond, leaving behind only a few small transparent circles. As victims of cruelty, the young girl and the donkey confront "a solidarity in evil,"[53] communal acts of violence that lead to lethal outcomes. Despite this thematic continuity, Bresson acknowledged his reluctance to make *Mouchette* as he strived to come up with a composition that might attenuate the harshness of the young girl's suicide.

On the other hand, the novella's young heroine seemed tailor-made for Bresson; Bernanos himself emphasized her automatic responses to the world and its torments: "Now that she had abandoned the struggle, Mouchette returned to her instinctive, unconscious animal-like resignation."[54] Mouchette, we read elsewhere, "was so overwrought that she could no longer hold a thought in her head, and obeyed mechanically [*machinalement*]."[55] Moreover, Bernanos's cinematographic narration depicts the physical and interior despair of this young girl from Pas de Calais in a way that seems to mirror Bresson's own narrative predilections: "Of course, thoughts never passed through Mouchette's mind in such a logical way. She was vague and jumped quickly from one thing to another. [*Elle reste vague, passe aisément d'un plan à l'autre.*] If the very poor could associate the various images of their poverty they would be overwhelmed by it, but their wretchedness seems to them to consist simply of an endless succession of miseries, a series of unfortunate chances."[56] A third-person perspective, rather than the heroine's point of view, "associates the various images" of a mind that "jumps quickly from one thing to another" or, as one might well glean from the French version, from one *shot* to another. The automatic associations of a young girl's mental wanderings, along with her animal-like reactions, seem ready-made for Bresson's theory of the model, but also for his practice of what one might call "responsive" montage, where one shot is linked to the next in the most gripping, yet logical way, rather than in a "series of unfortunate chances."

Mouchette is often silent; she expresses herself much more easily with her hands and feet than she does with words. When she speaks, the phrases that come from her lips inflect her facial expression and in that way both qualify and modify Bresson's resolve that his models deliver an "inner truth." As Rancière puts it, we have to wonder "what exactly is this 'truth' produced by the automatism of equal syllables enunciated in an even tone."[57] Indeed, Bresson's models do not always express themselves in monotone. Mouchette is insolent; her behavior is markedly similar to that of the good pupil Séraphita in *Diary of a Country Priest*. The latter dutifully recites the catechism not because she understands the meaning of the Eucharist, but because she and her classmates have conspired to make fun of the priest. As if she were mimicking a model, the young girl plays a prank and, in response to the priest's question whether she is eager for her first communion, gives the reason for her conscientious recitation, mechanically uttering the phrase "You have such beautiful eyes." In a similar vein, Mouchette says "Merde" to her father because it is the coarsest word she knows, even though she does not fully comprehend its semantic impact. Elsewhere, she knows that her pronouncement "Monsieur Arsène is my lover" will shock the gamekeeper's wife, although the gravity of such a claim remains ungrasped.

Bresson's aversion to "filmed theater" is a crucial element in his project of a pure art of the cinematograph, and his use of "models" figures strongly in his attempt to distinguish the cinematograph from the dramatic arts. Nonetheless, the flat voices only assume their full meaning within Bresson's logic of fragmented framing and reactive editing. A comparative analysis of the novella and its cinematic treatment demonstrates that Bresson's dialogues are "cinematographic" rather than theatrical, not because the models deliver the lines in a monotonous way, but because the lines perfectly correspond to the work's narrative and spatial fragmentation. In other words, Bresson can grapple with the traces of other arts because his cinematographic system sustains such a thoroughgoing autonomy.

The models' lack of affect challenges the expressive theatricality and professionalism of conventional cinema, but it only gains significance and credibility when accompanied by their blank voices, vessels of a speech that has come to be identified as singularly Bressonian. Whereas other film directors stage psychological melodramas, Bresson portrays filmic interiority and tragedies of the soul with visual spareness and expressionless demeanor. If Bresson's cinematograph so clearly formalizes its opposition to theater, it is because he positions his artistic enterprise in dialogue and continuity with the aesthetic concerns of his time and seeks to further them in his singular deployment of the cinematograph.[58]

As an example of the filmmaker's desire to guard the cinematograph from impure influences, *Mouchette* also reveals possibilities that are new and unpredictable (Bresson was fond of using the word "spontaneous"), among them an extreme expressiveness of the face. In the bumper car scene, which is Bresson's creation, the editing allows a brief release from the hunt scenario and inserts a rare touch of playfulness. Set in the sunny Vaucluse in the south of France, as opposed to the gloomy Pas de Calais of Bernanos's novel, the passage depicts the leisure time pursuits of a community otherwise crippled by poverty, alcohol, and humiliation. Having just gulped down a glass of gin that her father offers as a modest remuneration after taking her money, Mouchette enjoys a ride using the chip passed on to her by a stranger. The playground crystallizes the ludic potential in the girl's behavior of which we have only seen glimmers. There is no doubt that Bresson invented the scene for the sake of contrast and to provide a break; this interlude is above all striking because of Mouchette's animated face and its stirring palette of emotions. For a very brief moment, it is hard to believe that one is watching a Bresson film.[59]

The playfulness and lightness of this defiant smile signal a burgeoning erotic awareness. It is the same smile that we will glimpse very fleetingly when she comforts the poacher Arsène during his epileptic seizure by singing the tune we know from her classroom. Again, this is Bresson's addition; Mouchette performs the very same song that she could not get right and for which she is cruelly humiliated by her teacher. A variety of emotions become legible on her face as she caresses Arsène's body: the pleasure of striking the right note, the easy demeanor

Illustration 2.1: Mouchette Lights Up (*Mouchette*, dir. Robert Bresson, 1967)

of being by herself, as well as the erotic charge of touching the hair of a man with whom she identifies as an outcast and rebel. Bresson stages the tender scene as a site of contrast; it renders the rape that will follow all the more brutal and disturbing. To the punctuation sign "..." from Bernanos's novel, and the abrupt change of episode, Bresson responds with an enigmatic sigh that comes from Mouchette's now impassive body, and a very rare dissolve to black.

The film's second-to-last sequence, in which Mouchette faces the inquisitive women of the village as she goes to find milk for her baby brother after her mother's death adds another layer of complexity to the theory of the model. Hugging the milk can to her chest, she remains inert, unwilling to give away anything, not a word nor an expression, except for the mud of her ungainly shoes that she scrapes on the immaculate carpet in the living room of the vigil-keeping nun. This dynamic play of stifled expression and extreme withholding provides an embodiment of Bresson's theory of the model as "all face."[60] This dictum, argues Noa Steimatsky, does not endow "the entire body with a reflective, subjective expressivity." Rather, like the head of an animal, the face becomes "opaque, as resistant as a body, as if coated with the rough hide of a beast of burden."[61]

Given Bresson's harsh critique of canned theater and the expressive actor, the instances of "reflective" faces in *Mouchette* are certainly puzzling. After all, the

Illustration 2.2: Muddy Shoes (*Mouchette*, dir. Robert Bresson, 1967)

director has made a mission out of refuting the "habits that the cinema has cultivated to mediate anthropomorphic hierarchies, to synthesize expression and focalize subjectivity in the visual."[62] Along with Bresson's direction of models, his cinematographic composition, his singular framing and montage, and his organization of temporality all seek "to harness or deny expression, to withdraw the potentialities of the face."[63] Even when exposing physiognomies in all their expressiveness, Bresson still takes the image to "points of crisis and blockage" and thereby levels off animate characters and inanimate objects. It is this equality of all things that Bresson praises in his *Notes*: "Cezanne painting with the same eye and the same soul a fruit dish, his son, the Montagne Sainte-Victoire."[64] A similar leveling off of objects and human bodies certainly inspires Bresson's method. His work with the models does not translate directly in blank voices and unexpressive countenance, but informs his conception of the cinematic body. When he defines his models as "all face," he does not reduce them to their facial expression. In this sense, he refers the reader to Montaigne:

> A certain man demanded of one of our loytring rogues, whom in the deep of frosty Winter, he saw wandring up and downe with nothing but his shirt about him, and yet as blithe and lusty as an other who keepes himselfe muffled and wrapt in warme furres up to the ears, how he could have patience to go so. And have not you, good Sir, *(answered he)* your face all bare? Imagine I am all face. (Montaigne, Essays, I, chapter XXI)[65]

Cinema. All Body

Bodies are essential points of focus in Bresson's cinematograph; they bring together striking physiognomies, significant players, and evocative forms. Indeed, they play a crucial role in his dispositif, as well as in the texture of his cinematographic writing. Bresson's eschewal of the human body's customary unity is in keeping with his penchant for fragmentation. Take, for instance, *L'Argent*, where we see Yvon's hands while hearing the sound of his steps, or *Diary of a Country Priest*, where the priest's face is so often in the frame that is said to function as the "imprint of his soul."[66] Of course, this is not to say that Bresson presents dismembered bodies; nor do faces, hands, and feet function as metonymies for the entire body, or as metaphors for conceptual ideas. Only by breaking the unity of constituted bodies and objects, by displacing their ordering logic, can Bresson afford the body a special priority over consciousness. Within Bresson's project to promote and defend the autonomy of the cinematograph, the body takes on special meaning and renewed importance.

By understanding the body as an organic conglomeration of gestures, Bresson's cinematographic project obliterates the classical expressiveness of the drama as well as the psychological depth of the novel. Instead, it presents the instant manifestation of the automatic, that is, unconscious gesture, wherein the body succumbs to the gravity of its habits. It is by dint of such gestural mechanics that Mouchette, the priest, the pickpocket, the prisoner, and Lancelot the knight both establish and fathom their place in the world. Neither hypothetical consciousness nor external circumstances determine the articulation of a scene or, for that matter, the destiny of characters. The repetition of bodily gestures generates the materiality of cinematic space and time and provides the narrative energy of Bresson's films.

In Bresson's cinema the fleeting surface of the image does not suppress the texture; the images and sounds dispose of a heavy materiality, forcing the spectator to encounter this world afresh, unsullied by habits or conventions. Vincent Amiel, for instance, argues that this encounter is experienced and felt even before it can be named.[67] Among the most common examples we find is the sound of the donkey cart, so intensely present to our senses, in *Au hasard Balthazar*; its insistence makes itself felt before we even think of connecting it to agrarian work or opposing it to "signs" of modernity. In *Lancelot du Lac*, it is impossible to decipher the meaning of the banners that scan the jousts of the tourney. It is difficult to attach them to any distinct meaning (victory? defeat?); they are above all patterns, colors, and cadences. Bresson's images possess a distinct physicality; they don't seem to "signify" anything besides their material presence. The same holds for the characters' bodies that are rarely given in their unity, but are conceived, represented, and perceived in the repetition of gestures.

Cinematic space and time inhere in the simplest endeavors of these bodies and in the repeated gestures of writing, making coffee, tapping wine, or saddling horses. Gestures appear as movements, words assume the status of mere sounds, and the body becomes weight and volume in motion. Before we can assign an intention to these signs of life, we must face the amorphous fact of matter and the way in which it confounds our customary expectations. Above all, Bresson shows us sounds, colors, volumes, curves, and lines. In the primary sensuousness of human activity, the immediate concreteness of actions imposes itself without figuration. From *Diary of a Country Priest* to *L'Argent,* Bresson's work brings us in the immediate presence of figures rather than characters, of human bodies rather than complex psychologies. In this idiosyncratic cinema the body, in all its stark presence, provides the primary point of focus. No matter what the mission, the body remains our privileged guide, for embodiment is so strong and pervasive that it assumes the power of abstraction, not of an intellectual sort, but rather the abstraction of pure matter.

With Bresson fragmentation provides a "new form of feeling";[68] it is more than a technique or an element of style, but rather the effect of the body's gravity in its repeated gestures. This effect, in its stifling of intellectual response, becomes first of all evident in the realm of perception. In this sense, fragmentation rests at the core of Bresson's art; it dictates the rhythm of his cinematographic inscription. The priest's writing hand, for instance, impresses upon us the unfailing presentness of its gestures. When we see the hand fill an empty page with the priest's recollections, Bresson allows us to experience the present temporality of the body rather than the remembrance of the past. We become absorbed in the time of writing, which is the time of perception, and not in the time of intelligence and retrospection. When we see the priest open his notebook, we are drawn to the immediacy of his hand before we register the meaning of his words. In this regard, the conclusion of *Diary* is both poignant and striking. Dufréty's letter to Torcy, announcing the death of the young priest, marks an intrusion in the film's gestural logic: the letter arrives in a dactylo-typed envelope and its purely informative role appears in stark contrast to the nature of the priest's hand writing, to the weight of the hand in its automatic movement. As Bresson is fond of saying, quoting Montaigne, "Tout mouvement nous descouvre."[69]

In Bresson's filmic worlds, as Amiel points out, "perception, fragmentary and instantaneous, is not caught up by reason, which is concerned with totality and thus is atemporal or free of time."[70] This explains an approach to literary adaptation that reverses the order of the novel. Although Bresson dismissed appellations like *metteur-en-scène* or *cineaste*, he was glad to be called *metteur-en-ordre*. In his own order of cinema, the arbitrary unity of the body is dissolved and superseded by the inner logic of the gesture and its infinite repetitiveness. Amiel imputes this new order of the body to the power of montage which Bresson does not use as "a simple tool." In the director's own words from his *Notes*: "Because you do not have to imitate, like painters, sculptors, novelists, the appearance of persons and objects (machines do that for you), your creation or invention confines itself to the ties you knot between the various bits of reality caught. There is also the choice of the bits. Your flair decides."[71] The Bressonian cinematograph, as a function of choice, is a display of flair; as an aesthetic regime, it breaks with cinematic convention.

Bresson's cinematographic writing reassembles discreet elements through montage and in this way constructs a unique and autonomous world. It is performative, not in a theatrical sense, but in its pursuit of fashioning a world out of disparate elements, similar to how, as Austin and Searle put it, we "do things with words." Bresson "performs" his worlds by relying on the *mise-en-relation* of discreet elements submitted to the power of montage and the presentation of the "models." Cinematographic writing works not so much with images and sounds as it does with the "relationships between images and between sounds," as well as with the relationship between image and sound. It is this particular resolve that guides the way in which Bresson thinks of his characters and chooses his models, whom Michael Haneke so precisely describes as "icons of imposed forbearance," "projection screen[s], blank sheet[s] of paper, whose sole task is to be filled with the viewers' thoughts and feelings."[72] The theory of the models and the actual work with them find meaning only in the wider project of establishing the autonomy of the cinematographic narration face to face with the literary art, and in the modern aesthetic premises of the equality of all things, humans and objects. In other words, the three Bressonian "signatures" discussed in this chapter fulfill their role only when they work together in a specific permutation.

Style, in this understanding, is not a filmmaker's toolbox, but rather the result of the individual combination of aesthetic mechanisms. Style cannot be considered apart from its objects and the processes by which it is generated and apprehended; it cannot be extracted and investigated on its own. Instead, style inheres in the object's manner of appearance, in what we recognize in things and other people. Style is not merely a collection of ticks and patterns; and it is surely not just "a" certain style or a form of styling. In other words, for Bresson style is not technique. Style is not an emanation of the artist nor is it the effect of the written, painted, or filmed product. Rather, it dwells where signs give form to the world of experience or, as Merleau-Ponty put it, where signification becomes possible.[73] Style therefore cannot be an object; it becomes visible only in the perception of the work. The enactment of style is not to be found in the production of an object, nor in the invocation of a concept; it abides above all in the bringing into being of an orientation toward the world and one's own experience of the world.

It is within this unique approach to style that we come to understand why Bresson's "signature" does not function in the customary way. It is not a self-constitutive inscription that draws attention to itself. Nor is it announced by rhetorical embellishments, which Bresson abhorred. His approach was at once restrained—tightly woven in the texture of worlds created by cinematographic writing, every frame recognizable as his own, although no signature is visible—and emphatic, insofar as the relationships between images and sounds dictate our perceptive responses. But it is in his own positioning as an agent or mediator of the cinematograph as an expressive tool, and not as a demiurgic creator, that Bresson gave us the lead in understanding style as detached from the individual and yet intimately linked to it.

The auteurist rhetoric valorizes the exemplary individual whose clear style opens new creative paths that will inspire future artists. Of interest here is not so much the question of the influence, as that of confronting and overcoming that influence. By acknowledging the importance of their encounters with Bresson's films, the filmmakers that we call Bressonians also seek to signal that they have worked through the complex burden and anxiety of his influence. Jean Eustache for instance earned his reputation as Bresson's most faithful heir because his cinema pays tribute to Bresson's œuvre, from the recasting of Isabelle Weingarten from *Quatre nuits d'un rêveur* (*Four Nights of a Dreamer*, 1971) as a Bressonian player in *La Maman et la putain* (*The Mother and the Whore*, 1973) to the *Pickpocket*-like perspective in *Mes petites amoureuses* (1974). Even as he directly references Bresson, Eustache counters the master's elliptical montage, the tight framing, and the flat tonality of the characters' voices. Likewise, Maurice Pialat's preference for nonprofessional actors and his extreme usage of ellipsis figure nonetheless in a highly personal cinema that differs significantly, even radically, from Bresson's. This becomes especially apparent when the director of *Sous le soleil de Satan* (*Under the Sun of Satan*, 1987), in grappling with Bernanos's prose, confronts and works through the legacy of Bresson.

Bresson's influence in the world of cinema goes far beyond the realm of rhetoric. Instead it brings us back to the conceptual framework of aesthetics, understood here more broadly as *aisthesis*, as "an originary knot that ties a sense of art to an idea of thought and an idea of the community,"[74] rather than in the more restricted sense as the perception and judgment of works of art. To the extent that Bresson's method illuminated new possibilities for the cinematograph, it carried the emancipatory flag of an art in search of its aesthetic autonomy. As such, it ensured that its specific reconfiguration of the world "holds the promise of both a new world of Art and a new life for individuals and the community."[75]

Within this framework, Bressonianism is neither a school nor a movement, but an aesthetic community, or, in Rancière's understanding, a community of the senses that binds together "practices, forms of visibility, and patterns of intelligibility."[76] Rather than a collectivity shaped by a common feeling, explains the French philosopher, this community provides "a frame of visibility and intelligibility that puts things or practices together under the same meaning." Inscribing their own essence in their creative work, the Bressonians produce "this essence as a *community*."[77] For all their autonomy and singularity, these individual filmmakers do not function as monads. They come together, to use Pascal Quignard's formulation, in an idiosyncratic "communauté de solitaires." To be sure, it is difficult to elucidate the ways in which such a community is constituted, for, as Nancy laments, "there is no theory, ethics, politics or metaphysics of the individual that is capable of envisaging this declination or decline of the individual within community."[78] This will be the task of the following chapter.

Notes

1. Jousse, "Bresson souffle où il veut," 30–31.
2. Kent Jones in Nicole Brenez et al., "Robert Bresson—A Symposium," in *Robert Bresson (Revised)*, 612.
3. Jousse, "Bresson souffle où il veut," 30–31.
4. *Cahiers du cinéma* 543 (February 2000). See, for instance, the transcript of Bresson's 1955 intervention at the IDHEC, "Une mise en scène n'est pas un art," 4–9.
5. Jousse, "Bresson souffle où il veut," 30–31: "Dans le cinéma français, son influence se fait sentir très tôt, chez des cinéastes comme Melville. ... Mais c'est sans doute avec la Nouvelle Vague que l'ombre de Bresson commence véritablement à hanter le cinéma français. ... L'influence de Bresson sur la Nouvelle Vague n'est pas seulement formelle, elle est aussi morale. En quelque sorte, Bresson exige de ses disciples d'inventer leur propre forme. Dans le même ordre d'idées, il est sans doute avec Renoir, pour les cinéastes français au moins, le maillon le plus essentiel quant au développement du cinéma d'auteur. Dans les années 40, Bresson apporte la preuve en acte que le cinéma français est une réalité tangible, et c'est une leçon qu'un cinéaste comme Rohmer n'oubliera jamais."
6. Michel Ciment, "Éditorial: Bresson et Kubrick," *Positif* 468 (February 2000): 2.
7. Ciment argues that this formal influence can be found in films as different as Jean-Claude Brisseau's *Un jeu brutal*, Jean-Paul Civeyrac's *Ni d'Ève, ni d'Adam*, or Bruno Dumont's *L'Humanité*.
8. Ciment, "Éditorial: Bresson et Kubrick," 2.
9. Foucault, "What is an Author?," 131.

10. Jean-Luc Nancy, *The Inoperative Community*, ed. and trans. Peter Connor (Minneapolis: University of Minnesota Press, 1991), 3.
11. Ibid.
12. Ibid.
13. Ibid., 4.
14. Eric Rohmer, "Le Miracle des objets," *Cahiers du cinéma* 65 (December 1956): 42: "Ce n'est point qu'il répugne aux théories, bien au contraire: ses intentions sont claires et transparaissent nettement dans son œuvre sans qu'il ait besoin de les commenter. La première de ces idées est que le cinéma est un art difficile, rigoureux, épris de perfection, qualités qui ne se jugent qu'au résultat. Aucun mépris chez lui pour le public: celui n'a qu'à se montrer aussi exigeant que l'est, vis-à-vis de lui-même, le cinéaste. Il importe de se débarrasser de maintes habitudes fâcheuses, séquelles du théâtre dont les scories barbouillent encore l'écran. L'art cinématographique n'a pas encore trouvé son vrai ton, son vrai naturel. Parfois, à tel passage d'un film que nous aimons, qu'il vint d'Europe ou d'Amérique, nous avons envie de nous écrier: 'Mais c'est du Bresson!' Nous voulions dire que l'auteur rompait avec un certain clinquant, se passait résolument d'une indulgence dont nous aurions aimé nous savoir dispensés: 'C'est du Bresson,' preuve irréfutable de sa pureté, si nous en avions ailleurs d'autres de son génie."
15. Ibid.: "Nous sentions le cinéma tâtonner dans un sens que Bresson nous avait révélé comme possible. Ce classique, ce modeste faisait ainsi figure de précurseur, et si les œuvres les plus récentes des autres rivalisaient avec les siennes dans notre cœur, c'est de lui que nous tenions notre aptitude à les aimer."
16. Ibid.
17. Bresson, *Notes*, 5, 2.
18. Ibid., 27, my emphasis.
19. Bresson's formulations recall both Husserl's definition of style as a translation of the original relationship to the world as well as Merleau-Ponty's understanding of style as the "prose of the world."
20. The model for this dynamic goes back to Dante, who made ample use of self-commentary to establish himself as an Italian author. See Albert Russell Ascoli, *Dante and the Making of the Modern Author* (London and Cambridge: Cambridge University Press, 2008).
21. Louis Malle, "Avec *Pickpocket* Bresson a trouvé," *Arts* (January 1960), reprinted in Philippe Arnaud, *Robert Bresson: Éloge* (Paris: Cinémathèque Française, 1997), 35.
22. David Bordwell, *On the History of Film Style* (Cambridge: Harvard University Press, 1997), 4.
23. Ibid., 8; 4.
24. Ibid., 4.
25. Georges Bernanos, *Nouvelle histoire de Mouchette*, in *Œuvres romanesques suivies de "Dialogue des Carmélites"* (Paris: Gallimard, Bibliothèque de la Pléiade, 1991); English version appears as *Mouchette*, trans. J.C. Whitehouse (New York: New York Review Books, 2006).
26. The director spoke of his desire "to bind persons to each other and to objects by looks." See *Notes*, 6.
27. Sadoul, "Conversation plutôt qu'interview avec Robert Bresson sur *Mouchette*," in *Les Lettres françaises* (16 March 1967), reprinted in *Bresson par Bresson*, 234.
28. Rainer Werner Fassbinder, "Preliminary Remarks on *Querelle*," in *The Anarchy of the Imagination*, ed. Michael Töteberg and Leo Lensing, trans. Krishna Winston (Baltimore: Johns Hopkins University Press, 1992), 168.

29. Béla Balázs, "Die Einstellung ist die Einstellung," in *Schriften zum Film. Zweiter Band*, ed. Helmut H. Diederichs and Wolfgang Gersch (Munich: Hanser, 1984), 239.
30. Theodor W. Adorno, "Transparencies on Film," trans. Thomas Y. Levin, *New German Critique* 24/25 (Winter/Spring 1981-1982): 204.
31. See Aumont, *Les Théories des cinéastes*, 46.
32. Bresson resolutely distanced himself from the conception of *mise-en-scène* as écriture embraced by the critics of the *Cahiers du cinéma*. In the lengthy interview conducted by Godard and Delahaye in May 1966, Bresson admitted that he approached cinematographic composition in the manner of a painter: "I am scarcely a writer. I write, yes, but I force myself to write, and I write—I realize—a little as I paint, that is to say that I am unable to write a continuous strip. I am able to write from left to right, and thus to align some words, but I cannot do it for a long time, or in continuity." To these comments, Godard responded: "To make cinema, precisely, one has no need of that. It is the cinema in itself that constitutes the strip. One has it from the start; one absolutely no longer needs to concern oneself with it." "That is correct," Bresson replied, "but then you are speaking of the general composition of the film. As for me, when I write, I write as I put color: I put a little on the left, a little on the right, a little in the middle, I stop, I start again… and it is only when there begin to be some things written, that I am no longer annihilated by the blank page, and that I begin to fill the holes. You see: it is not at all a strip that I write." See Delahaye and Godard, "La Question," in *Robert Bresson (Revised)*, 642.
33. Bernanos, *Nouvelle histoire de Mouchette*, 1301; English translation, *Mouchette*, 60.
34. Ibid., English translation, 61.
35. Tony Pipolo, *Robert Bresson: A Passion for Film* (Oxford: Oxford University Press, 2010), 215.
36. Ibid.
37. Jacques Rancière, "Après la littérature," in *Les Écarts du cinéma* (Paris: La Fabrique Éditions, 2011), 50, my emphasis.
38. Quoted in Napoléon Murat, "Dix-sept ans après le *Journal d'un curé de campagne*, il revient à Bernanos. Bresson s'explique sur son nouveau film," in *Bresson par Bresson*, 227: "Chez Bernanos il y a peinture, il n'y a pas analyse et psychologie. L'absence d'analyse et de psychologie dans ses livres coïncide avec l'absence d'analyse et psychologie dans mes films. S'il y avait analyse et psychologie dans mes films, ce serait plutôt à la manière des peintres portraitistes. Ce qui me va aussi chez Bernanos (et cela a un rapport direct avec ses personnages), c'est qu'il fait son surnaturel avec du réel."
39. Ibid., 227: "Surprises au lieu de prises."
40. Ibid.
41. For a multifaceted analysis of Bazin's writings on Bresson, see Noa Steimatsky, "Incoherent Spasms and the Dignity of Signs. Bazin's Bresson," in *Opening Bazin. Postwar Film Theory and Its Afterlife*, ed. Dudley Andrew (Oxford, New York: Oxford University Press, 2011), 167–76. See also Hervé Joubert-Laurencin, "Sans rien changer, que tout soit différent," in *Le Sommeil paradoxal. Écrits sur André Bazin* (Paris: Éditions de l'œil, 2014), 178–85.
42. André Bazin, "*Journal d'un curé de campagne* and the Stylistics of Robert Bresson," in *What is Cinema? Volume 1*, ed. and trans. Hugh Gray (Berkeley: University of California Press, 1967), 127. Cf. Theodor W. Adorno, "Transparencies on Film," trans. Thomas Y. Levin. *New German Critique* 24/25 (Winter/Spring 1981–1982): 200. "Transparencies on Film" offers a complementary understanding of the challenges of literary adaptations and the "artistic difference between the media." Although Adorno does not share Bazin's faith in the

cinematographic medium, his interrogation of the distance between language and film provides an ideological reading of questions that are central to Bazin's ontological understanding of cinema. For Adorno, the logic of arbitrariness that rules natural language obviously affects literary writing. "Even when dialogue is used in a novel, the spoken word is not directly spoken, but rather distanced by the act of narration—perhaps even by the typography—and thereby abstracted from the physical presence of living persons. Thus, fictional characters never resemble their empirical counterparts no matter how minutely they are described. In fact, it may be due to the very precision of their presentation that they are removed even further from empirical reality; they become aesthetically autonomous. Such distance is abolished in film: to the extent that a film is realistic, the semblance of immediacy cannot be avoided."

43. Bazin, "*Journal d'un curé de campagne* and the Stylistics of Robert Bresson," 127.
44. Ibid., 128: "Des deux, c'est le film qui est littéraire et le roman grouillant d'images."
45. Yvonne Baby, "Le domaine de l'indicible," *Le Monde* (14 March 1967), reprinted in *Bresson par Bresson*, 224.
46. She follows him, writes Bernanos, "no more worried by the presence of this man than by that of some familiar animal, but without being really aware of it she had caught something false, something odd in the tone of his voice." See *Nouvelle histoire de Mouchette*, 1275; English translation, 21.
47. Ibid.
48. Jacques Rancière, *The Intervals of Cinema*, trans. John Howe (London: Verso, 2014), 46–47.
49. Ibid., 42–43. The aesthetic revolution in the realm of literature, argues Rancière, overturned fundamental principles of the classical representative order, namely the primacy of plot and its intelligibility, the ordering of actions according to necessity and probability, and the system of expressing emotions, feelings, and wishes through the codification of discourses and attitudes. It is the paradoxical unity of "a power of incarnation and a force of the disincarnation" that for him constitutes the depth of literature.
50. Ibid., 46.
51. See Steimatsky, "Incoherent Spasms and the Dignity of Signs," 169.
52. Delahaye and Godard, "La Question," in *Robert Bresson (Revised)*, 663.
53. Bresson, in *Au hasard Bresson*, Theo Kotulla's documentary about the making of *Mouchette*, supplement to the Criterion edition of the film.
54. Bernanos, *Nouvelle histoire de Mouchette*, 1271; English translation, 17.
55. Ibid., 1305; English translation, 77.
56. Ibid., 1271; English translation, 16.
57. Rancière, *Intervals of Cinema*, 56.
58. According to Rancière, the literary revolution of the nineteenth century brought an end to the traditional hierarchies of noble and common subjects. It thus became an arena of the political and as such affected the community of literature which would internalize this upheaval of aesthetic values. Rancière grants a crucial role to the triumvirate of cinematograph-theater-literature; he counters Bresson's vehement critique of cinema as "filmed theater," insisting that it is not the opposition to the dramatic form that motivates the director's aesthetic revolution. The speech of the models, argues Rancière, would not be perceivable as such had it not come "after literature," i.e., after Mallarmé and Flaubert, who as writers intervened in the political process of parceling out space and time, place and identity, the visible and the invisible, speech and noise. Bresson attempts to do the same thing in the realm of cinema by "resetting theater's speech to the time of literature, that of mute speech." Such speech "gives voice to silence by

deciphering the mute signs inscribed in the things" and "conceals by interiorizing the allure of imaginary sensuousness that it displays." See Rancière, *Intervals of Cinema*, 55–56.

59. The bumper-car scene appears in Hou Hsiao-Hsien's three-minute contribution to *Chacun son cinéma (To Each His Own Cinema)*, a film produced by Gilles Jacob in 2007 to celebrate the sixtieth anniversary of the Cannes Film Festival. The single-shot short shows a screening in a run-down cinema; we see how children in the audience become enthralled by the magic of Mouchette's expressive face and animated body.
60. Bresson, *Notes*, 16.
61. Noa Steimatsky, "On the Face, in Reticence," in *Film, Art, New Media: Museum without Walls?*, ed. Angela Dalle Vacche (New York: Palgrave, 2012), 165.
62. Ibid., 161.
63. Ibid., 160.
64. Bresson, *Notes*, 72.
65. Ibid., 16. In fact, the reference to Montaigne is wrong—the quote is not from the chapter indicated by Bresson.
66. Bazin, *What Is Cinema*, I, 133.
67. Vincent Amiel, *Le Corps au cinéma: Keaton, Bresson, Cassavetes* (Paris: Presses Universitaires de France, 1998), 37. Amiel's study is admirable in the way it rescues the cinematic body from conventional discourses and articulates the essential criteria at work in Bresson's method. See also Vincent Amiel, *Lancelot du Lac de Robert Bresson* (Lyon: Presses Universitaires de Lyon, 2014).
68. Bresson, *Notes*, 18: "Cinematography: new way of writing, thus of feeling."
69. Ibid., 67: "Every movement reveals us."
70. Amiel, *Le Corps au cinéma*, 42.
71. Bresson, *Notes*, 35.
72. Michael Haneke, "Terror and Utopia of Form Addicted to Truth: A Film Story about Robert Bresson's *Au hasard Balthazar*," in *Robert Bresson (Revised)*, 389.
73. See Maurice Merleau-Ponty, *The Prose of the World*, trans. John O'Neill (Evanston: Northwestern University Press, 1973), 115–16.
74. Jacques Rancière, "What Aesthetics Can Mean," in *From an Aesthetic Point of View*, ed. Peter Osborne (London: Serpentine, 2008), 33.
75. Jacques Rancière, "The Aesthetic Revolution and its Outcome: Emplotments of Autonomy and Heteronomy," *New Left Review* 14 (2002): 133.
76. Jacques Rancière, "Contemporary Art and the Politics of Aesthetics," in *Communities of Sense: Rethinking Aesthetics and Politics*, ed. Beth Hinderliter et al. (Durham: Duke University Press, 2009), 31.
77. Nancy, *The Inoperative Community*, 3.
78. Ibid., 4.

CHAPTER THREE
Kinsmen

> Originality is wanting to do as others do, but without ever succeeding.
> — Michel Delahaye and Jean Luc Godard,
> "La Question: Entretien avec Robert Bresson"

A Model Recast

When Isabelle Weingarten returned to the big screen in *La Maman et la putain* (*The Mother and the Whore*, 1973) shortly after playing a leading role in *Quatre nuits d'un rêveur* (*Four Nights of a Dreamer*, 1971), her appearance (as Gilberte, the lost love of Alexandre) prompted critics to speak of Jean Eustache as "indisputably the principal heir of Robert Bresson in France."[1] The ascription of such noble heritage, to say the least, seems inappropriate for this "blue collar dandy"[2] of proletarian background and with no academic pedigree, who in the early 1960s moved to Paris from his hometown of Pessac in the south-west of France. In Paris, he experienced the cinephilic frenzy of the Cinémathèque, while earning his life as a manual laborer, a railwayman or a garment deliverer. Married to Jeannette, one of the secretaries at *Cahiers du cinéma*, Eustache spent long hours in the journal's office where he made the acquaintance of the Nouvelle Vague directors, and either assisted them on their films[3] or edited them.[4] Between 1963 and 1981, he made thirteen films that maintain a unity of vision despite their heterogeneity: a notorious three hours-and-forty-minutes *film-fleuve*, shorts on assignment that he inflected with his inimitably rigorous signature, regional documentaries, medium-length fiction films, and a few shorts, as well as one 35mm feature shot in normal conditions. "Ethnographer of his own reality,"[5] Eustache created a highly autobiographical cinema, even as he alternated between documentaries about local rituals, "the most auteurist Parisian fiction ever created,"[6] and the provincial

Illustration 3.1 Isabelle Weingarten, as Gilberte (*La Maman et la putain*, dir. Jean Eustache, 1973)

Illustration 3.2 Alexandre Bressonian (Jean-Pierre Léaud and Isabelle Weingarten in *La Maman et la putain*, dir. Jean Eustache, 1973)

chronicle of a childhood. He referred to Dreyer, Mizoguchi, and Bresson as his models, but also recognized the influence of more popular filmmakers like Sacha Guitry and Marcel Pagnol. His suicide in 1981, though not surprising, triggered a lot of speculation. Whether it was because "cinema denied him," as Luc Moullet wrote,[7] or because his films, ruthlessly and bitterly personal, drained his vitality, in Serge Daney's assessment,[8] Eustache to the end remained the *cinéaste maudit* he could not help but be.[9]

Weingarten's status as a Bressonian player was well known; this past association granted an unequivocal allure to her appearance and Eustache's film itself drew attention to this nexus. "One falls in love with a woman," says Alexandre, the protagonist of his 220-minute feature, "because she's played in a Bresson movie." The choice of Weingarten for an important cameo role constituted a tribute; quite literally, Eustache invoked a Bressonian model. At the same time, following Bresson's lead and yet deviating from it, he broke out of the director's self-contained world.[10] For all of Eustache's misgivings about Bresson's later work, his act of reverence bore compelling witness to what Harold Bloom has called the anxiety of influence.[11]

The singular physiognomy[12] of Bresson's characters figures strongly in *The Mother and the Whore*. That this dimension was important to Eustache as a film director found further confirmation in his "euphoric reuse"[13] of other Bressonian figures. One recalls, for instance, the resemblance between Daniel (Martin Loeb) in *Mes petites amoureuses* and young Jacques in *Au hasard Balthazar* and, of course, the way in which Daniel's "little love" recalls Bresson's Mouchette (Nadine Nortier). By employing a Bressonian model in *The Mother and the Whore*, Eustache engaged in an exercise in imitation, but also, and more importantly, reconfiguration. The director set Gilberte apart from other characters in the film while rewiring her within a different network. Unlike the film's other post-68 destinies with their psycho-dramatic lives of disillusion and anxiety, Gilberte remains understated and oblique, very much in keeping with Bresson's inimitable minimalism. In Eustache's neurotic world, Gilberte stands out because she embodies "a sort of rigor and healthy constitution absent in the others," as Weingarten herself confessed upon the occasion of the masterpiece's fortieth anniversary. "She is really on the track" despite the palpable uncertainty and hesitation when Alexandre seeks to seduce her.[14]

As conspicuous and seemingly epigonic as the inscription of Weingarten is, Gilberte is on view for only a precious few minutes. Without a doubt, it is the performance of Françoise Lebrun as Véronika that stands out in *The Mother and the Whore*. Véronika's existence remains painstakingly confined to her presence on the screen, and the little that we learn about her comes from the stories she recounts *ad infinitum* in a dispassionate, monotonous voice fully of a piece with her languid body language. We never see her at the hospital where she works or in the nightclubs of Saint-Germain-des-Prés of which she claims to be a regular; the only times she appears without Alexandre are when she speaks on the phone. Her actions above all abide in verbal transactions. She is a "text,"[15] the function and sum of words and sentences that she delivers with Bressonian blankness and flatness. Unlike Alexandre, être *de littérature*, whose privileged mode is that of writing, reading, and quotation, Véronika is above all a speaking being. Eustache insisted that she modulate her voice to sound like certain actresses in French film classics—for example like Janie Marèse in Renoir's *La Chienne*, or Simone Simon in *La Bête humaine*. "From time to time," said Lebrun, "Jean was calling to read to me what he had written. He was not sending me the text, but instead was saying it, which allowed me to feel what he wanted… The precision and the exactitude, the truth of what was written, this is what I was supposed to render."[16]

Lebrun's unforgettable performance in the film derived from her "intuition of what Jean Eustache wanted," and from her own compelling awareness that her work "was to be a medium for someone else's dream."[17] As a vessel for Eustache's imagination, Lebrun in fact reenacts the theory of the model to which Weingarten's presence refers. Véronika's first encounter with Alexandre at the Café de Flore represents a stunning instance of the power of the model. She smiles vaguely before her face becomes an enigmatic point of focus in a one-minute close-up. As a model, to paraphrase Bresson, the actress is enclosed in her mysterious appearance. She is there, elusively present "behind that forehead, those cheeks."[18]

Although these quotations lead us back to Bresson, the project of *The Mother and the Whore* could not be further removed from the mesmerizing asceticism of, for instance, a work like *Pickpocket*. Eustache's film abounds with quotations and intertextual references; his characters, with the exception of Véronika,[19] constitute theatrical and cinephilic palimpsests, veritable echo chambers of French cinema and culture. The distance that Eustache puts between himself and Bresson is all the more significant since he appeals to the director of photography of *Four Nights of a Dreamer*, Pierre Lhomme. It is especially in its *mise-en-scène* that Eustache's *The Mother and the Whore* deviates from Bresson's example. To the latter's fragmented vision, Eustache stubbornly opposes the long take; to Bresson's

Illustration 3.3 Françoise Lebrun, as Véronika (*La Maman et la putain*, dir. Jean Eustache, 1973)

analytical decomposition, Eustache poses the unflinching duration of the shot; where Bresson employs montage to render the event in its absolute presentness and isolate it from the unforgiving fugitive movement, Eustache prolongs the gesture in an inexorable duration, expanding time to improbable limits, granting enhanced significance to the two exceptions in which the cutting à la *Bresson* stubbornly breaks the intensity of the long take.[20] As we have seen in chapter two, Bresson's use of the models assumes its full meaning only when combined with other crucial functions of representation, such as framing and editing. Indeed, as Steven Shaviro points out, in Bresson "cinematic space and time are themselves articulated as extensions or constrains of bodily rest and motion."[21] In grappling with Bresson's theory of the model, Eustache does not blindly simulate it, but in fact dismantles it before recasting it in his own configuration of cinematic space and time.

As an actress in Eustache's film, Weingarten's Gilberte provides a reading key for the movie: she is at once a Proustian creature and a Bressonian model.[22] In his exploration of cinematic time, Eustache shares Bresson's negotiation of temporality. The stakes in *The Mother and the Whore* are high; because "everything [is to] be told,"[23] and "nothing seen,"[24] the *mise-en-scène* assumes surprising and eccentric contours. Speaking about the long night that Véronika spends with Alexandre during Marie's trip to London, Eustache observed that

> *the entire sequence lasts fourteen minutes, and this night lasts fourteen minutes of fiction. I thought that the cutting implied a fictional time. Even a film supposed to be shot in real time implies a fictional time. Cinema implies a fictional time, and you might very well shoot an action as it takes place, sometimes it is longer than in the film, sometimes the fiction is longer than reality. A film by Bresson for example, is longer than reality, but most of the time, it is shorter.*[25]

Eustache was keenly aware of Bresson's montage and its radical effect on human gestures, its dissection and decomposition of bodies and actions. Like Bresson, who had unique ways of transforming "concrete time into symbolic temporality,"[26] Eustache was very sensitive to the impact of camera movements whose accelerations and decelerations disclose the "imperceptible" dimension of human affect. Seeking to forge a reality whose autonomy stems above all from its powerful temporal dimension, Eustache relied on the "scrupulous recording of emotion in long takes."[27] Like Bresson, Eustache transformed time into duration, and the materiality of the shot into a formal event. At once a celebration and a critique, *The Mother and the Whore* circulates among cinephiles, in Nicole Brenez's words, as the "profane reincarnation of Bresson, to the measure of its model."[28]

The Anxiety of Influence

If Weingarten's Gilberte both resuscitates an over-determined physiognomy and enacts Eustache's fascination with a special understanding of temporality, she does not straightforwardly attest to Eustache's Bressonianism. Unlike Bresson's color films, Eustache's most famous feature is verbose, theatrical, and rooted in the post-May 1968 tumultuous and disillusioned times. Eustache's next feature, *Mes petites amoureuses* (1974) represents his most overtly Bressonian endeavor. Like *Mouchette*, audacious and demanding, the film possesses a familiar austerity, as well as a resolute restraint. Unlike *Mouchette*, whose formal unity is stunning, *Mes petites amoureuses* seems to mock the repetition of identical patterns and insistently refuses to let despair or "predestination," to use a Bressonian term, figure in this childhood story. The film traverses the uncertain territory of pre-adolescence in which sexuality overcomes the body; solitude and humiliation provide a backdrop for this tale of sexual awakening in which Eustache's young hero experiences both puberty and poverty.[29]

The modest commercial success of *The Mother and the Whore* allowed Eustache to shoot in "normal" conditions for the first and only time in his life. Produced in the aftermath of May 1968, *The Mother and the Whore* focuses on Alexandre, another of Eustache's alter egos played by Jean-Pierre Léaud, who had previously appeared as Daniel in *Le Père Noël a les yeux bleus*. Written between these two films, *Mes petites amoureuses*, a tale of Eustache/Daniel's childhood similar in its thematics to *400 Blows*, was held up due to financial difficulties. Unlike Truffaut, whose debut feature both recounted his childhood and served to jumpstart a successful long career, Eustache would have to gain a hard-won base of operation in French cinema before he could make a film about his childhood.

Mes petites amoureuses follows Daniel as he finishes middle school in his grandmother's village and is taken by his mother to the city. Sent to work in a bicycle shop, his education is brought to an end. As the film chronicles Daniel's outings—to a café, to the movies, to the esplanade, to neighboring villages—Eustache replicates *The Mother and the Whore*'s brilliant method of offering at once a close-up of a character's personal story in all its everydayness, and a more panoramic view of a community, all this set against the background of postwar French society in the midst of rapid modernization. The somberness of the film testifies to the poverty, both material and emotional, experienced by the child Eustache, a condition that he thought of as a congenital fault that only cinema could cure.

Seeking to reshape what he considered to be his own existential plight into a work of art, Eustache relied on a Bressonian *mise-en-scène* very close to that of *Pickpocket*: voice-over for the narration, and especially for the commentary, direct views of opening and closing doors, omnipresence of the main character. Everything is seen through Daniel's eyes and each sequence represents a step in his quest for selfhood and a place in the world.[30] Daniel is the pickpocket at the age of thirteen, a masculine Mouchette, even a sort of Balthazar. The visual gravity, combined with the voice-over, the dissolves to black, the precise montage in which each shot corresponds to a single expression—these all figure in the film's first sequence, the site of a solemn communion that recalls not only Bresson's

Illustration 3.4 Daniel à l'église (*Mes petites amoureuses*, dir. Jean Eustache, 1974)

style, but his religious impetus as well—at least to a point. In one of the early scenes, we see the choir children advance toward the altar. As Daniel walks slowly behind a young girl, we find ourselves altogether unprepared for the bluntness of his declaration: "I felt my sex harden. I pressed myself against her."[31]

The investigation of the adolescent's sexuality employs Bresson's formalist principles so faithfully that the effect is overwhelming. One might even go as far as to say that the film teaches us more about Bresson than about his influence on Eustache. Nicole Brenez notes how spiritual problems become problems of the body, how that which usually pertains to morality becomes behavior: "*Mes petites amoureuses* transposes the Bressonian metaphysics in organic terms."[32] There is something aggressive in this inversion of spirituality and sexuality; the gesture also reverses the priority of the stylistic model, and forges a relationship beyond the homage and its reverent quotation.[33] Quite strikingly, Eustache's enterprise elucidates the method of his elder, demonstrating how Bresson's is a cinema of the body just as much as one of the spirit, how transcendental questions come to life in the minute details of filmed bodies. Bresson wanted his models to reanimate their bodies, to live *with*, indeed *in* them, rather than in the way of professional actors simply utilizing them as tools.

To say that Eustache's relationship to Bresson is neither unidirectional nor unequivocal is to confirm the tremendous degree of his creativity. Eustache's originality derives first and foremost, as Michel Estève pointed out, from the intimate relationship between the life he led and the films he made.[34] Daniel of *Mes petites amoureuses*, Daniel of *Le Père Noël a les yeux bleus*, and Alexandre of *The Mother and the Whore* offer cinematic variations on existential possibility. Eustache does not seek to remember his childhood, but rather to inscribe it in an absolute present. It is particularly in this distance from his self that he emulates Bresson.[35] Eustache resuscitates Bresson's work in order to recode it; it is for this reason that the girl who Daniel meets towards the end of the movie looks so very much like Mouchette. The iconographic quotation transforms its original and redirects it, for her destiny will surely not be Mouchette's. The story of this new "little lover" Mouchette is a painful story of childhood, as Eustache's film has us feel, but is much less unbearable than that of Bresson's heroine.

Illustration 3.5 Petite Mouchette (*Mes petites amoureuses*, dir. Jean Eustache, 1974)

In an ambience of sadness and bitterness, *Mes petites amoureuses* revolves around two privileged aspects of childhood narratives, desire and poverty. The display of desire recalls Truffaut's *Les Mistons* with its similar geographical surroundings and childhood longings. Truffaut's characters mischievously spy on and lust after a young girl, caressing and kissing and hoping for a little bit more than the mores of the times would allow. Eustache, however, is bolder and more serious. His project eschews Truffaut's evocative and nostalgic remembrance. His Daniel is not the child experiencing the story, nor the forty-year-old telling it. There is almost a "schizophrenic relation" in the character's perception of his life in the city, which contaminates his relationship with others. The poverty on view here, both material and emotional, resonates strongly with that of Maurice Pialat's *L'Enfance nue* (*Naked Childhood*, 1968).[36] As is the case in Pialat's film, there is no camaraderie, only sullen silence and painful solitude.

The comparison with *Les Mistons* brings to mind another crucial legacy that spans the history of French cinema and takes us back to Jean Renoir. The landscape, village life, and local customs—the young men swimming across a river to get the boat they will need to cross to the other shore on Sunday, Daniel's apparently definitive departure from the grandmother's house which his neighbors take to be a rite of passage—are imbued with a blend of earnestness, conviviality, and affection. The film's atmosphere recalls the work of Renoir from *Toni* to *Une partie de campagne*; in its social realism, class determinations inform the psychology and behavior of children and adults alike. Even secondary characters are subtly portrayed, like the neighborhood trafficker (his pockets invariably full of cash, always in his Sunday's best), the abandoned girlfriend (constantly passing by the terrace of the café in the hope of seducing her long lost ex-lover), or the Spanish stepfather reminiscent of *Toni*.

Other elements of the film have a less everyday aspect; indeed, they appear to be alien, uncanny, and inexplicable. They lack the fluidity and vitality of Renoir's realism. Indeed, their rigor and fragmentation lend an altogether different countenance to the visible. Unrelenting wide views of empty country spaces alternate with close-up images of Daniel's fixed, focused, and often unhappy gaze. Off-screen spaces assume a suggestive importance, as do the intervals between sequences, ellipses that evoke the invisible but undeniable presence of the empirical world. The characters speak "falsely" and dialogues are pointed, like a ping-pong exchange, a mode of speech reminiscent of Bresson, not Renoir.

Although *Mes petites amoureuses* offers a *mise-en-scène* of childhood memory, or rather remembrance, its impetus is anything but Proustian. With Eustache, there is no *madeleine* cookie that triggers taste, sensation, or association; his recollection is driven by the idea of memory, or better said, anti-memory. The beginning of the film makes this emphasis clear: as Daniel/Eustache sees himself in the past, he (and we) cannot see or hear his friends. What we partake of is their undeniable presence, the evidence of their bodies. These fragmented, abstract memories gravitate around something past rather than something concrete. They seem to belong to someone else, a third party who gives voice to them through the medium of Daniel or Eustache.[37] The same goes for the spaces, "spaces whatsoever," streets, places, and deserted houses, deprived of atmosphere and sensuality, "a past reality reduced to its idea."[38] The locations are never identified; one needs to know and recognize Narbonne if one is to gain a sense of spatial orientation.

This ascetic treatment of people and places subdues any realist project, and it grants all that it encompasses the weight—imprecise, faded, and almost abstract—

Illustration 3.6 Daniel Pickpocket (*Mes petites amoureuses*, dir. Jean Eustache, 1974)

Illustration 3.7 Daniel Pickpocket, Hand 1 (*Mes petites amoureuses*, dir. Jean Eustache, 1974)

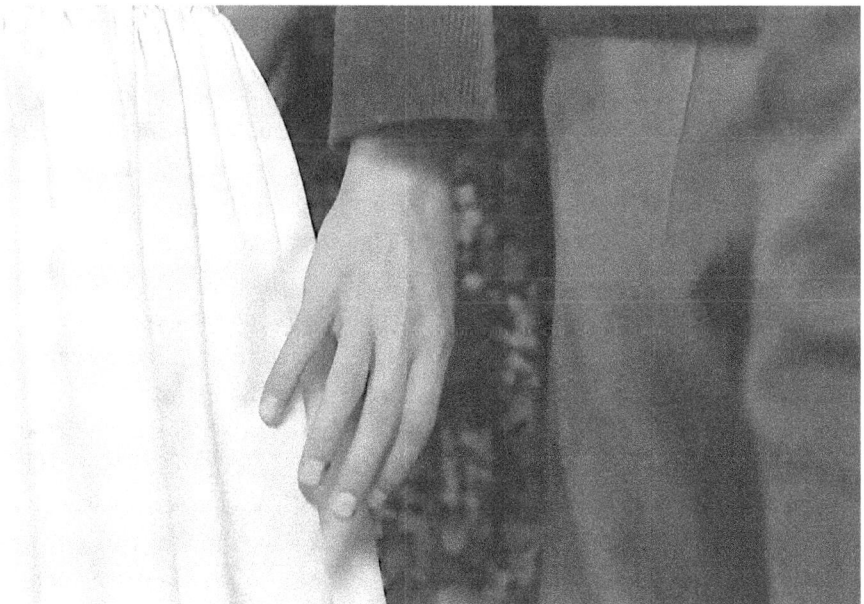

Illustration 3.8 Daniel Pickpocket, Hand 2 (*Mes petites amoureuses*, dir. Jean Eustache, 1974)

Illustration 3.9 Pickpocket at Work 1 (*Pickpocket*, dir. Robert Bresson, 1959)

of things past that are being recollected. Unlike Bresson, whose presentness never falters, Eustache writes Daniel's story as if it had emerged from a dense fog threatening to engulf his memories. The regular dissolves to black, as well as the unpredictable length of shots, mark the individual episodes as the disconnected and unlinkable pieces of a narrative, tightly framed tableaux with an occasional primitive theatricality that put on display the throes of a burgeoning sexuality, the injustices of the working world, and the awakening of a social consciousness.

Nothing testifies more strongly to Eustache's deference to Bresson than the scene at the civic fair in *Mes petites amoureuses* in which Daniel listens to girls in a choir sing "T'es bien trop petit mon ami," a sequence that replicates the famous beginning of *Pickpocket*. The young girl in a white dress, next to Daniel, both responds and does not respond to his daring touch. The choreography of shot-reverse shot alternates between Daniel's hungry stare and the choir performance, between his fixed gaze and his wandering hand. The girl's mother, taking note of the transgression, grabs her daughter and departs in a huff. The scene features no totalizing point of view, nor does it elucidate the narrative; it separates this

Illustration 3.10 Pickpocket at Work 2 (*Pickpocket*, dir. Robert Bresson, 1959)

moment from its viewer, sustaining an impossible dialogue that poignantly accentuates Daniel's solitude.

Eustache's method, at once more empirical and less rigorous than Bresson's, discloses the powerful and moving coexistence of that which is palpably true and painfully present as well as that which is just as undeniably inconsistent, atonal, and false. And there is no tension between the two registers of experience; the salient truth does not (and, for Eustache, cannot) redeem the presence of the false. In Bresson, the body is the architecture of the soul. Matter informs and governs the spirit, the soul vibrates in the concrete flesh and the flesh resonates with the graceful vibration of the soul. In Eustache, the noble and the true oblige us to accept (rather than reject or seek to overcome) the abject as a symmetrical equal. This is evident in the content of his films as well as in their singular form.

The variances between these two filmmakers, who employ different means to similar ends, are perplexing. Does Eustache, in deferring to Bresson's example, seek to defy its rigor? If his act of borrowing suggests a filiation, one is left to wonder whether it fosters a legacy grounded in the rejection of actors' performance in favor of models' iconography and filmic fragmentation. How are we to understand Eustache's resistance to the master's lessons? Beyond the apparent straightforwardness of the quoting gesture, which might have been Eustache's overt intention, the reference surely also provides, as stated, a cinematic enactment of the "anxiety of influence." With Eustache, Bressonianism functions in a transparent way at the level of quotation, informing a complex nexus of principles inherited from and influenced by Bresson's cinema.

"Un Marginal du Centre"

Eustache's *Mes petites amoureuses* features the French film director Maurice Pialat as the friend of the mechanic in whose shop the main character Daniel works. At one point the mechanic and his friend criticize the education system for passing on abstract and worthless knowledge, instead of *savoir-faire* and practical sense. Daniel, who has had to quit school, is asked to recite the alphabet ("a – bé – cé – dé – eu") only to be brutally mocked (the alphabet is "a-beu-seu-queu-deu-eu-feu-gueu"). Everything takes place as if Pialat and Eustache, in an act of working-class solidarity, had united to rebuke the official system, seeking to stake a place of their own in the French film world apart from the intellectual proclivities and bourgeois pretensions of the Nouvelle Vague as well as at a remove from the contemporary mainstream cinema.

There are a number of resemblances between the two filmmakers, both in terms of subject and execution. Luc Moullet, who produced Eustache's *Numéro zéro* and offered him work on the editing set of his own films, is keen to mention the friendship that linked him to Pialat whom he greatly admired: "Two excessive, short-tempered, fiery filmmakers, who distinguished themselves by their rejection of big, complex, dramatic constructions and exploitative situations, by their keen observations of human behavior, and by a certain dislike of plasticity."[39] In his monograph on Jean Eustache, Alain Philippon mentions his attempts to get the Eustache-Pialat-Rozier trio to collaborate, referring to them as "Renoir's children."[40] Philippon's efforts were in vain, for the initiative to create a movement (or a school) was hard to repeat after the stunning success of the Nouvelle Vague. Pialat and Eustache, and with them Jacques Doillon, Philippe Garrel, and Jacques Rozier, would figure in a constellation of filmmakers linked to and yet directed against the Nouvelle Vague. Drawing on the problems of proletarian and middle-class populations, their films transgress the border between populist cinema and the *cinéma d'auteur,* and in that way follow Renoir's lead. However, if Renoir's films are accessible, well crafted, and inviting, the films of his "children" are difficult, demanding, and elusive. What unites these filmmakers is not so much an approach to filmmaking, but rather a radical understanding of film's potential that takes recourse to less popular and conventional methods. For that reason the impetus of such marginal filmmaking will also have significant ramifications in matters of production, distribution, and spectatorship.

After the popular success of Pialat's 1983 film *À nos amours,* film critics extolled his greatness. Alain Bergala located his work within a "marginal[ité] du centre," pointing both to its centrality within French film culture and its marginal status in the critical scene during the early days of the director's career, especially in comparison to the Nouvelle Vague's wide acclaim.[41] Not enjoying the international reputation of his more visible contemporaries, but attracting far larger audiences than they ever would, Pialat's career was in equal measure idiosyncratic and eccentric. He abhorred the cinephilic playfulness of his colleagues,[42] and because he had to wait much longer than they did to finish his debut feature, resented what he deemed to be the ease with which his peers had been able to fund and make their first films.[43] From the opening shot of a workers' demonstration in *L'Enfance nue* to *La Maison des bois,* with its chronicle of everyday life during the World War I, Pialat's entire œuvre fixes on the class differences and social inequities of a postwar nation catching up with the effects of modernization. To the Parisian landscapes mapped and embraced by Truffaut, Godard, Rivette, and Rohmer, Pialat opposes the ugly countenances of the *banlieues* and the unglamorous confines of provincial landscapes.

If the Nouvelle Vague filmmakers by and large drew their intertextual references from the world of cinema, Pialat came with a different point of orientation: the universe of painting understood not as culture, but as practice. He saw himself as a worker for whom filmmaking was a manual exercise and a labor, and not a theoretical or critical enterprise. His references are mostly French, and, with the exception of Bresson with whom he shared his training as a painter,[44] derive to a great extent from popular cinema, especially the Saturday night screenings of his childhood. He admired Pagnol, Carné, and the early Renoir, but his essential point of reference was the Lumière Brothers. Pialat's background differed from that of most Nouvelle Vague directors as did his affect and aspirations. He was relentlessly self-deprecating and, at the same time, ceaselessly demanding of those with whom he worked, with actors, technicians, and above all himself.[45]

Pialat's reputation as a difficult director who abused his collaborators preceded any other epithet or praise that one might grant his films.[46] Although he was obstinate and mercurial, Pialat enjoyed much popular success, especially in the 1980s; four of his films (*À nos amours*, *Police*, *Sous le soleil de Satan*, and *Van Gogh*) attracted over four million viewers, a spectatorship that in sum surpassed that of all of the films by Nouvelle Vague directors put together.[47] Unceasing self-doubt went hand-in-hand with Pialat's profound distrust of the established film industry as well as his virulent resentment of the Nouvelle Vague. Truffaut may have supported the project of *L'Enfance nue*, but he did so in spite of Pialat, who saw a downside in everything, even in the prestigious Jean Vigo Prize awarded to his first feature in 1969. This was the second institutional recognition of his career after the Louis Lumière Prize in 1961 for his short *L'Amour existe*.

A profound awareness of class distinctions and social inequities drives Pialat's narratives. His characters face acute material exigency and the emotional hunger that attends it. On occasion they briefly succeed in overcoming their material difficulties only to face a cruel turn of fortune and the renewed prospect of failure. These heartbreaking narratives take on formal shape in bleak compositions that emphasize the harsh realities of hard lives. There is an intense (and at times even melodramatic) melancholy in Pialat's excruciatingly long takes and revealing deep-focus shots. Even though his films follow paths to ruin, humiliation, and sometimes death, an indefatigable survival instinct abides in their players' acts of obstinacy and resistance. Pialat suspends the laws of narrative chronology, often effacing temporal marks so that time becomes protracted, the world seemingly unchanged and, by implication, unchangeable. Despite the passage of six years in *Nous ne vieillirons pas ensemble* (*We Won't Grow Old Together*, 1972), for instance, Jean and Catherine do not visibly age or seem to alter their wardrobes. Change is unlikely in a world where time seems to stand still, where people remain the captives of their limited circumstances and their narrow perspectives. At the end of *À nos amours*, Suzanne leaves for California with a new lover knowing all too well that he is not going to make her happy. *Loulou*'s main character disappears into the night, facing the undeniable prospect of his continuing misery. Mangin of *Police* and the priest of *Under the Sun of Satan* likewise will surrender to the painful certainty of their finitude. Despite their self-destructiveness, Pialat's characters cling to life even while marching to their ruin. Only Van Gogh, in his act of suicide, will fully succumb to the allure of disappearance common to so many of Pialat's personages. The essential thing for the director is not the inevitable fatal outcome but the struggle that comes before the end. As he puts it, "every creative work is a battle against death."[48]

Uncommon Sensibilities

Pialat's work has inspired many comparisons with that of Bresson. In a certain respect this is surprising, for their sensibilities diverged greatly. The argumentative, unpredictable, and resentful Pialat had an altogether different personality than the composed, confident, and seemingly self-possessed Bresson. Nonetheless, they shared a background as painters that would strongly inflect their self-understanding as filmmakers. Both disdained conventional psychological drama and stagey cinema; each often made use of nonprofessional actors. And the two directors embraced the cinematic medium as a vehicle to probe the real and fathom what they considered to be its more profound and often hidden truths. Nonetheless, as we read in Marja Warehime's recent monograph on Pialat, "nothing could seem further from the 'naturalism' (although Pialat rejected the label) of Pialat's work, where eros, love, hate and death have an overwhelming material reality, than the 'spiritual style' of Bresson's films."[49] Indeed, the paradigm of a transcendental cinema used by Schrader and others to apprehend Bresson's work does not serve one well in encounters with the instinctual needs and material depravations of Pialat's films. Bresson's characters, one might say, plot their salvation and eternity while Pialat's simply try to navigate the prison house of mortality.

A strong unity of form and content links the work of Pialat to that of Eustache and, in the propensity for narratives rooted in a world ruled by doubt and chance, also to that of Bresson. With Pialat, however, the painful awareness of every aesthetic choice is played out before our eyes; the cinematographic process is dismantled, torn to pieces, and shredded like a fatal illusion. Pialat cannot help but expose the medium as he digs deeply into the inner reaches of his characters. Be it in the framing, the editing, the choice of angles or the combinations of words and images, everything is unveiled as it takes place. Pialat often sacrificed the formal beauty of his images, retaining "shots that were less than perfect, technically or otherwise, where the image was slightly out of focus, under- or overexposed, where a microphone was visible in the frame."[50] This was, however, not a price he paid in order to capture the messy lives of his characters and the harsh terms of their circumstances, but rather a calculated way of making sure that he could find the formal means to match them. Pialat's cinema offers a vision of naked truths and worlds stripped to the bone, revealing what people look like behind all their defenses and disguises. The aesthetic smoothness of Bresson's dramas of the spirit finds a striking counterpart in the formal nakedness of Pialat's tragedies of the flesh.

In his work with actors, Bresson preferred lengthy rehearsals and many takes, as Theodor Kotulla's documentary of 1967 on the shooting of *Mouchette* demonstrates.[51] Unlike Bresson who required his models to follow his detailed instructions with utter exactitude, Pialat's approach was more instinctive. He relished having his actors grow into and merge with their characters so that they might put their own personas, with all their fragilities and imperfections, into their roles. This is why the men and women in Pialat's films are all so different in their bodily constitution, physical expression, and star status, while Bresson's players in comparison appear strikingly homogenous. If Bresson seeks to evoke what belongs to all of us and unites us, Pialat celebrates the mad, disruptive, and buoyant differences within the spectrum of human possibility.

There is also a marked variance in their work's negotiation of temporality. In Bresson's films fragmentation serves the narrative economy, as we have seen in the analysis of *Mouchette*. In Pialat the concerted use of fragmentation and ellipsis makes it at times difficult to reconstitute the relationship between individual scenes or determine the duration of events. We are often left to wonder how much time, if any, has passed between shots and sequences. Above all, Pialat suspends the temporal logic of the film and emphasizes its weight and gravity. Time is absorbed, space feeds off its materiality, creating a magnetic field that both attracts and confounds the spectator. The singular fragmentation of space and time is essential to Bresson's films and altogether out of keeping with Pialat's intense cinema of duration. Whereas Bresson fractures the continuity of time and space and the integrity of bodies in brief shots that collide with each other, Pialat (even when shooting scenes indoors) privileges the long take, wide composition, and depth of field. The long take generally respects the duration of the event, and the wide frame allows for optimal insertion of the characters in their milieus.

The Shadow of Grace

When Pialat set out to film Georges Bernanos's *Sous le soleil de Satan*, he realized well that he would have to reckon with a formidable novel as well as with the imposing standard set by Bresson's rendering of the writer's other work.[52] As a literary adaptation, the film offers an engaging point of reference for the purposes of our discussion. It is in fact the only feature by Pialat not based on an original script; the director maintained that the project occupied his mind well before he made his first film. Bernanos's novel abounds with inner monologue and contains little dialogue. The adaptation was conducted under the constraining supervision of the writer's heirs, who were very protective of the original text. For the first time, a film by Pialat gained its narrative shape in the process of writing rather than during shooting. The feature's strength above all derives from Pialat's choice of actors, especially Depardieu in the role of Donissan and Sandrine Bonnaire as Mouchette. Their stark physical presence transforms the supernatural story of the novel into a realistic, even naturalistic narrative.

Pialat's script streamlines and condenses the three parts of Bernanos's novel. Menou-Segrais (Maurice Pialat), priest and Dean of Campagne, a village in the north, is the superior and spiritual advisor of the priest Donissan (Gérard Depardieu). The young man, whose abruptness scares the parishioners, lacks the ease and eloquence of his superior. Troubled by doubts about his vocation, he punishes himself with brutal mortifications of the flesh. One of the parishioners, the sixteen-year old Mouchette (Sandrine Bonnaire), pregnant with the child of Marquis de Cadignan (Alain Arthur), kills her lover when he refuses to flee with her from Campagne. Determined to escape to Paris, she admits the crime to her other lover, only to face incredulity as well as his refusal to leave his wife and abandon his station of social privilege as doctor and deputy. Dispatched by Menou-Segrais on a mission to the neighboring village Étaples, Donissan loses his way and is rescued by a horse-trader in whom he recognizes Satan. He is tempted by the devil's promise of a deeper self-knowledge and the power to see within the souls of others. On his way back to Campagne, he encounters Mouchette and, reading her mind and realizing that she has committed a crime, begs her to repent. When Mouchette later slits her throat, Donissan places her corpse on the church's altar and claims that it was her dying wish. In response to this act of desecration, Menou-Segrais sends the priest to a monastery. Years later Donissan resumes his parish work, but remains torn between the vocation of sainthood and the temptation of Satan. His self-doubts cause him to neglect a dying child; arriving after the boy has expired, he begs for a miracle, sacrificing the salvation of his soul for the youth's resurrection. Hailed as a saint by the elated mother, he returns to the church and the waiting parishioners before dying of a heart attack. Menou-Segrais seeks him out and stands before him in a confession booth, closing the eyes of the tormented priest.

One cannot help but wonder how Bernanos's "spiritual" and "surreal" explorations, which could not be further removed from Pialat's materialistic and profane proclivities, could have piqued the filmmaker's interest. Contrary to one's expectations, the film treats the supernatural dimensions of the book with an unabashed straightforwardness, without any dramatic touches or special effects. This becomes strikingly manifest in the film's set piece, the priest's walk from Étaples to Campagne. The trip in Bernanos's novel represents a journey into darkness and a passage into the uncanny. The stranger is felt before he is seen; once he appears, he shifts shapes and moves from one side of Donissan to the other as if he were a fantastic creature. At one point he pitches ahead as if driven by a fast forward; at another he assumes the countenance of the priest's double. Indeed, Bernanos's *Sous le soleil de Satan* possesses all of the cinematic allure that Rancière has also discovered in the writer's *Mouchette*.[53] In Pialat's adaptation, the walk remains a long trek through wintry fields in inclement weather. The nocturnal

Illustration 3.11 Arduous Walk (*Sous le soleil de Satan,* dir. Maurice Pialat, 1987)

Illustration 3.12 Erotic Encounter (*Sous le soleil de Satan*, dir. Maurice Pialat, 1987)

route is rough and uneven; it takes the priest through muddy paths and plowed fields. In the encounter with the stranger, there is no generic border-crossing into the territory of the horror film. There are no shock cuts, no sudden changes of appearance, and no disorienting shifts of place and perspective. The confrontation with the devil, which becomes a veritable psychomachia in Bernanos, remains in Pialat's tableau a dialogue with a stranger, who appears out of nowhere and later departs. The only tonal remnant of the novel's uncanny encounter in the film is a chilling kiss and erotically charged embrace.

    A striking example of the substantial variance between the novel and the film comes in the cut that links the narratives of Donissan and Mouchette at the beginning of the film. Giving the sacred Eucharist to churchgoers, Donissan raises his eyes and looks at the cathedral door. As we follow his gaze, we see a young woman entering, only to catch ourselves as we realize that Mouchette has not stepped into the church, but rather her lover's mansion. The novel, organized in three parts, is altogether different in its negotiation of the two destinies. It begins with "The Story of Mouchette" without a single mention of the priest. The second story, "The Temptation of Despair," focuses on Donissan's development under the tutelage of the Dean of Campagne, and ends with Mouchette's suicide and the priest's attempt to "give her back to God" by carrying her corpse to the church

Illustration 3.13 Priest in Church (*Sous le soleil de Satan*, dir. Maurice Pialat, 1987)

Illustration 3.14 Mouchette Enters Room (*Sous le soleil de Satan*, dir. Maurice Pialat, 1987)

altar. This desperate act occasions a harsh response and the priest is sent packing to a Trappist monastery.

In the film, Mouchette commits suicide after her encounter with Donissan at the end of his long night during which he sees "through" her body into her inner soul, recognizing the murder she has committed and her utter despair. Unlike the scene in Bernanos's novel, their meeting has nothing surreal or supernatural about it; the earlier cut with its conspicuous eyeline match has already anticipated the encounter and intimated an affinity between these distraught souls. When Donissan predicts Mouchette's suicide and arrives at her house shortly thereafter in the hope of rescuing her soul, there is no great surprise. In this way, the film forges an unholy alliance between the two cursed figures. Mouchette dedicates herself to the forces of evil yet wants to return to God; Donissan commits his soul to a holy vocation, but is interrupted and sidetracked by Satan's temptations. Setting the tone for the adaptation, and establishing Pialat as a master of his own medium, the elliptical cut between the doomed characters is not only a sign of an adaptation's narrative economy, but also a way of negotiating and neutralizing the metaphysics of faith so present in Bernanos's prose.

Much about the film is reminiscent of Bresson: the austerity of the shots, the elliptical construction, and the fragmentation of body parts. Rendering Bernanos's prose in a filmic form, Pialat followed Bresson's lead in crucial regards. There is

Illustration 3.15 The Dead Priest (*Sous le soleil de Satan*, dir. Maurice Pialat, 1987)

Illustration 3.16 Death Mask (*Sous le soleil de Satan*, dir. Maurice Pialat, 1987)

nothing strikingly visual or picturesque in his images, not even in the wide agrarian landscapes saturated with fresh green color. On the other hand, the dialogues and the way in which they are integrated in the visual economy of the film could not be more different. A comparison of the divergent ways in which Bresson and Pialat adapted the closing sequences of Bernanos's novels about the travails of priests is instructive. In *Diary of a Country Priest*, we see the weary and distraught priest on his last legs. The camera then cuts to a letter that, in a voice-over, provides a chronicle of the poor man's last hours and his final words "What does it matter? All is grace." that are uttered before the screen empties out and its whiteness is filled with a large grey cross. In *Under the Sun of Satan*, the tormented Donissan expires in a confession booth. Pialat's lighting is precise and stark, shrouding the priest's face in darkness. Menou-Segrais will come into the space and close the deceased's eyes. The film leaves the viewer with a striking final image of a corpse that has become a death mask. There is no grace; there is only the fact of one man's life of suffering which has finally come to an end.

It is above all the virulent disparity in the conception of and approach to bodies that separates the two filmmakers. In *Under the Sun of Satan*, Depardieu's body becomes the "stage of the most violent struggle, culminating with the last heart attack, when Donissan seems to receive in his chest the stabs of an invisible opponent."[54] Depardieu's performance is formidable. The large actor gives life to an inner torment without the slightest grimace or convulsion. He uses slight contractions of the jaw and a large range of breathing sounds, from conspicuous sighing to excessive panting. He has an unforgettable way of carrying his stocky frame, corseted in a constant imbalance, slightly leaning to one side or the other depending on where he is standing. Heavy and maladroit, Depardieu seems to disappear into the landscape when he meets the horse-trader who embodies Satan. The ungainliness of his physique, the fierceness of his struggle with the devil, the difficulties he has in articulating his thoughts: everything here serves to provide the drama with a physical ground, to divest it of any mystical or metaphysical dimension, and to grant the film an undeniable corporeal intensity.

Renowned for his cruelty, Pialat demanded his actors' full commitment, even if it meant psychological or even physical violence. If his films feel like open wounds, it is because they issue from sites of duress, from acts of violence sustained by the director to penetrate what he deemed to be the truth concealed in the depth of his actors' beings. Like Bresson, Pialat spoke of a quest for profound truth; unlike Bresson, he sought it in the weight and gravity of moving—and suffering—bodies that were forced to bear tortures catalyzed by the filmmaker's own pain and despair. This method was certainly not easy on Pialat's teams. To this day his difficult relationship with his actors remains the source of many painful and bitter memories.

The Torment of Truth

The abstract and fantastic story of a priest's doubts, somber and surreal, so different from what one might expect from a filmmaker whose previous films explode with the force of pent-up human emotions, *Under the Sun of Satan* bears Pialat's inimitable signature. Like the film's protagonist, Pialat's cinema itself lingers in a constant state of uncertainty, ever second-guessing itself, constantly distancing itself from the security of the tried-and-true and the straightforward. In his undeniably profane way, Pialat combats what Bernanos terms "the satanic temptation of despair." Afraid of achieving the "success" that he desired more than anything, Pialat made work difficult on the set and in the editing room, for the people he worked with and above all for himself. As if echoing the novel's plot, the film captures the traces of this fight with the Satan of cinema, the devil in one's ear who ceaselessly whispers that it is purposeless to fight the good battle and try to be different. This doubt afflicts filmmakers of various sorts regardless whether they are mainstream directors or consummate *auteurs*. The concepts of *auteur* and cinema themselves falter as they face the task of the original moment. For Pialat this original moment derives from the Lumière Brothers and the utter transparency of their realism.[55] "Men and women recorded by an apparatus they knew nothing about," Pialat avers, "gave away a moment of their lives and since then all the actors have done the same. When it comes to the fantastic, Lumière outmatches Méliès."[56]

Pialat's travail and torment as a filmmaker can be projected onto Donissan's struggle with his faith. That Menou-Segrais, who guides Donissan, is played by Pialat himself opens the film to a reading that centers around the mixture of despair and hope experienced by the characters, but above all, the Mephistophelian pact that the filmmaker might be ready to sign in order to find his true artistic vocation and gain popular recognition. The casting choice also signals the filmmaker's self-destructive doubt, his fear of conformity, and the dangers of cowardice. "A strange character that combines strength, contained rage and tenderness,"[57] Menou-Segrais plays the role of an "enabler." It is he who takes responsibility for this errant spirit in spite of the young priest's awkwardness and inability to preach the word of God. It is the elder who plots his counterpart's manifest destiny by dispatching him on a journey into the night and toward a fateful meeting with the devil. The ensuing virulence of doubt serves more to reveal Menou-Segrais's weakness than confirm the inevitability of Donissan's demise. The priest will remain the chief executor of Donissan's fate, there at the bitter end to close his eyes.

Should we see in Pialat's relationship with Donissan/Depardieu an embodiment of the dynamic between creator and creation? To be sure, Pialat was not wont to allegorize the filmmaking process. For this reason, it is more plausible to see in *Under the Sun of Satan* a psychodrama, or better yet, a psychomachia, an enactment of the director's anxieties, desires, and doubts. In this way, Pialat addresses the question of religious faith on his own terms, all the better to confirm his belief in cinema's realist potential. A book about the mystery of faith becomes a film about faith in and doubt about cinema. Bernanos's book is metamorphosized into a secular tale, beautiful and enthralling, without losing the grace and poignance of the religious novel. Pialat's approach to grace, although different from Bresson's, suggests a common preoccupation of the two filmmakers, namely the gravity of cinema and its ability to fathom the weight of being.

As Menou-Segrais leads Donissan to his struggle with Satan, Pialat himself fights to elude the grip of Bernanos's text and to impose his own signature—and in the process also to distance himself from Bresson. The text poses formidable resistance to this willful spirit's attempts to remold it, to divest it of the surreal and fantastic trappings that are so out of keeping with Pialat's more secular interests and instincts. The intense stakes in this altercation might well account for the extreme conditions of the film's production, the physical dangers and vicissitudes that Pialat imposed on the actors and the team who were forced to work in a bitter cold and often to sustain long and complicated dialogues in one take. Trying to forge a space and a time that owed nothing to the novel, that belonged entirely and utterly to his film, Pialat drove himself as well as his collaborators to great extremes. *Under the Sun of Satan* abides as the remarkable and stirring work of a maniac of truth.

Joël Magny refers to Pialat's "denudation of the actor," in which both the soul and the body become divested of "protecting layers" so that one might penetrate "the shell of habits and propensities."[58] To reveal what he considers to be the truth of his characters, Pialat does not let Bresson's model (and the director's treatment of models) guide him. He does not divest his players of intention; on the contrary, he insists that the intent of their words and actions be radically embraced. He asks that actors fully inhabit their characters so that they might externalize the unconscious energies and darker motivations that drive them. Where Bresson insists on a rebirth that forces his models to forget lived experience, Pialat requires that actors transcend their selves and plumb the deepest depths of their beings with all their contradictions and imperfections, to follow the disturbing and messy trajectories of anxieties, resentments, and torments no matter where they might lead one. Whereas Bresson strives for simplification and purification, Pialat seeks to present the extremes and abysses of human existence without embellishment or compromise.[59] Eustache once said that he does not create anything; he simply films actors engaged in a creative process. For him creation passes through the word, enunciation, and discourse, a disposition that remains faithful to Bresson. This approach differs markedly from that of Pialat; in his case creativity emanates from within his actors' bodies; they anchor his films and grant gravity to his endeavors.

"Bresson is a dangerous master for his imitators," wrote Luc Moullet in his assessment of *Mes petites amoureuses* and its Bressonian frame.[60] Rather than a model that one emulates, Bresson serves for the Bressonians as a *revenant*, a singular author whose works "are not tombs, pyramids and sepulchers, but indefinitely iterable."[61] That two such seemingly incompatible concepts as canonical singularity and iterability might be mentioned in the same breath attests to the estimable role of Bresson's example in furthering a more expansive understanding of the *auteur* tradition as a site where singularity and community commingle. As we have seen, the two terms coexist and cooperate in the history of film authorship, both in the process of legitimating artists and furthering artistic practices. At the same time, the coexistence of such terms attests to a *return to* a practice of origin, in Foucault's understanding, albeit "not to restore the theme of an originating subject, but to seize its function."[62] The recourse to Bresson's stylistic patterns serves, I would argue, less to commemorate an author than to probe and at times question the value and criteria of authority that regulate access to and recognition by the professional community. In this sense, Eustache and Pialat do not defer to Bresson as disciples, but rather as "kinsmen," to use Alexandre Kojève's term from *The Notion of Authority*, a book that investigates the conceptual framework that has dominated discourses of authorship. While the authority of the Master or of the Leader can be unassailable, claims Kojève, a model of authority shared by a community of "kinsmen" offers a less strict disposition. Kinsmen "love one another according to their degree of kinship." Above all, they love "their common kin, their ancestors, the source and origin of the being to which they attribute a positive value. And if they recognize an Authority, it is the Authority of that 'kinsman' par excellence that they recognize, and it is the Authority of being as such who is recognized also by non-kindred members of the Family."[63]

For all their differences, Bresson, Eustache, and Pialat might be seen as kinsmen; they share a fervent belief in the possibility of cinema as a source of deeper truth (however one might want to define it) as well as the enduring awareness that this possibility can at best be approached but never realized. This shared belief is enacted in markedly different ways. Bresson, the absolute author, believes in the cinematograph as the enabler of grace and a revealer of truth and in himself as a chosen mediator. Eustache's belief in the cinema is lived differently; it abides even in the deep doubts that ensue from recognizing the limitations of the medium and his own filmic endeavors. As for Pialat, he never doubts the possibility of cinema, only himself as a filmmaker. Bresson, with his resolute poise and self-assurance, became and remained the author he wanted to be; Eustache and Pialat had a far less easy time of it in careers full of rifts and disturbances.

In the wake of Bresson, two formidable challenges to French film authorship would surface; the following chapters discuss how the Bressonians and their contemporaries confronted the crises surrounding the death of the author and the end of cinema.

Notes

1. Nicole Brenez, "Approche inhabituelle des corps," in *De la figure en général et du corps en particulier: L'invention figurative au cinéma* (Paris: DeBoeck Université, 1998), 68.
2. Moullet, "Blue Collar Dandy," 38–43.
3. He worked as an assistant on Rohmer's *La Boulangère de Monceau* and *La Carrière de Suzanne*, Jean Douchet's *Le Mannequin de Belleville*, and Jean-André Fieschi's first feature *L'Accompagnement*. See "Les Années d'apprentissage," in Alain Philippon, *Jean Eustache* (Paris: Cahiers du cinéma, coll. Auteurs, 2005), 11–20.
4. Eustache worked as a film editor for Luc Moullet and Jacques Rivette; he also edited his own films.
5. Antoine de Baecque, "Introduction," in *Le Dictionnaire Eustache* (Paris: Éditions Léo Scheer, 2011).

6. Moullet, "Blue Collar Dandy," 41.
7. Ibid.
8. Serge Daney, "Le fil," *Libération* (16 November 1981), quoted in de Baecque, *Le Dictionnaire Eustache*, 9: "Son cinéma était impitoyablement personnel. C'est-à-dire impitoyable d'abord pour sa propre personne, arraché à son expérience, à l'alcool, à l'amour. Faire le plein de son réel pour en faire le matériau de ses films, ceux que personne ne pourrait faire à sa place. Seule morale mais morale de fer: parvenir à transcrire ce qui le travaillait, les femmes, le dandysme, Paris, la campagne, la langue française. C'était déjà beaucoup."
9. Until the recent death of Chantal Akerman, Eustache was the only major French filmmaker to commit suicide. One can also count the name of Max Linder, who came from the same town of Pessac as Eustache.
10. It is surprising that Eustache decided to hire the "model" of *Four Nights of a Dreamer*, a film that he had spoken of as "inept" in an interview where he otherwise acknowledged his deep admiration for *Pickpocket* and Bresson's earlier work as well as his keen disappointment with the *auteur*'s later features. Towards the end of his life, Eustache would come to regret and retract these comments, praising *L'Argent* for its artistic achievements. See the interview with Serge Toubiana in Alain Philippon, *Jean Eustache* (Paris: Éditions de l'étoile, 2005), 96.
11. Harold Bloom, *The Anxiety of Influence: A Theory of Poetry* (Oxford, New York: Oxford University Press, 1973).
12. Paul Schrader deems Bresson's emphasis on his models' physiognomies to be the unmistakable signature of the director's "transcendental style." The proclivity, claims Schrader, has a long history and can be traced back to Byzantine iconography.
13. Brenez, "Approche inhabituelle des corps," 67.
14. Didier Morin, Interview with Isabelle Weingarten in "Les 40 ans de *La Maman et la putain*," *Mettray* (September 2013), n.p.
15. Barthélémy Amengual, "Une vie récluse en cinéma ou l'échec de Jean Eustache," *Études cinématographiques* 153 (1986): 103.
16. Jean-Claude Guiguet, "Entretien avec Françoise Lebrun," in Colette Dubois, *'La Maman et la putain' de Jean Eustache* (Paris: Yellow Now, coll. Long Métrage, 1990), 93. Luc Moullet's confessions about Eustache's work on the script of *The Mother and the Whore* point to the importance granted to voice and sound. See Moullet, "Blue Collar Dandy," 40: "[Eustache] was obsessed by this autobiographical project, and constantly dreamt about it. In 1971, lacking funds and with nothing else to do, he offered to edit my film *Une aventure de Billy the Kid*. In front of the Moviola, he would recite the dialogue he had written in his big notebook the night before, without pausing from his editing."
17. Morin, "Les 40 ans de *La Maman et la putain*," n.p.
18. Bresson, *Notes*, 7.
19. It was Françoise Lebrun's first leading role, and only her third film after *La Ville-bidon* (Jacques Baratier, 1971) and *Le Château de Pointilly* (Adolfo Arrieta, 1972).
20. In this enterprise, we find two further (albeit fleeting) cuts à la *Four Nights of a Dreamer*: (1) Interior: Alexandre borrows the keys of a young woman's car followed by a high-angle shot as Alexandre begins to walk down the stairs, then a cut to an exterior view of the car being parked on the street (with the sound of car engine starting links the two shots). (2) Alexandre and Gilberte sit on a bench in the Jardin du Luxembourg; in a series of oblique close-ups in shot-reverse shot, she talks about going to a café to eat something. The camera cuts to a parallel

medium-shot of the bench seen from the back, then cuts again to a similar set-up, with the couple no longer in the image.
21. Steven Shaviro, *The Cinematic Body* (Minneapolis: University of Minnesota Press, 1998), 249.
22. We see Alexandre sit in a café and read Eustache's fetish book, Proust's *The Remembrance of Time Past*. The author also had a notable impact on other Eustache films, most significantly on *Le Père Noël a les yeux bleus*, which the director spoke of in reference to Flaubert's *Sentimental Education*.
23. Moreover, it is in the use of sound and voice, in the dialectic between image and sound that, as we shall see in the fourth chapter, Eustache reveals Bresson's most poignant lesson.
24. Eustache in an interview with Sylvie Blum and Jérôme Prieur, "Scénario," *Caméra/stylo* (September 1983), reprinted in Philippon, *Jean Eustache*, 117–18.
25. Ibid., 118: "La séquence entière dure quatorze minutes et cette nuit dure quatorze minutes de fiction. J'ai pensé que le découpage impliquait un temps fictif. Même un film supposé être en temps réel implique un temps fictif. Le cinéma implique un temps fictif, et on a beau filmer une action qui se déroule, parfois c'est plus long que le film, parfois la fiction est plus longue que la réalité. Un film de Bresson par exemple, c'est plus long que la réalité, mais la plupart du temps, c'est plus court."
26. Brenez, "Approche inhabituelle des corps," 67.
27. Ibid., 67.
28. Ibid., 68.
29. The title refers to Arthur Rimbaud's poem: "Ô mes petites amoureuses/ Que je vous hais!/ Plaquez de fouffes douloureuses/ Vos tétons laids." ("O my little lovers/ How I hate you!/ Plaster with painful blisters/ Your ugly tits"). They are indeed young, these little lovers, a choir of girls between twelve and fourteen years who sing at a fair, "T'es bien trop p'tit mon ami," while Daniel tries to "touch" the girl next to him. The song is not innocent and in keeping with the film title's poignant meaning: the boy is too young to love, but not too young to suffer.
30. Marc Cérisuelo, "*Mes petites amoureuses*," in de Baecque, *Le Dictionnaire Eustache*, 191.
31. "Je sentais mon sexe se durcir. Je me suis serré contre elle."
32. Brenez, "Approche inhabituelle des corps," 69, my translation.
33. In Brenez's view, one can even speak of a *détournement*; the subversive imitation perpetuates the model, showing how a style of allegorical vocation can be the best way to describe the here and now of a common experience. See Brenez, "Approche inhabituelle des corps," 69–70.
34. "Jean Eustache présenté par Michel Estève," *Études cinématographiques* 153 (1986): "Jean Eustache ou le cinéma comme nécessité vitale, au sens propre du terme."
35. Amengual, "Une vie récluse en cinéma," 89.
36. Pialat plays a small role in the movie that attests to the class solidarity between the two filmmakers.
37. Amengual, "Une vie récluse en cinéma," 79. Amengual invokes "the imperious necessity of cinema as a Pascalian pastime (divertissement)." See Jean Eustache's interview in *Cahiers du cinéma* 187 (February 1967): "Bons films ou pas, l'indispensable est de tourner." "Le cinéma sauve mal et par d'étranges détours. 'Je crois que c'est en vivant qu'on fait acte de création. Pas en filmant. Si dans mes films il y a une création quelle qu'elle soit, elle vient du personnage, pas de moi. C'est le personnage qui en vivant fait création. Je filme cette création, c'est tout."
38. Amengual, "Une vie récluse en cinéma," 111.
39. See Moullet, "Blue Collar Dandy," 43.
40. Alain Philippon, *Jean Eustache*, 19.

41. Alain Bergala, "Maurice Pialat, un marginal du centre," *Cahiers du cinéma* 354 (1983), 20.
42. In a special issue taking stock of the Nouvelle Vague, French film director Noémie Lvovsky justified her lack of enthusiasm for Pialat's films because they do not possess the "playfulness" of features by Truffaut and Godard. See Olivier Assayas, Claire Denis, Cédric Kahn, and Noémie Lvovsky, "Quelques vagues plus tard," *Cahiers du cinéma* (Special Issue, 1998).
43. Maurice Pialat, "Entretien," *Cahiers du cinéma* 304 (1979): 15: "Vous savez, j'en veux (je dis bien: j'en veux) à la Nouvelle Vague."
44. See Serge Toubiana, *Maurice Pialat: Peintre et cinéaste* (Paris: Cinémathèque française, 2013).
45. Joël Magny, *Maurice Pialat* (Paris: Éditions de l'Étoile, 1992), 10.
46. See Antoine de Baecque, "Pialat, l'emmerdeur," in *Maurice Pialat, l'enfant sauvage*, ed. Sergio Toffetti and Aldo Tassone (Torino: Lindau, 1992).
47. *Le Retour du cinéma*, ed. Antoine de Baecque and Thierry Jousse (Paris: Hachette, 1996), 56.
48. Maurice Pialat, *À nos amours: scénario et dialogue du film* (Paris: L'Herminier, 1984), 14.
49. Warehime, *Maurice Pialat*, 8.
50. Ibid., 9.
51. See *Au hasard Bresson* (1967), included as a special feature in the Criterion 2006 DVD edition of *Mouchette*.
52. Pascal Mérigeau, *Pialat* (Paris: Grasset, 2002), 254.
53. See Rancière, *The Intervals of Cinema*.
54. Magny, *Maurice Pialat*, 103.
55. Jean Eustache also spoke of his desire to emulate the Lumière Brothers' first recordings of the world. See de Baecque, *Le Dictionnaire Eustache*, 11: "Je voudrais être révolutionnaire, c'est-à-dire ne pas faire des pas en avant dans le cinéma, mais essayer de faire des grands pas en arrière pour revenir aux sources. Le but que j'ai essayé d'atteindre depuis mon premier film, c'est de revenir à Lumière. Je suis peut-être réactionnaire, mais je crois être en cela révolutionnaire."
56. Quoted in Mérigeau, *Pialat*, 278.
57. Magny, *Maurice Pialat*, 105.
58. Ibid., 25–26.
59. Ibid., 28: Pialat's procedure seems in fact closer to that of Roberto Rossellini, for instance when he led Ingrid Bergman to "deliver her truth by relinquishing her stardom and embracing her womanhood."
60. Moullet, "Blue Collar Dandy," 41.
61. Burke, *The Death and Return of the Author*, xiii.
62. Foucault, "What is an Author?," 137.
63. Alexandre Kojève, *The Notion of Authority (A Brief Presentation)*, ed. François Terré, trans. Hager Weslati (London, New York: Verso, 2014), xv.

CHAPTER FOUR
The Ethics of Duplicity

> I will tell you that in this art that relies on images, the spectator has to lose the notion of image.
> — Robert Bresson, "Entretien avec François-Régis Bastide"

The Death of the Author

The question of authorship has been central to the development of film criticism since the 1950s; the ascription of a single, unified, and identifiable author to a film or a body of films has become inextricably bound to the status of film as an expressive form. Even though the medium would assume firm institutional shape as a collaborative, commercial, and narrative enterprise already in the 1910s, it would not be taken seriously as a legitimate art until it generated its own version of authorship. The auteurist movement became a significant factor not only for film theory, but also within the twentieth-century history of ideas. Nonetheless, its great success seems curious in light of what Colin MacCabe calls two "massive contradictions."[1] The first had to do with the collective nature of film production regulated by the legal determinations of a complex process that had led, as we have seen in the first chapter, to the law of 1957. By its very nature filmmaking is, in John Caughie's words, a "collective, commercial, industrial and popular" enterprise.[2] The multiple agencies involved in the making of a film are so diverse[3] and the process so intricately organized around a variety of specialist trades and professions that "for all practical purposes" film authorship seems impossible to assign.[4] Yet the victory in the long run of the *politique des auteurs* and the subsequent *auteur* theory was so considerable that this contradiction remained at best a quibble.

The second paradox stemmed from the simultaneous circulation of conflicting discourses on authorship. When classical auteurism seemed to be at its peak, cutting-edge work in linguistics, psychoanalysis, and the social sciences proclaimed the departure of belief in authority, intention, and creativity, a sentiment that found a resonant expression in "the death of the author," the title of Roland Barthes's famous essay. Barthes's manifesto formulated strong critical reservations about the institution of literary authorship, as well as recommending that criticism move beyond the "man-and-the-work" analyses and focus on the nature of the text in and for itself. Reiterating his desire for a more systematic approach to literature,[5] Barthes argued that the removal of the author is not just a critical strategy to approach literary texts in a systematic way, but that it represents a property of the discourse itself. Barthes was not alone in this resolve. In a similar vein, Claude Lévi-Strauss declared that "the goal of the human sciences is not to constitute man, but to dissolve him,"[6] formulating what would be seen as the "slogan of the decade" for France in the 1960s.

As Roland Barthes, Claude Lévi-Strauss, and Michel Foucault, to name just the most prominent voices, increasingly stressed the social and ideological construction of subjectivity, *auteur* theory continued to rely on a conception of unified agency. The notion of authorship in film criticism and film studies remained quite resilient, even as the author met with demise in other branches of humanities. "One prefecture of French culture," quipped Robert Carringer, "was reinventing the idea of authorship while another one was trying to kill it off."[7]

"A little like Hegel's *Phenomenology of Mind*, which was composed within earshot of gunfire from the Battle of Jena," notes Seán Burke, "'The Death of the Author' has found a perfect setting against the background of May-time Paris in intellectual revolt."[8] In spite of its circumscribed scope, Barthes's essay came to be cited in connection with the crisis of authority in a variety of discourses, including film criticism. The social upheavals that led to the events of May 1968 had a substantial impact on the discourse and the practice of film authorship. Under the guidance of Jean-Louis Comolli, *Cahiers du cinéma* ran an issue that reevaluated the famous *politique des auteurs* only a few months after Barthes's intervention. The *Cahiers* editors reconsidered the rhetoric of the *politique* and took issue with the journal's legacy of cinephilic ocularcentrism. They questioned the values of concepts like "mise-en-scène" and "signature," lamenting and deploring the inflated usage of such terms in discussions of American cinema.[9]

Retrospective accounts of authorship took measure of the twenty years between Alexandre Astruc's "Caméra-stylo" essay of 1948 (which was seen as an essential precursor to the *politique des auteurs*) and "death of the author" discourses. In the revised edition of *Signs and Meaning in the Cinema*, Peter Wollen sought to cope with and incorporate theoretical challenges in a more expansive understanding of authorship.[10] Tracing a theoretical path from the idealized construction of a filmic author to a structuralist critique of authorial subjectivity, Wollen distinguished the cine-structuralist idea of film authorship from the Hollywood cult of personality. The director should not be seen as an "individual" who "expresses himself or his own vision in the film" but should instead be viewed as a subject whose "preoccupations" allow for "unconscious, unintended meaning" to be decoded in the film. This revised understanding of auteurism involved the "tracing of a structure (not a message) within the work, which can then *post-factum* be assigned to an individual, the director, on empirical grounds."[11]

The various turns in authorship theory after May 1968 would generate a significant amount of theoretical work. But the year of *les événements* greatly impacted cinema practices as well, forcing filmmakers to question the "truth" and the "reality" of the image, to confront the politics of representation, and the challenge of television. The demise of the author was linked to these significant challenges. The former critics at the *Cahiers*, each of whom had initially fashioned himself as an *auteur*, would experience the crisis of authorship in seismic ways. Militant cinema was a most radical response from Jean-Luc Godard, who would go on to form the Dziga Vertov Group; at the same time the "Left Bank" filmmakers Alain Resnais, Chris Marker, and Agnès Varda would rally under the aegis of the Medvenkin Group.[12] Jacques Rivette, in 1961 a firm believer that the *auteur* was the necessary holder of the point of view,[13] emphatically claimed years later, in September 1968, that "there is no author in a film,"[14] and continued to make features that focused on artistic communities faced with the inevitable absence of the master.[15] Eric Rohmer, the *politique*'s most fervent advocate, now turned cineaste, would have to confront the departure of the authorial figure, if only to affirm cinema's status as the "art of the present."[16]

Despite its imposing challenge to conventional understandings, the "death of the author" discourse marked new possibilities and provided writers and filmmakers with the opportunity to craft their creations with a novel sense of freedom, releasing them from the burden of the *auteur*'s former obligations. Far from just catalyzing acts of mourning, the death of the author in fact gave rise to a provocative array of expressive enactments, among them that of the author's disappearance, doubt, absence, dissimulation, dissemination, or duplicity. The authorial signature that conferred upon the *auteur* the prestige of being right was relinquished and elusive creators now enjoyed a newly found autonomy in the power to lie, hide, or vanish.

The former Nouvelle Vague filmmakers and—if we accept that this movement represents a critical category[17]—those who do not belong to it and worked either against it, or on its fringe, all made use of this new authorial license (for if the author is dead, he no longer is subject to laws that had previously bound *auteurs*). In the wake of the challenges to authority and truth, and despite radical differences in approach and style, filmmakers strived to redefine the ontological status of cinema and to reckon with the moral consequences of new orientations. If the author has disappeared and the source of film's truth has vanished, what world will the camera lens capture and how will the newly empowered spectators (for in the wake of Barthes reading/viewing has become a form of creating) trust its representations?

At this point, let us return to our Bressonian thread. The filmmakers considered in the previous chapter, by dint of negotiating their place in the wake of the "master," shaped cinematic works in which the authorial figure is compromised. Both Eustache and Pialat made anti-auteurist pronouncements and professed their anti-Nouvelle Vague sentiments. Eustache's case elucidates the dramatic changes of the late 1960s: their presence is tangible not only in his moral attitude towards the medium, but also in the stories told by his films. Diminished or dismissed, the figure of the author in his cinema gives way to an avatar, the narrator, a relic of an ancient world. The striking terms of Eustache's response particularly stand out when viewed vis-à-vis the work of another filmmaker who installed the narrator in the center of the cinematic project, namely Eric Rohmer. Incidentally, Eustache was an assistant (though not credited) on the set of Rohmer's first two *Moral Tales*.[18] In both projects, the narrator's strategies—elusive and seductive—superseded the author's former mission of truth-seeking, assigning to the spectators the role of a moral council.

The Erasure of Authorship

To embrace the *politique des auteurs* was one thing; to practice it was another. "What I have done is very easy," Jean Eustache once confided:

> I "erased," put myself less and less in the films, I tried to do away with the film author. I started out in cinema with this idea upheld by the old Cahiers in mind, the politique des auteurs, *that there are no films, there are only* auteurs. I was

convinced... Of course, as soon as one shoots, one often does the opposite of what one had intended to do.[19]

The illusory promise of authorship and its artistic sovereignty gave way to serious doubt. If the author is a myth, so too is the vision of the *auteur*. "To speak of the 'gaze' of the filmmaker," claimed Eustache, is misleading—and trite. "First of all, it's very easy, because all films, no matter how bad, are always created by the 'gaze' of a filmmaker."[20]

Eustache justified his anti-auteurism by referring to the impossibility of grasping the relationship between film and reality, and rendering one's holistic, uninterrupted experience of the world. "It is impossible to reconstitute the real," maintained Eustache, "because one cannot film everything: there are blanks, and only because one has to recharge the camera."[21] Because Eustache wanted cinema to be larger than life, his only recourse was to take measure of the reality provided by "the recorded material, and not the event that [he] witnessed." This rift between the event that takes place and the one that is recorded, between reality and the image, lies at the heart of Eustache's cinematic enterprise. Unsurprisingly, it deeply affected Eustache's conception and treatment of the image, as well as of sound, be it ambient sound, enunciation, dialogue, or music. Among his strategies of coping with the image's loss of authoritative truth vis-à-vis reality, one counts the utter denigration of the author and the unabated celebration of the narrator and storytelling. This emphasis on narration as a vehicle of granting expression to the experience of the world, to human community, to political reality was hardly a surprise in the late 1960s and early 1970s. *The Mother and the Whore*, Eustache's best-known feature, constitutes a detailed lesson in how film characters come to life when they speak and tell stories. In fact, Eustache deliberately went so far as to record long conversations and accounts of events that often replaced the filmed actions.[22]

The erasure of the author went hand in hand with the empowerment of the narrator whose functions continued the ritualistic tradition at the very core of Eustache's work; almost all of Eustache's films attempt to bring French rituals to life.[23] Faced with the intrinsic limitations of the mechanical apparatus that could not capture and fully render the world, Eustache took heart in the belief that reality—that which is recorded by the camera—will reveal its "truth" if the recording is treated as a ritual, meaning by virtue of its repetition. This repetitive pattern is enacted in *La Rosière de Pessac*, the title in fact for two different movies made a decade apart, in 1968 and 1979. Both films document a festival during which, under the guidance of the mayor and in accordance to a longstanding local tradition, the inhabitants of Pessac, Eustache's birth city, elect their virtuous maiden, or as they call her, a "Rosière." The temporal gap between the two documentations of this civic ritual reflects the event's abiding centrality to the life of the city, but also demonstrates the impact of postwar French modernization on communitarian activities in danger of disappearance. This representation twice repeated demonstrates the festival's importance as well as its tenuousness. Only a "ritual" repetition can sustain the semblance of the event, whose ephemerality haunts Eustache and his cinema.

The fragility of the representation vis-à-vis the vivid nature of memory will also figure in Eustache's last film, Les Photos d'Alix (1980), a fifteen-minute short in which a photographer speaks with a friend (played by Eustache's son, Boris) as she shows him a collection of images. With fascinating clarity, Les Photos d'Alix displays a filmmaker's personal struggle with the limits of visual representation, a struggle that will come to seal the reputation of cinema as Eustache's "profession of life."[24] Robert Bresson, as a "maniac of truth," already provided the role model of granting subjective expression to the universal by retrieving traces of the soul with the "miraculous tool that is the cinematograph."[25] Eustache would take this resolve seriously, which would lead to a tragic, indeed fatal conclusion. Les Photos d'Alix is the poignant last work of the filmmaker as well as the end of the road; having wrestled with cinema until he could go no further, he, or it, ended his life.

The project of Les Photos d'Alix seems almost simplistic in its straightforwardness; it seeks to show the rift between the photographic/filmic trace and the spectator's perception, to unveil the dissemblance and tortured invalidation of photography's indexicality.[26] The consequences of such a daring quest would shake Eustache's very existence. He explained his project in these terms:

> *Alix tells her friend what she wanted to accomplish. She remembers every painstaking detail, but he does not always recognize what he sees. He takes a guess, strays off, seizes a resemblance, gets lost among images and legends presented by Alix, so sure of herself...... Equally sincere, each character perceives and recounts differently that which we do not see, or what we see differently, with a different eye. As the conversation unfolds, the resemblances come undone.*[27]

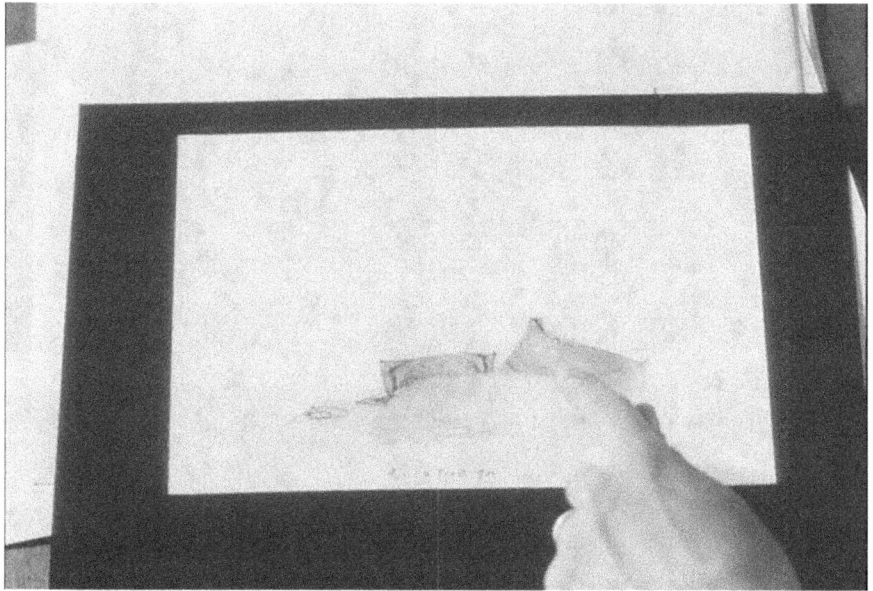

Illustration 4.1 Index (*Les Photos d'Alix*, dir. Jean Eustache, 1980)

The voice-over commentary animates the images, but it also loosens and ultimately undoes the ties between the filmed reality and its representation.

The breach between the visual traces of the world and the world itself grows larger, to the point that the only event the camera is able to capture is the disappearance of the traces—and of the world itself. Blurring the limits of perception in order to record this disappearance, Eustache's fascinating visual mechanism of disintegration challenges the stability of meaning and representation. As images lose their analogical power and words become divested of their meaning, the project of representation is revealed as an altogether fraught enterprise. How does one make sense of a world whose every manifestation discloses its shortcomings, its limitations, and its flaws? Eustache's film explores the archeological laboratory of representation, pointing to the compelling impact of dissemblance and doubt.[28] In this way, his little film enacts the precepts formulated in the diary of the photographer, Alix-Cléo Roubaud: "Aesthetic goal: disappearance."[29]

In the opening scene, Boris sees an image on the wall and wonders what it might be. "It is a childhood photograph," responds Alix, before adding that "in a certain way, every photo is a childhood photo." Asked a few minutes later whether

Illustration 4.2 Infinite Frames (*Les Photos d'Alix*, dir. Jean Eustache, 1980)

she is the woman in the picture, she prevaricates. Yes and no, "toutes les photographies c'est moi," as if to suggest that the complexities involved in expressing oneself with the means of cinema/photography are always a personal matter. From Daniel's childhood in *Mes petites amoureuses,* passing by (again) Daniel's youth in *Le Père Noël a les yeux bleus,* and moving on to the adventures of Alexandre in *The Mother and the Whore,* one could well argue that Jean Eustache's cinema resembles "a childhood photograph." For further confirmation one might add the documentary lucidity of *La Rosière de Pessac* with its images of Eustache's birth town, and especially *Numéro zéro,* the heartfelt uninterrupted account of his grandmother, filmed during one February day in 1971 in his own modest apartment that he shared with her and with his son Boris.[30] As if to assess the subjective charge of such an enterprise, the storyteller's words in *Une sale histoire* poignantly summarize Eustache's attitude: "I am not telling my personal stories, or if I do, it is because I am convinced that they are not personal, and will become comprehensible to everyone." As in *La Rosière de Pessac,* the "ritual" part of a lived story animates the representation and imparts meanings that transcend the life of an individual.

Soiled Stories

Une sale histoire is dazzling and disarming in its representations of a small town ritual at different moments in time. With its *mise-en-scène* of a double and duplicitous discourse, this original film is organized around the act of storytelling and, in this way, recalls Scheherazade's strategy in *The Arabian Nights*. The project links the pleasure of storytelling with the sensual pleasure of the experiences recounted by the narrator. This comes with a hitch, however, for exuberance confronts its necessary double, the compromise that inheres in the adage that with pleasure comes pain, "pas de plaisir sans peine."

The film opens up with the carefully framed image of a corpulent filmmaker played by Jean Douchet, a meaningful choice that indicates that he might be an *auteur*. However, *Une sale histoire* relegates the figure to a secondary role, as we soon learn that the *auteur* is quite unable to find an apposite form for his story. As if to suggest that only he who has experienced the event might be qualified to recount it, the filmmaker appeals to an unnamed character, played by Michael Lonsdale: "I would like you to tell me that story. I wanted to piece it together, illustrate it, I even started to write a script, but it does not work. I prefer it when

Illustration 4.3 Jean Douchet (*Une sale histoire*, dir. Jean Eustache, 1977)

you tell it." Because he insists on presenting the unfiltered truth, the filmmaker faces the prospect of "telling abject stories" instead of producing art that celebrates "greatness and beauty."

Negotiating this tension between noble art and abject narrative, the storyteller begins his tale, which happened "once upon a time, maybe nine years ago in a café near Motte Piquet-Grenelle." In the establishment's bathroom door he discovered a peephole that gave him "direct visual access" to the sight of women's genitals. He soon becomes addicted to the locus, in spite of the difficult position he must assume (literally a "dirty" one, since the "position of the Muslim prayer" required that he keep his face on the floor, which made his hair filthy with excrement). This hole is a "cylinder of vision"[31] that connects the eye of the seer with the sex of woman. "Instead of a hole or opening dug by a voyeur," writes Laurent de Sutter,

> there was a kind of lack of a door, a lack as inaugural as the idea of sin would be. And as soon as it was impossible to know that it was an act of chance, or of will, this lack presented itself as an oracle. This thing, this uncertain impersonality of the hole, is that which, before everything, provoked the call.[32]

This "cylinder of vision" renders the view of the intimate part an abstraction, removing it from the regime of spectacle or dramatic display. For this reason the experience assumes a singular, indeed defamiliarizing, aspect when the protagonist starts to match sexes with the faces of the women he looks at. To do so, he claims, is to subvert "the hierarchy of the body that was reinforced by four thousand years of human history." The experience is not motivated by a quest for physical or moral beauty, but only by a desire to view the sex, the "origin of the world," independent of the "cultural consensus" and the "état de parole" that interfere in acts of amorous seduction and conjugal sex.

What does the eye see? "Consider this carrot of vision as a sort of precipitate of the Real onto itself, about which it would have told the truth," argues de Sutter. "This truth would have been that of a double cesspool: the female sexual organ and the place from which it offers itself to be seen directly." But Eustache does not ascribe to the female genitals the privileged status of the origin of the world, the locus of the unattained, or the uncompromised truth of the real. The vision granted by the voyeur's opening is in fact the opposite of truth; it is the lie plain and simple. "There is nothing true, nothing of the Real in a direct view," notes de Sutter. "All of this is only a form, a cylinder of the same type as a kaleidoscope or a telescope, that is to say, a simple tunnel. For there to be illumination, this tunnel would have had to open onto an elsewhere, while in Eustache, it opens onto nothing. Vision is blocked by the eye pressed to the opening."[33]

The dispositif chosen by Eustache is stunning in its suggestiveness. Because the character discovers that "sex (and not the face) is the mirror of the soul," the story needs a mirror to verify its truth. The narrative does not represent an end in itself, but the means to address the audience, to involve listeners in a symposium about desire, sexual practice, and sexual difference. It is a story that bothers women, Lonsdale's character remarks, because it produces *jouissance* through the sense of hearing which, according to Sade, is the primary sensual organ. In 1978, with the now legalized porn theaters freely displaying sexually explicit X-rated features, Eustache's intervention aimed to irritate and agitate, all the more since the voyeurism of the anecdote never finds visual expression. The camera lingers in the room and lets the discussion take its course. In this way, *Une sale histoire* provides a minimalistic display of cinematic visuality while reflecting on the ultimate level of exposure granted by pornography. If Eustache refers to Sade's "certain reputation in the matter," it is not only to acknowledge a line of thinking, but above all to localize the ways in which cinema can absorb, rework, undo, and demolish regimes of visual and sensual pleasure.

These meditations on cinematic representation are acute and astonishing. Eustache erases the *auteur* and in its place installs the storyteller (the endorser or signatory of the ritualistic power of narration), denigrating the sacred notion of the cinematic gaze by emphasizing its artificial and fabricated constitution, its affirmation by "cultural consensus" and circumscription by morality and propriety. But this is only the "content" part of the lesson, for Eustache employs a novel formal framework. As the story comes to an end, the spectator realizes that this "one" dirty story is in fact part of a diptych in which the "same" event will be told twice, each time by a different voice with each of the two versions lasting roughly twenty minutes.

The second version starts *in medias res*, without the prelude that established the chief roles in the story. Michael Lonsdale's place is assumed by Jean-Noël Pick, and among the listeners we recognize Eustache himself, along with Françoise Lebrun (from *The Mother and the Whore*). The polished 35mm footage from the initial version contrasts sharply with the careless framing and sluggish camera movements of the 16mm sequel, whose imperfect lighting recalls the aesthetics of direct cinema. A sketch, a home video of a dinner party, replaces the fictionalized

Illustration 4.4 Michael Lonsdale (*Une sale histoire*, dir. Jean Eustache, 1977)

Illustration 4.5 Jean-Noël Picq (*Une sale histoire*, dir. Jean Eustache, 1977)

Illustration 4.6 Jean-Noël Picq 16mm Frame (*Une sale histoire,* dir. Jean Eustache, 1977)

atmosphere of the first sequence; recognizable professional actors give way to an entourage of Eustache's friends and acquaintances. This second version, it becomes clear, is the "original" one, the true dirty story recalled by the protagonist as opposed to the cinematic version, whose smooth presentation glosses over the purpose of representation.

Brought together in this mise-en-abyme of filmmaking, the documentary-version and the fiction-version reflect on and unmask the creative process. Eustache reverses the order of events, beginning with the "representation" that is followed by the documentary-version, undoing the relationship between reality and representation, between the real and the unreal. The gap between the two stories and the mental images they trigger correspond to the central motif of the "dirty story," *le trou*, the "(peep)hole" in the bathroom that opens onto another hole, the sex of the woman: "I have the impression," says the narrator,

> that first of all there was the hole/opening, that it was built first, then the door above it, then the café was built, and in the café there was a cashier, three boys, two pinball machines, sauerkraut, cold cuts, all of the drinks usually served.

> *There was all of this, but it only worked for the hole/opening, and that everything else was just for show.*[34]

As Alain Philippon puts it, the film calls

> *for a metaphorical reading: if there is a peephole, it is that of the camera or of the projector, the original peephole of the cinematograph, and around it, the theater, the cashier, the box office assistants and—incidentally—the films. It might make us smile that popular cinema appears in this discourse in the guise of sauerkraut and cold cuts imagined in a place that is not very high-end, but it gives a good idea of the disgust that Jean Eustache felt for the majority of the cinema created around him.*[35]

The hole is not a human creation; the origin of the hole does not stem from the action of a human agent. There is no author, rather the hole is the organizing principle and origin of the world. Cinema, as a cylinder of vision, as an original hole, is the "medium of immediacy of vision" and the "medium of the agnostic knowledge of the world," a medium of *jouissance* (not of desire).

The two versions of *Une sale histoire* involve an intertwined relation between spoken language or story and image, but also between original and copy.[36] Eustache denies the author any privileged relation to the real, and sustains a process, much like a ritual, that goes to bitter ends and leaves us with a bitter ending. For Eustache the truth is unbearable and cinema is as close as one can come to it. The plain truth, however, is that cinema cannot reveal the truth of the world; what it reveals is that this truth cannot be told or shown. *Une sale histoire* resists the "mise-en-images" and refuses to be screened; its story is already the "screen" of truth. As the story unravels, the *trou*, the origin of everything, becomes a marker of foreclosed representation. The truth of cinema, the film demonstrates, is that it is a "corked" art. In Eustache, narration (the spoken word) speaks the truth of the image's incapacity to convey truth, and the narrator laments the author's impotency. Eustache discovers contrivance and fakery with surprise and despair. Taken aback, he cannot resist these conclusions and their disarming inevitability.

Maybe the most painful and humbling lesson of Eustache's cinematic project is that the flawed and corrupted nature of filmic representation is not a matter of ontology. His purpose all along has been ethical, in the sense that he is not concerned with the essence of things, nor their photographic representation, but with the filmmaker's moral duty when faced with the flawed nature of the cinematic medium. The visionary hole provided by the camera only reaffirms the opacity of perception. Confronted with the compromised constitution of cinematic representation, the filmmaker has a sole recourse: to multiply the point of view in the ritual repetition of a story and in this way break off the illusion of representation and confound the arrogance of the singular gaze. Duplicity is a compromise, but it is the only ethical option, the only way to confront the menace of transience and death.

"Cinema First of All IS"

Eustache's disenchantment with the image embodied the disillusionment of the post-May 1968 years, and the match between his aesthetic project and the political mood of the time led critics to name him one of the most influential French filmmakers of the 1970s.[37] Compared with Eustache's deep despair, Eric Rohmer's utter confidence in the cinematic medium provides an obvious contrast and, for that reason, perhaps an all too schematic point of reference. Unlike Eustache, Rohmer firmly believes that film enjoys an objective relation to reality; both his critical writings and his films champion a "transparent visual style and a conception of *mise-en-scène* rigorously bound to the real."[38] As early as the 1940s, writing in Sartre's journal *Les Temps modernes* and Camus's *Le Combat*, Maurice Schérer/Eric Rohmer praised cinema for being "the only possible means of expression," stressing that "only the rough, inorganic language of the screen has been able to make epic the most ordinary events, a feat to which literature has been vainly aspiring for several centuries."[39] While literature can only "rest [its gaze] on the absurd and chaotic spectacle of appearances" and at best explain it, cinema alone can "show" this spectacle, reproduce it, and in the process "discover man."[40]

The cinematographic reproduction, however, is not superficial, in the literal sense of photographing the surface; it is not the sign or the symbol of a world out there. Rather, it is part of this world, image and sound, from ambient noise and spoken dialogues to music. "Cinema is cinema," observes Rohmer, striking an ontological note.

> Let those who still mourn the loss of an imagined purity do what they like with this secret… The characters in silent films perfected a subtle method of letting

us into their hearts. Everything became a sign or a symbol. Flattered by the compliment to his intelligence, the spectator worked on understanding and forgot to see. Now the screen, liberated from this foreign task since the advent of the talkies, should go back to its true role, which is to show and not to tell.[41]

Rohmer's first piece in the *Cahiers*, "Vanité que la peinture,"[42] which borrows its title from Pascal's *Pensées*, praises cinema as the only art able to reveal the "truth that these things [nature, the external world] are as they are, regardless of how we see them." The task of the painter is vanity, and if "in the past, Cézanne, Picasso, Matisse, gave us new eyes to see the world," the filmmaker's task is one of humility.[43] Thus, he says, "art is paying its debt to nature. It makes beauty out of ugliness, but *would beauty be truth* if it did not exist despite, almost against, us? Art's task is not to enclose us in a sealed world. Born of the world, it brings us back to it."[44] Unlike the other arts, "the cinema flashes a whole scene before our eyes, from which we are free to extract one of many possible significations."[45] This mechanical medium enables the viewer to produce signification, while other arts, unable to "imitate" are nonetheless able to signify. In cinema "meaning is extracted from appearances, not from an imaginary world of which appearances are only the sign."[46]

Very different from the purely descriptive and highly subjective film criticism of Truffaut and Godard,[47] Rohmer's contributions as the editor of *Cahiers* from 1956 to 1963 sustain an idealist aesthetic theory. More than any other critic at the *Cahiers*, Rohmer continued Bazin's legacy, that he likened to the Copernican revolution, "for it set cinema apart from the other arts under whose shadow it had long remained."[48] For Rohmer, as for Bazin, the arrival of sound reinforced the link between cinema and the real. That is to say, elaborates Paul Willemen, "there is something which is being reproduced and therefore there is an unfilmed world before the camera came along and pointed to it, some of which (and the more the better as far as Bazin is concerned) transpires into the recorded and projected image."[49] Sound enhances the physical connection between the thing represented and its representation. Sound and speech are important for they allow a more poignant manifestation of the real. Even if they contain impure elements, they are not less filmic, for they do not diminish cinematic specificity. Defending Bazin, Rohmer insists that cinema

> *first of all* IS. *It is this being that must be examined, no matter the appearance it takes, silent or spoken, black and white or in color, be it called western, comedy*

or documentary. What matters most is not what brings it closer to other arts, but what distinguishes it from them. For Bazin, it is this mechanical quality of the reproduction that makes the originality, the genius of cinema.[50]

Speaking with Jean Narboni in 1983, Rohmer once again emphasized that "the important thing in a film—to repeat what Bazin said—is ontology, not language. Ontologically, film says something that the other arts don't say."[51]

Despite being an advocate for film's ontological specificity and its superiority over the other arts, Rohmer often faced the criticism that his features were uncinematic because they were too "literary." In his long career as a film critic, and even longer as a filmmaker, he defended his position with an inimitable elegance as well as a firm insistence. Concerned with cinema's specificity, or what he believed to be the "truth of cinema," as well as with the critic's moral view of the world, Rohmer maintained that "truth" inheres in the phenomenological *appearance* of reality. The screen, "liberated since the advent of the talkies,"[52] should go back to "its true role, which is to show, not to tell. In the talkies, the appearance is the essence."[53] And in a more literal way, cinematic truth is to be found in the speaking image. With the coming of sound, the spectator relearns how to see thanks to the spoken word. Cinema can finally take leave of theatrical conventions that rely on words as bearers of truth; in sound film truth lies in the appearance of the world, and words, like appearances, can be deceptive. While admitting that "the discourse of my characters is not the discourse of my films," Rohmer also insisted that the moral tale abides in the cinematic representation of the world, in the "discourse of the film" drifting away from the "discourse of his characters."[54]

As a critic, Rohmer correlated the appreciation of ontological objectivity with "la critique des beautés," the positive relation to films and filmmakers that led critics to write only about the films they venerate. As a filmmaker, he pursued this objectivity as he examined the machinations of human subjectivity. Couching his *Moral Tales* in first-person narratives, Rohmer endeavored "to explore the most absolute subjectivity without compromising anything of the cinematographic objectivity." In 1962 Rohmer affirmed that "cinema, since its early beginnings, has attempted to show what happens inside people's mind, to go from objectivity to subjectivity. What I would like to express in my tales is, if I may say so, a pure relationship to the self (*un pur rapport de soi à soi*)." To this end, "in a form more *agreeable than austere*," Rohmer delved into "hidden worlds of the inner life, of the soul."[55]

Moral Tales

Throughout his work, Rohmer probed the credibility of cinema's narrative dispositif; in that way he complicated the medium's relationship with "reality" and "truth," terms that would come under particularly strong attack at the end of the 1960s. In his defense of talking cinema, he stressed that "a means must be found to integrate words not into the filmed world, but into the film, whether into the shot in which they are spoken or into a preceding or following sequence."[56] This well-known argument would later take an interesting turn, with Rohmer making a case for cinema as the only medium that can be deceptive, that can, put bluntly, tell lies. "There are not enough lies in cinema, except perhaps in comedies," Rohmer had already noted in 1948. This "formidable power of speech" should be put to use in cinema—not, "as was believed, [to] make the significance unimportant, but, instead, [to] make it *deceptive*."[57] In other words, one should enhance the "gap between the signification of speech and that of the visual element, the counterpoint of the text and that of the picture."[58] This project of deception could not but be backed up by the profound belief that Rohmer had in the medium and his love for its classical beauty. It stood in stark contrast to Eustache's emphasis on the soiled nature of a medium that has been compromised by cultural consensus.

"My intention was never to film pure events," Rohmer said in the preface of the booklet that accompanies his *Moral Tales*, "but the story into which they were transformed by characters. Told by someone else, the story would have been different, or it would not have been at all. My heroes, a bit like Don Quixote, believe they are the characters of a novel, but maybe there is no novel at all."[59] The narrator of Rohmer's moral tales sets the tone of a project that will define Rohmer's filmmaking career. He relates a series of events, mostly secrets that take on meaning by dint of the order in which they are presented; were they sequenced otherwise, the episodes might lead to an altogether different conclusion. Assuming a false distance towards his characters, the narrator's moral perspective seems generous, at times even lax. The film takes place in the interval between the signified and the signifier, or as Rohmer put it in his response to a critic, "my characters' discourse is not necessarily my film's discourse."

Present throughout Rohmer's work, this important distinction informs the project of the *Moral Tales*. While the first two allowed the transition from his first typical Nouvelle Vague endeavor, *Le Signe du lion* (*The Sign of the Leo*, 1962), to an *auteur*'s universe of common themes and formal patterns, it is with *Ma nuit chez Maud* (*My Night at Maud's*, 1969) that Rohmer becomes the cineaste we know.[60] After *Maud*, with the main character's voice-over narration that tells the story of his relationship, the next film in the series, *Le Genou de Claire* (*Claire's Knee*, 1971), adopts a noteworthy structure. The diplomat Jérôme (Jean-Claude Brialy) is spending his last summer as a bachelor and runs into a former flame from Bucharest, the writer Aurora (Aurora Cornu) who has retired to Annecy to work on a novel. Cozily settled in the lakeside residence of Madam Walter, she teases Jérôme about his forthcoming marriage and submission to bourgeois convention, especially given his Don Juanesque past and his flirtation with her landlady's teenage daughter, Laura. "Why would I tie myself to one woman if I were interested in others?" he asks. Certain of his own feelings, he agrees to try out Aurora's romanesque ideas about desire by engaging in a play of seduction with Laura. Things get more tantalizing with the arrival of Laura's long-legged, blonde stepsister Claire. At the end of a tennis game with a group of friends, Claire's boyfriend Gilles puts his hand on her knee, a gesture that inflames Jérôme's desire and generates a moral crisis. Aurora challenges him to demystify (and sublimate) his enamourment with the young and beautiful Claire by speaking about it, in other words by transforming it into a narrative. The exchanges between Aurora and Jérôme are registered in careful and precise words, and every stage of his passion is chronicled, dissected, and mulled over.

The story of *Claire's Knee* provides an intriguing nexus of forms and plots. The event that takes place before our eyes is "doubled," that is, articulated by Jérôme's voice-over. Taking seriously the role prescribed to Rohmer's narrators, Jérôme interprets the story as he recounts it to the writer Aurora, who will formulate it in her own words before proposing the subsequent course action. Everything is submitted to this ritual of story-telling, and Rohmer's subtle *mise-en-scène* brings about a moment of sensual intensity that at first seems altogether improbable, at best the function of a fervid male fantasy. Even the most ineffable moments undergo a verbal doubling, as is the case, for instance, in Jérôme's stunning discovery: "In every women, there is something particularly vulnerable: for some, the base of the neck, the waist, the hands, for Claire, in this position, in this light, it was her knee."[61]

Rohmer, frank and forthright about his "method," admits that he "first presents the facts in a direct, objective manner, while leaving [his] character's thoughts unknown." Only later, "during a conversation, I have my character tell his thoughts directly to the critical and amused novelist." If a verbal account follows the visualization of events, he explains, it is because Jean-Claude Brialy's Jérôme experiences something that "was written in its novelized version, in the manner of Saint Jerome, describing the progress of the protagonist's thoughts." How might one otherwise "show this purely internal emotion on the screen?" Defending his film against the reproaches of visual purists, Rohmer emphasizes the distance between the objective image and the subjective commentary.[62]

> *The commentary was necessary, but superimposing it on the image seemed to me even more useless and artificial because at the beginning of this thought process was a single event whose uniqueness made it valuable. Here, it was no longer possible to play on the gap between the tense (in the grammatical sense of the word) of the action and that of the thought. Showing an action and giving the exact thoughts of the person involved, at the very moment when he performs the act—is that "cinema" or not?*[63]

In his "Letter to a Critic (Concerning My Moral Tales)," Rohmer responds to a commentator's disapproval that his films might be too literary, and for that reason not truly cinematic. Much like the characters in his films, Rohmer addresses the question of taste, and reiterates "la critique des beautés."[64]

> *My cinema, you say, is literary: The things I say could be said in a novel. Yes, but what do I say? My characters' discourse is not necessarily my film's discourse. There is certainly literary material in my tales, a pre-established novelistic plot that could be developed in writing and that is, in fact, sometimes developed in the form of a commentary. But neither the text of these commentaries, nor that of my dialogues, is my film: rather, they are things that I film, just like the landscapes, faces, behavior, and gestures. And if you say that speech is an impure element, I no longer agree with you. Like images, it is a part of the life I film.*[65]

More than a quarter of century later, and this time as a filmmaker, Rohmer would reiterate thoughts from his earlier seminal essay: "It was quickly noticed that the word was a *sound before it was a sign*, and, as an immediate consequence, it was agreed that speech had to be treated as a way of being, not of revealing."[66] Language, he maintains, has an ontological dimension; it not only reveals the world, but it supplies, just like the image, a physical or indexical link between the world and the cinematic representation.

It is essential for Rohmer that one rethink the customary binary between image and sound that consigns sound and speech to a subservient status.[67] This spurious antinomy, he suggests, derives from the "distrust the best directors show toward the one power of language that is essential to it, that of *signifying*," a distrust that is understandable given that "film took more than thirty years to learn to manage without speech."[68] Films by the *auteurs* consecrated by the *Cahiers*, especially those of Cocteau, Renoir, Bresson, Hawks, and Welles, added to the discoveries of *mise-en-scène* the possibility of seeing how language might reveal "its true function."[69] In this "liberated cinema" the word becomes integrated into and part of "not the filmed world, but the film."[70] In the conclusion of "For a Talking Cinema," Rohmer insists that "the words maintain a relationship, not with the image, but with a *purely cinematic element*: the dynamism of the shot."[71] Further down the road, Rohmer will apply this lesson to his own cinema, subtly creating a dynamic space both for the eye and for the ear.[72] This space acquires an almost discursive dimension, allowing for an objective point of view that will delay or contradict the subjective discourse of Rohmer's characters. The voice-over, continuous and confident, self-conscious and sophisticated, adds to the images its own distinct rhythm.

Blindfolded Authors

Claire's Knee displays the *mise-en-scène* of a double-folded enterprise; the tale is twice-told, once by Jérôme, the protagonist of events that he himself plots, and a second time by Aurora, the professional writer, who presumably transforms those events into publishable prose. More importantly, however, the film's construction and organization make explicit the story's double constitution: for the characters who debate about the orientation of their lived story, but also for the viewers who are invited to make sense of what they see and hear as they draw their own conclusions. The moral intervention of the viewer is of course essential to the structure and effect of the *Moral Tales*. The narrators of *Ma nuit chez Maud* and *L'Amour l'après-midi* (*Chloé in the Afternoon*, 1972) duly warn the audience about the possibility of organizing the onscreen events into a different story that would contradict the validity or truth of the one that is being presented. *Claire's Knee* prolongs this duplicitous attitude and plants the seeds of doubt among the characters themselves. The film's manifest story hides, or rather veils, a second one that runs counter to the one that is being narrated. Rohmer is a storyteller, his is a cinema of endless tales with endings that leave us with secrets unresolved by his narrators.

In a universe where what is unsaid is just as relevant as what is spoken, the viewer assumes the role of an investigator. Yet the detective genre does not fully apply to Rohmer's cinema, because unlike Sherlock Holmes's adventures referenced by the characters in *La Femme de l'aviateur* (*The Aviator's Wife*, 1981), in his *Moral Tales* (as will later be the case of *Comedies and Proverbs* and the *Tales of Four Seasons*) there may well be no truth at all. Since the story is being told by an uncertain, duplicitous, forgetful narrator, or sometimes by several narrators who are equally equivocal and hypocritical, it is as if there were no definitive story. The narrator embarks (and takes the viewer with him) upon a tale that is more or less his own. The subjective nature of the experience explains why the innocence of the tale might be lost, corrupted by doubt and suspicion, and ultimately irrelevant. While these narrators might appear as mind-game masters, one should not forget a crucial detail, namely their personal investment in the story, their passion, which is the blind spot of their very status as narrators. Because of this subjective investment, they ignore, overlook, forget or misinterpret the facts. The viewer, endowed both with empathy and critical judgment and working from a distance, is enabled to reconstitute the events and resolve the enigma. The key to the story is not some obscure truth, but rather the very fact that the narrators are blind or blindfolded in their quest for a truthful explanation. Rohmer's characters do not appear to suffer from moral scruples. Aurora, the writer character in *Claire's Knee*, admits as much, seeing the ignorance of heroes as their virtue: "the heroes of a tale are always blindfolded," otherwise they would not act at all and the plot would not advance.

The pattern is recognizable in almost all of Rohmer's films. In *Chloé in the Afternoon*, Frédéric's certitude that Hélène is virtuous is the crucial factor that drives the film's plot.[73] If he were to know that she had been unfaithful to him, there would be no story between him and Chloé. However, just as Frédéric can submit to the allure of a beguiling young woman, his lawful wife, of whom he is so certain, becomes herself involved in a plot of desire. Certain of her and himself, blinded by his self-assurance, Frédéric will devote his entire attention to his own moral meanderings and believe all the while that he controls the strings of the show. In the end, aware of the "coulisses" in the couple's life, the viewer will suspend the faculty of critical judgment and assume a more sympathetic perspective. Frédéric's arrogant certitude will cost him his ignorance, which in turn, appears to be the virtue that ensures the continuation of the story. With Rohmer, this sort of moral dilemma becomes a recurrent pattern. *Les Nuits de la pleine lune (Full Moon in Paris,* 1984) is likewise organized around a young woman's firm belief in her boyfriend's fidelity as she pursues her desire for freedom. Throughout the film, Louise carries on about the importance of an active social life, of which she feels deprived in the new and very spacious apartment shared with her boyfriend in residential but quiet suburbs. Responding with increased vanity to the boyfriend's protests that she keep a small Parisian studio, she does not suspect that he, who is overtly jealous and possessive, might have a secret—and a secret life—of his own.

In Rohmer, ignorance and oblivion are the motors of narrative action, with his protagonists deeply involved in a quest for a certitude that eludes them. This quest surely involves a moral dilemma, and a plethora of secrets and mysteries, but the structure of cinematic spectacle inevitably yields an unexpected dénouement. This principle of incertitude is at odds with cinema's virtue of "showing," of testifying to the presence, the existence (if not the truth) of what is being screened. Rohmer is, of course, very aware of this dynamic, defending the image as a medium of "monstration" and not of signification, the latter being the property of spoken language. This gap between showing and saying, between image and speech, generates the doubt and suspicion that constitute the dramatic engine of Rohmer's cinema. Opposed to the eschewal of speech and dialogue in favor of a purely visual language, Rohmer does not reinforce the gap between image and sound, but proves that it is precisely the dialectic between the two registers that most strikingly reveals cinema's arresting force. In this way Rohmer defiantly contradicts the interpretation that he might privilege spoken language over cinematic representation and reenacts his earlier defense of talking cinema.

Pascal Bonitzer defines the narrative dynamic of Rohmer's films as one in which "the camera *records* encounters that the narrator *interprets* as he pleases."[74] In this light, the moral tales, comedies and proverbs would be the sublimated versions of detective stories and enigmas, in the Sherlock Holmes style, as Lucie and François of *The Aviator's Wife* like to believe. Seeking to identify the mystery woman who appears with the aviator, Lucie and François follow the couple around Paris, gathering clues that they playfully interpret while earnestly defending their obsession with "truth." In this game, the camera becomes a character, an "absent point of view," whose function is to recognize fissures and blanks, things that do not fit into the stories under construction by errant and often less than savvy investigators. In *Claire's Knee*, Jérôme sees Gilles, Claire's boyfriend, with another woman, and chooses to interpret the incident to his advantage; he invents a scenario that is sure to upset Claire, while at the same time allows him to pursue his own scheme, and under the pretext of comforting her, to act on his desire to caress her knee. The true nature of Gilles's meeting with the other woman is irrelevant; what matters here is that the incident provides the means to propel events in the desired direction.

The interpretation is flawed by errors, and the narrators' ability to turn these errors to their advantage, to bounce back and to continue the plot, sustains the trajectories of Rohmer's films. Unlike Eustache, who is disconcerted, unsettled, and ultimately defeated by the blanks in the visual continuum, Rohmer is undeterred and enterprising, playing the game of interpretation that he cherishes more than anything. It is the false perception, or the false interpretation of what one sees, that precipitates the story unexpectedly, similar in that way to the classic scheme of jealousy in Shakespeare's *Othello* where Cassio's handkerchief accidentally picked up by Desdemona will drive the delirious eponymous character to murder. Rohmer's films, in spite of or because of their classical "transparency," make formidable use of false clues, ambiguities, intrigues, and machinations.

The pivotal element here, once again, is the notion of truth. Rohmer's narrators appear confident that the truth of the tale lies in their telling. Rohmer the filmmaker inscribes their doubts and the shortcomings of their perspectives in the film's plot, as well as in the film, that is within its formal construction. Doubt, dissimulation, duplication, incertitude, blindness, ignorance, even hypocrisy abound in Rohmer's narrators, but they are not the moral of the tale. The moral lies in the appeal to the audience, in the opportunity granted to viewers to fathom for themselves the truth of the tale within the maze of the story. As Pascal Bonitzer submits, the *Moral Tales* are the result of such a dialectic: "The reality of the event finds its only comfort in the fragility of the tale. The pivot of this dialectic, of this paradox is the narrator."[75] In other words, there is no story, the story is only a pretext for the function and existence of the narrator; any ultimate truth in the tale becomes the product of the viewer's own reflection.

Not only is Rohmer's narrator "blind"[76]; this blindness, reminiscent of Proustian ignorance, becomes the very engine of signification. "The task of the image is not to signify, but to show," insists Rohmer. Signification is produced through "an excellent tool, the spoken language."[77] However, language does not signify the truth, but the act of speaking. If his characters speak, insists Rohmer, it is because "I most often have been inspired by people who talk... Situations in which no one talks are the exception. It has nothing to do with literature, but, rather, with reality."[78] Given the way in which exchanges in Rohmer's films skirt the truth, spawn uncertainty, and give rise to ambiguity, it is often said that his cinema is, as stated, a classical one that privileges the play of words over the power of images. But Rohmer's is not an easy cinema and one cannot simply say that by emphasizing the act of speech it disables the force of the image. In fostering verbal miscommunication and confusion, Rohmer probes the dialectic between what is shown and what is signified. This is why the function of the narrator is essential in his cinema; being only a voice, articulating the story as it takes place, this agent fabricates a "truth" that arranges the elements of the story in a certain order, aiming not to convince, but rather to seduce the audience.

To be sure, Rohmer's cinema of false turns, enigmas, and deceptions discloses the playful distance between image and sound, between showing and signifying, but also between cinema and literature. If his heroes pretend to be characters in a novel, the narrator in charge of telling their stories has to negotiate his new power of being a film narrator. The literary narrator has the absolute authority of delaying, even failing the formation and display of the world it attempts to build. The cinematic narrator, on the contrary, claims his authority not from the delay, but the immediacy of this display and revelation. The memory and sensibility of the character-narrator are inflected with subjectivity, and as such they differ from the inanimate, unconscious, and disinterested camera. It is from the interplay of personal bias and objective disinterest that Rohmer's moral tales appeal to the viewer. Rohmer's narrator ultimately shares the creator's impetus, revealing the fragility of cinema in general, as well as the tenuousness of its defense mechanisms, be they blind as in Cervantes, ignorant as in Proust, or joyfully overcome as in Marivaux. Immersed, as if by accident, in a story that he must report as faithfully as he can, Rohmer's narrator, Rohmer, and cinema itself face the evasion of truth, the vicissitude, even the impossibility of revealing the exact, verifiable, and unique truth. But since Rohmer, unlike Eustache, shares Bazin's assurance, he does not despair in his mission; he trusts the power of the image and grants to it the potential of truth. The indirectness of the discourse and the directness of the image coexist, for truth is recorded automatically by the eye of the objective.

The Author in Abeyance

In their fondness for interpretation, Rohmer's narrators resemble detectives, with the decisive difference that their discourse is only one element in an entangled mélange of objective certainty and subjective deceit and ignorance. The constant ambivalence, indeed duplicity, rehearsed in singular ways by the cinematographic projects of Rohmer and Eustache bring into play energies that compensate for the absent author. There is someone, Roland Barthes said in reference to Jean-Pierre Vernant's reading of Greek tragedy, "who understands each word, in its duplicity, and who, in addition, hears the very deafness of the characters speaking in front of him, this someone being precisely the reader (or here, the listener)."[79] And, one might add, the spectator.

Barthes's "The Death of the Author" called into question the relationship between author and literary text;[80] the author is supposed to exist before the work of art in "the same relation of antecedence to his work as a father to his child."[81] By empowering the narrator, both Eustache and Rohmer enact their uneasy relation to authorial power, relying on a figure "born simultaneously with the text."[82] For Rohmer, this figure resembles the detective, the exegete, while for Eustache, it assumes a more primitive and shamanic role, that of a mediator, very much in keeping with Bresson. Unlike Bresson, however, who wished to "express himself"[83] originally and singularly, Eustache and Rohmer install "a multidimensional space in which a variety of writings, none of them original, blend and clash."[84] Such a dynamic space comes into view in Eustache's juxtaposition of the two versions of the tale in *Une sale histoire* as well as in Rohmer's reiterations and reinterpretations of single events.

Eustache faces the conundrum of making and watching films while believing that cinema cannot capture, much less reveal, the entire truth. Despite the equivocation of their narrators, Rohmer's films come to far less uncertain and unsettling conclusions. To be sure, in *Claire's Knee* and throughout Rohmer's cinema, viewers are positioned not to trust the inscribed narrators. Rather, they are called upon to solve mysteries on their own, guided, of course, by frequent tips and clues from a "neutral" and absent point of view that coincides with the camera's presumably objective perspective, which in fact points us back to Rohmer himself as the ultimate *metteur-en-scène*. Indeed, play is an essential part of the equivocation in Rohmer's films; his intelligence remains in the wings, guiding what we see and what we know and, as such, abiding as the force that determines where his films will ultimately lead us.

Responding to the dilemma posed by the death of the author, Eustache and Rohmer deploy the incongruity between sound and image to generate a double story as well as a double interpretation. The former divests authorship of what Barthes speaks of as its divine "hypostases—reason, science, law."[85] On the other hand, Rohmer, in his plays of narrative deceit and deception, goes so far that one might say the author is just playing dead. The shared duplicity of this odd couple leads us to quite different ends, but most surely not the end of cinema, which is the subject of our final chapter.

Notes

1. Colin MacCabe, "The Revenge of the Author," in *Film and Authorship*, ed. Virginia Wright Wexman (New Brunswick: Rutgers University Press, 2003), 40.
2. John Caughie, *Theories of Authorship: A Reader* (London: Routledge, 1981), 13.
3. Andrew Bennett, *The Author* (London: Routledge, 2005).
4. Jack Stillinger, *Multiple Authorship and the Myth of the Solitary Genius* (Oxford: Oxford University Press, 1991), 174.
5. For at least five years before writing "The Death of the Author," Barthes formulated his skepticism towards the institution of authorship, especially in *On Racine* (1963) and *Criticism and Truth* (1966).
6. Claude Lévi-Strauss, *The Savage Mind*, trans. George Weidenfeld (London: Nicholson, 1966), 326. Cf. Jonathan Culler, *Structuralist Poetics: Structuralism, Linguistics and the Study of Literature* (London: Routledge, 1975), 32. See also Seán Burke, *The Death and Return of the Author: Criticism and Subjectivity in Barthes, Foucault and Derrida* (Edinburgh: Edinburgh University Press, 1998), 13. Burke argues that the concept of the dissolution of man is promulgated in direct opposition to Sartre's notions of individuality and dialectical history.
7. Quoted in Sarah Kozloff, *The Life of the Author* (Montréal: Caboose, 2014), 7
8. Burke, *The Death and Return of the Author*, 19.
9. Jean-André Fieschi, Jean-Louis Comolli, Michel Mardore, André Téchiné, Gérard Guégan, Claude Ollier, "Vingt ans après. Le cinéma américain, ses auteurs et notre politique en question," *Cahiers du cinéma* 172 (November 1965): 18-31.
10. Peter Wollen, *Signs and Meaning in the Cinema*, 3rd rev. edn (Bloomington: Indiana University Press), 1972.
11. Peter Wollen, "The Auteur Theory," in *Theories of Authorship*, 146.
12. See Gérard Leblanc and David Faroult, *Mai 68 ou le cinéma en suspens* (Paris: Éditions Syllepse, 1998). See also Emmanuel Barot, *Caméra politica: dialectique du réalisme dans le cinéma politique et militant* (Paris: Vrin, 2008).
13. Jacques Rivette, "De l'abjection," *Cahiers du cinéma* 120 (June 1961).

14. Jacques Rivette, "Time Overflowing," Interview by Jacques Aumont, Jean-Louis Comolli, Jean Narboni and Sylvie Pierre, *Cahiers du cinéma* 204 (September 1968), in *Rivette: Texts and Interviews*, ed. Jonathan Rosenbaum, trans. Amy Gateff and Tom Milne (London: BFI, 1977), 31.
15. See Hélène Frappat, *Jacques Rivette, secret compris* (Paris: Cahiers du cinéma, coll. Auteurs, 2001), 184.
16. Maurice Schérer, "L'âge classique du film," *Combat* (June 1949), reprinted in translation as "The Classical Age of Film," in Eric Rohmer, *The Taste for Beauty*, trans. Carol Volk (Cambridge: Cambridge University Press, 1989), 41.
17. Jill Forbes's account of the "post-Nouvelle Vague" posits the Nouvelle Vague as a powerful critical category that, linked to the "auteur film" as a genre, functions as a landmark in determining the place of contemporary or future filmmakers. In this sense, for instance, visible filmmakers like René Allio, Jacques Doillon, Jean Eustache, Philippe Garrel, or Maurice Pialat are ascribed a place in French film history only vis-à-vis the Nouvelle Vague. See Forbes, *The Cinema in France. After the New Wave* (Bloomington and Indianapolis, 1992), 3–4, 125–52. See also Alison Smith, *French Cinema in the 1970s. The Echoes of May* (Manchester: Manchester University Press, 2005), especially chapter 3, "The New Naturalism," 74–112.
18. See "Les Années d'apprentissage," in Philippon, *Jean Eustache*, 11–20.
19. Quoted in Georges Sadoul, *Dictionnaire des cinéastes* (Paris: Seuil, coll. Microcosme, 1982), 181.
20. Amengual, "Une vie recluse en cinéma," 82.
21. In "Propos de Jean Eustache," recueillis par Michel Contat, *Cahiers du cinéma* 306 (December 1979): "On ne peut pas reconstituer la réalité puisqu'on n'a pas tout filmé: il y a des trous, ne serait-ce que parce qu'il faut recharger la caméra. Alors j'ai pris comme la réalité le matériel enregistré et non pas l'événement dont j'avais été témoin."
22. Speaking about a scene when Alexandre and Véronika, after a night spent together, are about to listen to an early morning radio show, Jean Eustache commented: "My first idea when I wrote the script was that he should say (to her): 'Let's go to a café where great things happen,' a café that opens at 5:30 in the morning. But I thought it would break the rhythm of the movie to film what happened somewhere else, and instead of doing that, I preferred to have him tell the story. It seemed more accurate than to introduce a certain number of actions... It's the stance of the film that everything be told and that nothing be seen." See interview with Sylvie Blum and Jérôme Prieur in Philippon, *Jean Eustache*, 126. It is, to be sure, noteworthy that in Eustache's filmography Alexandre is similar to a Rohmerian hero who fashions himself as a novel character, a figure who will ultimately be worn out by life and humbled in a violent crash.
23. The list includes the disembowelment of a pig (*Le Cochon*), the election of the Rosière, suburban dance parties (*Les Mauvaises fréquentations*), Christmas traditions (*Le Père Noël a les yeux bleus*), the rites of adolescent flirting (*Mes petites amoureuses*), even the café conversations in Paris's Saint-Germain-des-Prés (*La Maman et la putain*).
24. Amengual, "Une vie recluse en cinéma," 79.
25. Robert Bresson, Interview with François-Régis Bastide, *Le Masque et la plume*, France Inter (30 April 1966), reprinted in *Bresson par Bresson*, 163.
26. Ari Blatt argues that Eustache's film intimates a dialogue with photographic theory and criticism that was circulating around the same time. His argument suggests that *Les Photos d'Alix* mobilizes a cinematic reflection on "the indexical ontology of the photograph," as well as "the link between photography, personal memory and collective history." See Ari Blatt, "Thinking Photography in Film, or The Suspended Cinema of Agnès Varda and Jean Eustache," *French Forum* 36.2–3 (Spring/Fall 2011): 183.

27. Excerpt of the film synopsis, "La Photo fait son cinéma," *Photogénies* 5 (Paris: CNP, Ministère de la Culture, 1984), no page numbers, my translation: "Alix lui explique ce qu'elle a voulu faire. Elle se souvient de tout, mais lui ne reconnaît pas toujours ce qu'il voit. Il devine, s'égare, saisit une ressemblance, se perd à nouveau entre les images et les légendes d'Alix qui est toujours tellement sûre d'elle... ... Avec la même sincérité, chacun perçoit et raconte différemment ce que nous ne voyons pas, ou ce que nous voyons autrement, mais d'un autre œil. Au fur et à mesure de la conversation, les ressemblances vont se défaire."
28. See Barbara Le Maître, "Défaire la ressemblance: *Les Photos d'Alix* (Jean Eustache, 1980)," in *Entre film et photographie: Essai sur l'empreinte* (Saint-Denis: Presses Universitaires de Vincennes, 2004), 35–36.
29. Alix-Cléo Roubaud, *Journal 1979-1983* (Paris: Seuil, 1984), 137.
30. See Marie-Anne Guérin, "Numéro zéro," in de Baecque, *Le Dictionnaire Eustache*, 215–17.
31. Laurent de Sutter, *Théorie du trou. Cinq méditations métaphysiques sur 'Une sale histoire' de Jean Eustache* (Paris: Léo Scheer, 2013).
32. Ibid., 37.
33. Ibid., 21–22.
34. My translation: "J'ai l'impression que d'abord il y avait le trou, qu'on a construit le trou d'abord, puis la porte au-dessus, puis qu'on a construit le café, et que dans ce café il y avait une caissière, trois garçons, deux flippers, de la choucroute, des assiettes froides, toutes les consommations servies habituellement, qu'il y avait tout ça mais que ça ne fonctionnait que pour le trou, et que tout le reste c'était de la frime."
35. Philippon, *Jean Eustache*, 59.
36. We recall the claim of Alexandre's friend in *La Maman et la putain* that Zarah Leander, the Nazis' stand-in for Marlene Dietrich, is more authentic and truly more interesting than the original. In order to analyze the intricacies and temptations of "falsehood," one needs a strong and stable point of reference for what constitutes the "truth."
37. See Phil Powrie, *The Cinema of France* (London: Wallflower Press, 2006), 133.
38. Schilling, *Eric Rohmer*, 59.
39. Maurice Schérer, "Nous n'aimons plus le cinéma," *Les Temps modernes* (1949), translated as "The Romance Is Gone," in Rohmer, *The Taste for Beauty*, 34.
40. Rohmer, "The Classical Age of Film," in Rohmer, *The Taste for Beauty*, 41.
41. Ibid., 42, my emphasis.
42. Eric Rohmer, "Vanité que la peinture," *Cahiers du cinéma* (1951), translated as "Such Vanity is Painting," in Rohmer, *The Taste for Beauty*, 44.
43. Schilling, *Eric Rohmer*, 72.
44. Rohmer, "Such Vanity is Painting," in *The Taste for Beauty*, 44 (my emphasis).
45. Ibid., 46.
46. Ibid., 46.
47. With willful élan and subjective panache, they lingered on memorable scenes and privileged moments. Their written responses to films, observed film scholar Paul Willemen, were highly impressionistic, "in T.S. Eliot's terms, an 'evocative equivalent' of moments which, when encountered in a film, spark something which then produced the energy and the desire to write." See Paul Willemen, *Looks and Frictions* (Bloomington: Indiana University Press, 1994), 235.
48. See Rohmer's essay, "André Bazin's *Summa*," in Rohmer, *The Taste for Beauty*, 97. Sketching an argument that will be more fully fleshed out in his famous *plaidoyer* for talking cinema, Rohmer

prophetically claims that "in the talkies, the appearance is the essence, and it draws upon itself the substance of an interior world, a world of which it is the incarnation, not the sign."

49. Paul Willemen, "Through the Glass Darkly: Cinephilia Reconsidered," in *Looks and Frictions*, 243.
50. Ibid.
51. Jean Narboni, "The Critical Years: Interview with Eric Rohmer," in Rohmer, *The Taste for Beauty*, 10.
52. Rohmer, "The Classical Age of Film," in *The Taste for Beauty*, 42.
53. Ibid., 42.
54. Eric Rohmer, "Lettre à un critique (à propos des *Contes moraux*)," *La Nouvelle revue française* (March 1971), translated as "Letter to a Critic (Concerning my Moral Tales)," in *The Taste for Beauty*, 80.
55. Quoted in Antoine de Baecque and Noël Herpe, *Eric Rohmer: Biographie* (Paris: Stock, 2014), 136 (my emphasis). De Baecque quotes extensively from the "Interview with Eric Rohmer," in *Nord-communications* (1962, IMEC Fond Eric Rohmer): "Nous assisterons donc à une peinture incessante des arrière-pensées. Enfin, pour débarrasser l'histoire de toute scorie dramatique, je prendrai bien soin de ne conter que de l'anodin, me cantonnant dans le domaine des rapports sentimentaux, ce qui ne veut pas dire que je me désintéresse du décor, du milieu physique, social."
56. Eric Rohmer, "Pour un cinéma parlant," *Les Temps modernes*, 1948, translated as "For a Talking Cinema," in *The Taste for Beauty*, 31–32.
57. Ibid., 32–33 (my emphasis).
58. Ibid., 32.
59. Eric Rohmer, *Six Contes Moraux* (Paris: Editions de l'Herne, 1974).
60. See de Baecque and Herpe, *Eric Rohmer*, 178.
61. "Dans toute femme, il y a un point plus vulnérable: pour les unes, c'est la naissance du cou, la taille, les mains, pour Claire, dans cette position, dans cet éclairage, c'était le genou."
62. Rohmer's keen distance between what is shown and what is said is reminiscent of Bresson's careful usage of sound, not in "formal," but in "moral" terms. See Bresson, *Notes*, 28: "When a sound can replace an image, cut the image or neutralize it." "A sound must never come to the help of an image, nor an image to the help of a sound." "If a sound is the obligatory complement of an image, give preponderance either to the sound, or to the image. If equal, they damage or kill each other, as we say of colors." "Image and sound must not support each other, but must work each in turn through a sort of relay."
63. Rohmer, "Letter to a Critic (Concerning My Moral Tales)," 80.
64. Ibid., 80. If in *La Collectionneuse* (1967), the Platonist symposium on beauty and friendship goes together with a Nietzschean discourse on the nature of art, Rohmer's letter relies on "his colleague's natural taste for beauty" to avoid "a sterile battle of words, of which our common love of film would risk being the first victim."
65. Ibid., 81.
66. Eric Rohmer, "For a Talking Cinema," in *The Taste for Beauty*, 29–30 (my emphasis).
67. Ibid., 29: "If talking film is an art, speech must play a role in conformity with its character as a sign and not appear only as a sound element, which though privileged as compared with others, is but of secondary importance as compared with the visual element." Cf. Schilling, *Eric Rohmer*, 66: "'Pour un cinéma parlant' is a compact manifesto provocatively claiming that despite the introduction of sound, the cinema has yet to learn how to talk. Filmmakers must not reduce speech to literary dialogues that lie halfway between theatre and the novel. In a novel,

dialogues conjure up a world that is present only in the reader's imagination; transposed in the sound film, those same dialogues become redundant, since their referent is visible onscreen. Ideally, speech should intersect with, rather than duplicate the film world."

68. Rohmer, "For a Talking Cinema," in *The Taste for Beauty*, 29.
69. Ibid., 31.
70. Ibid., 31–32.
71. Ibid., 31 (my emphasis).
72. This strategy becomes particularly transparent in the beginning of *L'Amour l'après-midi* (*Chloé in the Afternoon*, 1972), where the exchange between Frédéric's gaze and that of the women he observes in the train creates a dynamic space that the ear and the eye respond to differently.
73. Cf. Frédéric's voice-over in the opening sequence: "Oui, c'est vrai, du temps de Miléna j'avais un bandeau sur les yeux, j'étais esclave. Maintenant, sûr d'Hélène, comme elle l'est de moi, je peux regarder le monde qui m'entoure."
74. Pascal Bonitzer, *Eric Rohmer* (Paris: Éditions de l'étoile, 1991), 24.
75. Ibid., 14.
76. Ibid., 17: "L'aveuglement est donc le principe même de l'action. Les films de Rohmer ne décrivent pas des personnages lancés dans des aventures physiques, mais obscurément travaillés par un objet qui se dérobe, et qui est de nature morale. Il y a quelque chose qui intéresse le spectacle en tant que tel, la structure de l'appareil cinématographique, caméra et projection."
77. Eric Rohmer, "Entretiens," in *Cahiers du cinéma* 172 (November 1965): "L'image n'est pas faite pour signifier, mais pour montrer ..., pour signifier, il existe un outil excellent, le langage parlé."
78. Narboni, "The Critical Years," 16. Some films in particular seem to exhibit the act of speaking, the characters driving the plot by criticizing and contradicting each other, as they fiercely defend their opinions and values, always involving a moral choice. *Pauline à la plage* (1983) and *Le Beau marriage* (1982) are examples of a strategy that will govern the *Tales of Four Seasons*.
79. Roland Barthes, "The Death of the Author," in *Image, Music, Text: Essays*, trans. Stephen Heath (New York: Hill and Wang, 1977), 148.
80. It goes without saying that Barthes's comments on literary criticism should not be directly projected onto the understanding of films, particularly given the critic's reluctance to write about cinema, and his declared "resistance," indeed mistrust of the seventh art. See Philip Watts, *Le Cinéma de Roland Barthes*, trans. Sophie Queniet (Paris: De l'incidence éditeur, 2015). See also Jean Narboni, *La Nuit sera noire et blanche. Barthes, 'La Chambre claire', le cinéma* (Paris: Les Prairies ordinaires et Capricci, 2015).
81. Ibid.,145.
82. Ibid.
83. Bresson, "Une mise en scène n'est pas un art," *Cahiers du cinéma* 543 (February 2000): 5.
84. Barthes, "The Death of the Author," 146.
85. Ibid., 147.

CHAPTER FIVE
Working Artists

> Your film—let people feel the soul and the heart there, but let it be made like a work of hands.
> — Robert Bresson, *Notes on the Cinematograph*

The Crisis of Cinema

The Cannes festival is a highly publicized event in which, for twelve days each year, competing imperatives such as art and commerce, *auteur* cinema and popular genres, French film and Hollywood, enjoy a tenuous and not always amicable coexistence. Its reputation as a haven for *auteur* cinema has not prevented it from becoming a major locus for transactions between filmmakers and financiers. The French festival is, in Colin MacCabe's words, a "French state business"; it has become involved in national cultural and political affairs, with the presence of domestic films in the competition program never a simple matter and the constitution of the jury invariably a complicated affair. For a festival historian observing the sixtieth anniversary of the event, "Cannes is, and always has been, a volatile nexus of aesthetic idealism, commercial opportunism and hard-nosed geopolitics," animated by the never-ending conflict between art and capital.[1]

Since its inception, the Cannes Film Festival has provided a major forum for French cinema and a visible venue for the promotion of a national film culture. Without a doubt the presence of Hollywood stars and movies, red-carpet spectacle, endless parties, and lucrative deals figure strongly in the festival's splashy image. Nonetheless, Cannes has played a fundamental historical role in elevating the ideas of film art and the *auteur* to quasi-religious heights. In a lengthy reflection on the festival in 1955, André Bazin characterized the Cannes spectacle as a "holy order."[2] As glamorous and cosmopolitan as the festival might appear to outsiders, for critics like Bazin and other cinephiles the festival represented a "particularly intense and intensive communion with the art of cinema."[3] The annual ritual pilgrimage to the Riviera brought together the faithful to worship film art—and to express their dismay at the way in which money changers were invading the temple.[4] "The essential goal of the festival," lamented François Truffaut, "is to bring paying customers into the hotels and casinos at a time when business is poor."[5] Even as it has energized the local and national economy, Cannes has served as the most influential bastion of *auteur* cinema. The festival is essential to the film world, "setting agendas, influencing other festivals, unearthing new talent, and propelling selected directors to global attention."[6]

As in previous iterations, the 1991 edition of the festival gave rise to the inimitable tensions between art and commerce, while nonetheless confirming the centrality of *auteur* cinema in French film culture. With the exception of a few American productions, the majority of the films in the competition program had received French financial backing, either in their entirety or by way of coproduction.[7] In the face of a marked disparity between big-budgeted entries and films supported by more modest means, critics like *Positif*'s Michel Ciment spoke of a renewed "international crisis of cinema,"[8] especially for an *auteur* cinema struggling more than ever to stay alive, both at home and elsewhere in the world. The economic constraints invoked by Ciment's exposition of the festival's 1991 official selection signaled a larger concern with the future of cinema. Only a few years later, a group of French and Anglo-American intellectuals would lament people's loss of faith in the "right cinema," or "the decay of cinema" itself, in what would become a collective plea to defend an ideal art of moving images—known as *auteur* cinema—that has cultivated a standardized cinephilic praxis.[9] However, as André Gaudreault suggests, the crisis of cinema is clearly linked to the end of cinema's aesthetic hegemony,[10] and, I would add, to the understanding of the relationship between art and money as intrinsically fraught.

This aesthetically bound discourse dates back to when Nouvelle Vague's *politique des auteurs* held sway, and is to a large extent the effect of such powerful cinephilic discoveries as *Rear Window*, with its inscribed photographer as a surrogate *auteur*. Classical allegories of authorship frame the history of the Nouvelle Vague, from Godard's *Le Mépris* (1962) to Truffaut's *La Nuit américaine* (1973), dramatizing threats to filmmakers' artistic integrity and confirming their priority status vis-à-vis producers, scriptwriters, and stars. In their redemptive approach to Hollywood luminaries like Alfred Hitchcock, Howard Hawks, and Otto Preminger, the exponents of the Nouvelle Vague hailed these *auteurs* for maintaining a singular vision and a directorial integrity despite material constraints and pressures from studios. Their very status as *auteurs* rested in their resistant energy, their remarkable ability to create films that transcended the impersonal workings of the industrialized system from which their features issued. The *auteur*, in this understanding, retained his inimitable signature and artistic integrity no matter where he worked and regardless of the conditions. As such, *auteurs* distinguished themselves from filmmakers who remained subservient to the industrial machine and functioned as *metteurs-en-scène*.

Asked to address the so-called malaise of cinema in the early 1990s, French director Arnaud Desplechin provided a surprising response in the form of a frank dissenting opinion: "I would say that there isn't as much a malaise of cinema as there is a malaise of film criticism." Indeed, for him any malaise is a function of critical incapacity and intellectual failure. Film critics, he argued, "do not understand the films any longer, cannot place them in relation to one another, or in a history, or integrate them in their historical context, and thus cannot say anything to the viewers."[11] A telling sign of this critical myopia, according to Desplechin, lay in the "ill-fated influence of the Nouvelle Vague." Critics fail to realize "that the filmmaker with the strongest and most steadfast impact on the young French cinema is not Jean-Luc Godard, but Maurice Pialat, and, as a secret cousin Jean Eustache, with John Cassavetes as the American friend."[12] Desplechin's words recalled the centrality given to the Nouvelle Vague, as film criticism and film historiography face the challenges of cinema's new developments.

Crisis commentators reflected on the inequalities at work in the film world at a variety of levels. However, instead of focusing on the ways in which different national film industries and production schemes have coped with the pressures of economic viability and the criteria of profitability, discussants insistently turned to the question of the endangered artist. Indeed, this theme served as the centerpiece of the year's competition program which featured many films whose main characters were artists. There was, for instance, the eponymous protagonist of *Van Gogh* (Maurice Pialat, France), the painter of *La Belle Noiseuse* (Jacques Rivette, France), the writer of *Barton Fink* (Ethan and Joel Coen, United States), the poet of *Life on a String* (Chen Kaige, China), the musicians of *La Double vie de Véronique* (Krzysztof Kieslowski, Poland/France/ Norway) and *Bix* (Pupi Avati, Italy), author Ingeborg Bachmann in *Malina* (Werner Schroeter, Germany, Austria), the photographer of *Hors la vie* (Maroun Bagdadi, France), the TVreporter of *The Suspended Step of the Stork* (Theo Angelopolous, Greece, France), and Jacques Demy as the filmmaker-hero of *Jacquot de Nantes* (Agnès Varda, France, screened out of competition).

These films, with their emphasis on the fragile status of the artist and the difficult pursuit of art, both confirmed and responded to renewed critical concern about cinema's creative function. There was an acute focus on the question of artistic identity and the place of the artist in society at large. Entries in the official competition that dramatize the disparity between artistic endeavors and economic determinations surely provided further fuel for the "crisis" discourse of film critics. A century into its history, with legal battles of authorship long settled and debates regarding film's viability as an art resolved, it was not surprising that commentators would return to the question of the medium's sustainability and contemplate whether the death of cinema was upon us.

The Vicissitudes of Singularity

After the second half of the 1980s, especially as heritage cinema surfaced, the self-referential penchant known well from the Nouvelle Vague features found renewed expression in representations of painters. Indeed, commentators at the time would frequently note how painting was now serving as a prominent metaphor for the cinema.[13] In a radical shift, Godard, for instance, turned to painting as a model for cinema; although *Passion* (1982) marks the turn, his *Allemagne année 90 neuf zero* (1991), in Daniel Morgan's reading, presents a meditation on media history that posits cinema as following directly from painting, and not photography.[14] As the art of images potentially liberated from the dictates of verisimilitude, painting also serves to enact the autonomy of the film director as a creator of visual artifacts. In this way, the profusion of films on painters and painting in the late 1980s and early 1990s would become inextricably bound to the self-assertion of filmmakers as *auteurs*. Jacques Rivette's *La Belle Noiseuse* and Maurice Pialat's *Van Gogh* were seen as significant examples of such a proclivity and their selection in the official Cannes competition in 1991 surely confirmed this theme's international presence and contemporary pertinence.

La Belle Noiseuse and *Van Gogh* would often be spoken of in the same breath as works that explained the relationship between painting and cinema. Each film addressed the role of the art market as well as the place of creative endeavor in the world at large. Pialat tells the story of the famous painter who cut off his ear, but withholds the obligatory scenes and the well-known anecdotes. In demythologizing the artist, Pialat takes pains to situate Van Gogh in the gritty realities of labor and commerce. Rivette's *La Belle Noiseuse* (based on Balzac's novella, *Le Chef-d'œuvre inconnu*) pathologizes an artist-genius, a formidable presence in the art world, courted by dealers and idolized by young painters. His struggle with the limits of visual representation is excruciatingly painful and in many ways destructive. Rivette depicts the artist's quest for a singular vision and in the process, so many critics argued, reflects on the persistence of this quest for the film medium. The director's well-known affiliation with the *politique des auteurs* and the Nouvelle Vague prompted the inevitable claim that *La Belle Noiseuse* was part of a "dialogue of French film culture with itself."[15] Rivette made an *auteur*'s film, submits Thomas Elsaesser, "but one in the full knowledge that it has to be an *auteur*'s film, for reasons of survival, not only as bulwark against the anonymous output of TV, but also so that it can be shown at Cannes." The film's classicism and "its apparently solemn affirmation of the spiritual values of great art" must be regarded less as "a polemical re-statement of the *politique des auteurs*, and a rather more subtle or nuanced intervention in present-day cultural politics."[16]

Despite the apparent similarities between their two Cannes entries, Pialat and Rivette diverged in fundamental regards. Rivette, a former critic and editor-in-chief at the *Cahiers du cinéma*, and the interlocutor of such intellectual heavyweights as Roland Barthes and Claude Levi-Strauss, is in fact a far cry from Pialat. According to Gilles Jacob, Pialat did not think well of Rivette. He referred to his colleague as "the worst French director" and became livid when he learned that his *Van Gogh* would appear in the Cannes program along with *La Belle Noiseuse*.[17] With an acute knowledge of working-class destinies and everyday milieus, as well as a down-to-earth, anti-theoretical, and anti-cinephilic sensibility, Pialat had no sympathy whatsoever for what he considered to be the bourgeois stuffiness of Nouvelle Vague rhetoric. When he received a Palme d'Or for *Under the Sun of Satan* in 1987, much of the audience was none too pleased; indeed, the award ceremony has gone down in history as one of Cannes's most infamous scandals. "All your boos and hisses make me happy," snapped the hyper-sensitive Pialat. "And if you don't like me, I don't like you either."[18]

For all the undeniable differences in their personalities, the directors' shared thematics would prompt responses from film critics ever eager to defend the artist out of principle. The social status of the artist is seen as fragile; the fatal destiny of the genius becomes a passion play with contemporary implications. And the work of art, as the singular expression of the artist-genius and eternal reservoir of creativity, gains its power and authority precisely due to the incompatibility between artistic vocation and the surrounding socio-economic environment. Film critics sought to defend as well as to maintain cinema's artistic status against the specter of market forces. Artists, and by extension *auteur* cinema as the production of artists in the pursuit of singular expression, are celebrated for their creative triumphs despite imposing odds.

To be sure, the hallowing of the artist as a model human being is hardly singular to film auteurism. Discourses that position the artist as the embodiment and realization of the exemplary self have a venerable place within French as well as European cultural history and date back many centuries. The Renaissance themes of God as an artist (Marsilio Ficin) and of the artist as the holder of divine power (Leon Alberti) resonate with the rhetoric of film critics who reduce creation to an aesthetic phantasm and foreclose its social dimension.[19] The opposition between artists and artisans has left indelible marks in the perception of film authorship—so much so that other discourses have been practically dismissed, even though the relationship between artistic creation and professional endeavor has a long and complex history. Auteurism's prism remains narrowly focused on films and filmmakers; its focus needs to be expanded beyond a mere fixation on aesthetic factors if one is to appreciate the profound ways in which films also reflect—and reflect on—the realities of working artists.

The Art of Collaboration

With its four-hour duration in which, unlike other Rivette films, there are no playful shifts of time and space, *La Belle Noiseuse* has a classical structure. It readily lent itself to readings in which an isolated artist provided a "mise-en-abyme" for the embattled *auteur* as well as offering an allegorical representation of the relationship between painting and cinema. No doubt, if one is to "salute the artist and his inimitable signature,"[20] it helps to know Rivette's other work, his other films and especially his critical writings.[21] Whereas his earlier features frequently employed theater as a key point of impetus and orientation (as performances being rehearsed or preparations for plays in whose course characters must confront obscured and often painful truths), *La Belle Noiseuse* turns to painting. In fact, the narrative of the film was anticipated in a brief scene from *La Bande des quatre* (*The Gang of Four*, 1988) that relates the plot of Balzac's story. An advocate of cinema's rightful place among the arts, Rivette had devoted much of his time as the editor of *Cahiers du cinéma* to discussing the relationship between the art of cinema and other artistic practices.[22] He remained convinced that cinema's "truth" is revealed only from a contemplative distance and above all through another medium.[23] The relationship between painting and cinema was one of Rivette's chief obsessions as a film critic, as manifested by the links he made between the work of Griffith and Giotto, Rossellini and Matisse, Chaplin and Fautrier, Resnais and Braque.[24]

In *La Belle Noiseuse*, the art dealer Balthazar Porbus (Gilles Arbona) brings the young painter Nicolas (David Bursztein) and his girlfriend Marianne (Emmanuelle Béart) to visit the studio of the secluded famous artist Frenhofer (Michel Piccoli), who lives with his wife Liz (Jane Birkin) on a beautiful estate in the South of France. Suffering from a prolonged creative crisis, Frenhofer allows himself to be persuaded by Porbus to resume *La Belle Noiseuse* whose ambitious project of rendering painting's "absolute truth" was abandoned a decade earlier. In a display of admiration and devotion, young Nicolas offers his own lover to the master as a model. Although outraged by what she deems to be an immodest proposal and none too eager to play a role in the project, Marianne returns to the studio during the following three days and the painting is completed. The experience will test her relationship with Nicolas, as well as Frenhofer's with his spouse (the original model of *La Belle Noiseuse*). After long periods of demanding and painful posing, Marianne recognizes herself in the canvas and, so taken aback that she is unable to resume her previous life, she will ultimately decide to leave Nicolas. Liz secretly enters the studio and, chagrined that her face in the original painting has been replaced by Marianne's, inscribes a black cross next to the painter's signature. When the painting is put on display, Frenhofer unveils what he calls his "first posthumous canvas," that, to Liz's great surprise, is not the image she saw in the studio. The painter has interred the real *Belle Noiseuse* behind a wall of bricks; presumably, it will be hidden from the public for all eternity. The marks it has left on the lives of those involved in its making will nonetheless remain undeniable.

The film won the Grand Prix at Cannes and received widespread critical acclaim. It represented an ideal object for auteurist appreciation, providing ample opportunity for the well-known critical game of recognizing personal themes and formal obsessions, of spotting allusions and ferreting out cross-references and intertexts. The thematic topoi traversing Rivette's other films were duly noted and appreciated: the opposition between life and art, between classical order and the messiness of personal relations, between formal discipline and the anarchy of *l'amour fou*. La Belle Noiseuse generated a plethora of auteurist readings that gravitated around the mythical role of the artist as a bearer of the "shadow of sacrifice and the sacred."[25] In such an understanding, the film dramatizes and mourns the death of the author at a time when economic determinants have suffocated the noble aspiration to "truth." Rivette, faced with "the impossibility of the *auteur* and yet the necessity of being one," bears witness, in Thomas Elsaesser's assessment, to the "end of cinema."[26] This exercise in *Trauerarbeit* figured within a larger tendency, especially among directors eager to sustain their own careers, to present "the death of cinema" as "a grand melancholic theme."[27] In this way *La Belle Noiseuse* offered a statement about the contemporary state of cinema by presenting a "postmodern conception of the fully commodified artwork, an object of exchange whose value fluctuates with the vagaries of the market."[28] This claim, to be sure, invokes the working of market realities in the film but does so in very general terms; such a reading in fact does not truly address or explore how material concerns figure and function within the film's textual workings. From a "postmodern" testament to the end of art and its transformation into a commodity, to a classical "act of resistance" and the "anticipation of another form of vision,"[29] the film becomes a *cri de cœur* for the lost values of art and a grand tribute to artistic greatness.

Such auteurist approaches, despite some degree of difference in their emphases, privilege a painter and his creation and reduce the narrative to a creative drama. In so doing, they pay far less attention to the complex dynamics of the artist's labor and its function within and consequences for a larger constellation of players. In fact, much of the film's running time is dedicated to transactions among the film's six principal characters in a host of configurations, between for instance an art dealer and two painters and his former lover or between an established painter and the young artist who admires him. We partake of the strained relations between a married couple caused by the painting as well as the growing disaffection between two young lovers and the ultimate separation that is occasioned by the creative undertaking. There is also the almost incestuous intimacy between Nicolas and his sister Julienne who takes care of his business affairs, the often tense exchanges between the artist's model and his jealous wife, the unfriendly words between Marianne and her boyfriend's sister, and of course the arduous and uneasy encounters between the master painter and the willful model. If the film is about art, it surely does not sanctify artistic sovereignty. If anything, it problematizes the extremes of aesthetic endeavor and demonstrates the ways in which creative self-involvement, in its quest to rise above the world, can foster self-doubt as well as wreak havoc on the lives of other people. Indeed, rather than valorizing the quest for the ultimate vision of artistic truth, *La Belle Noiseuse* pathologizes the pursuit of art that takes a dire toll on a community.

Rivette scrutinizes the process of artistic creativity by isolating the artist and the model in his studio. Staging the genesis of imagination and creative power, Rivette's *La Belle Noiseuse* reminds us of Clouzot's documentary *Le Mystère Picasso*.[30] Focusing more on the painting than the painter, it also brings to mind Minnelli's *Lust for Life*. Gruffly and often coarsely, with little regard for the discomfort he is causing, Frenhofer forces Marianne into painful and tortuous poses in order to extract from her the "truth of woman." "I want to see," he insists:

The whole body, not just some pieces. I don't care about your breasts, your legs, your lips. I want more. I want everything. The blood, the fire, the ice. All that's inside your body. I'll take it all, I'll get you out of you and put it into this frame. In this blank. Like that. I want what is beyond the thin surface. I want the invisible.

Frenhofer manipulates Marianne's body into grotesque shapes and does so in the name of art that transcends his person and her being anything else. "It is not me who wants," he insists.

It's the line, the stroke. Nobody knows what the stroke is. And I'm after it. I'm running, running, running. Where am I going? To the sky? Why not... No more breasts, no more stomach, no more thighs, no more buttocks! Whirlwinds! Galaxies, the ebb and the flow... Black holes! The original hubbub, have you never heard of it? That's what I always wanted from you.

For this reason he promises to crumble her so that she comes apart. His desire is unessential, what matters is what the painting wants. "You and I," he says to Marianne, "we're just involved. It's going to be a whirlwind, a cataract, a maelstrom. Faster, faster, until you see nothing, feel nothing. Mach 1, Mach 2, Mach 3." In the thick of the process, Marianne admits not being able to feel her body anymore, just as Frenhofer loses possession of his physical self. He is ready to surrender himself so that he might become the hand of a visionary eye: "That's almost it. Almost. I'm just beginning to see you. Go further to the point of no return. That's what I cannot reach. It is better to stop."

In this adventure of creation, however, the artist ultimately will come to rely on the help of the model. Indeed, it is only when the master-slave dynamic between the two gives way to a collaboration between equal parties that a breakthrough becomes possible and the painting can be completed. When Frenhofer seems to be at his wit's end and ready to capitulate, Marianne insists quite adamantly (for much is at stake for her as well) that he see things through. Rather than having him continue to treat her like a malleable prop, however, she insists that he step back and permit her feelings and her memories to guide them. "Let me move like I want. Let me be myself." Eschewing Frenhofer's contorted postures and aggressive gestures, she intuitively finds her way to the pose that has eluded the artist. Recasting her role in the creative process and renegotiating her relation to the artist, Marianne relinquishes all artificial play and displays what she considers to be the essence of her corporeal being. And this will help to yield that which Bresson sees as the final end of representation, namely to pin down an image intact so that it is neither deformed by the model's intelligence nor by the artist's. At this point she delivers herself, her "truth," the all-important truth of the model vis-à-vis the artist articulated in Bresson's *Notes*: "Model. Their way of being the people of your film is by being themselves, by remaining what they are. (*Even in contradiction to what you had imagined.*)"[31] This is not to say that Rivette's method is in any way akin to Bresson's; nor does the film in any way detract from Emmanuelle Béart's stardom, as Godard's *Le Mépris* commentated on that of Brigitte Bardot. Rather, as it is thematized in *La Belle Noiseuse*, the collaboration between artist and model dispossesses the genius from his hegemonic access to truth. On a metatextual level, it recasts Bresson's apodictic theory of the model with a decided twist. The model becomes something akin to a Derridean *pharmakon*, the philter used by the artist to overcome his self-doubt and affirm his genius, but also that which ultimately destabilizes his autonomy.[32]

If Frenhofer achieves a breakthrough, it is because he has chosen his model well; it is Marianne who will lead him where he wants to go.[33] With his wife Liz, he stopped because he became frightened by the gravity of what he was doing and remained inactive for a full decade. It is as if he sensed that the price of continuing would be too dire, the consequences too grave. Artistic endeavor, as Klaus

Theweleit elaborates, so often involves a creator's use and abuse of his partner. "Author husbands marry typists, writers for the stage marry actresses and singers, painters pick models, filmmakers marry film editors." The creative bonds of artist couples are relations of production with special terms for which the story of Orpheus and Eurydice provides an organizing paradigm. In Theweleit's account, however, the master scenario "is not so much about the tragic failure to call back the beloved as about a deliberate program of delivering the woman's body to Hades. In reanimating the body of the dead woman, the man produces new possibility—in other words, 'art.'"[34] In order that he might succeed, the artist literally undoes the body of his partner; the death of the woman (usually a spouse, but often also a partner or a model) brings life to the artistic creation. Theweleit's kings of pop, literature, and art, in Klaus Mladek's formulation, "suck their victim's blood, incorporate and consume them, force their 'medial women,' helpers and beloved into suicide or death, leave or ruin them, in order to be able to bear witness then to their unbearable suffering from the loss of the lover."[35]

A feminist reader of *La Belle Noiseuse* argues that the film reduces women to the mere objects of use and exchange in homosocial pacts that solidify male bonds.[36] This analysis, however, stops short and does not consider the narrative in its entirety. Without question, an agreement between Nicolas (who is eager to win the master's favor), Porbus (who very much wants a new masterpiece from the legendary artist), and Frenhofer (who has remained inactive for ten years) enables the resumption of the project. Marianne, who is not consulted, is to serve as the model for a renewed attempt to complete the painting. Throughout the sessions in the studio, Marianne meets the painter's grumpiness and self-absorption with a blend of impassiveness, intensity, and a hint of defiance. When he is ready to give up, she compels him both to carry on as well as to modify his approach. The fundamental change of course forecloses the lethal terms of the Theweleitian dynamic, allowing her "truth" to become a crucial part of the "truth" that the painting wants to capture. Looking at the completed image, she is initially taken aback, for she sees "a thing cold and dry. It was me." This disarming prospect fosters a self-awakening, the recognition that she does not want to be the partner of an artist, that she needs to move on, even if it is unclear where she will go. She has gained the power of negation that will enable her own self-re-creation. It stands to reason that the last word she speaks in the film, which itself is the film's final word, is "No," a response to Nicolas's entreaties that she stay with him. She has learned from the process to defend herself, to fight back, to be a creator and not a *bricoleuse*, not another Liz who resigns herself to a lonely life in a big mansion with nothing to do but stuff rare birds.

Thomas Elsaesser maintains that the "vanished" painting in Rivette's film functions as a truth revealer. The authority of the "real painting" opens our "inner eye,"[37] he submits, and it will augment our appreciation of everyday life. In fact, though, everyday life plays a very small role in the film; if anything, the feature poses a formidable gap between life and art. *La Belle Noiseuse* recedes into a theatrical setting and closes on a "No," after which there is only silence. It is tempting to twist Rivette's narrative into a fable about the end of film and the future of cinema, but such a reading is complicated by Marianne's decisive exclamation. What lies ahead, in Marianne's words, "you will not find out tonight." An expression of the ostensible crisis of cinema and an intervention in discussions about the so-called death of art film, Elsaesser's interpretation is an eloquent statement of latterday auteurism. For him Rivette's film stands as a financially successful instance of European cinema. His reading focuses on the theme of the artist as a genius and conspicuously overlooks other possible interpretations, especially ones that might probe the ways in which the working conditions of painters come into view and receive painstaking scrutiny.

Maurice Pialat's *Van Gogh* appeared along Rivette's portrait of an artist in the 1991 Cannes competition program. Despite their common subject matter, the two films offer different emphases and sustain dissimilar tones. To the imposing silence of Frenhofer's studio, *Van Gogh* juxtaposes the outdoor landscapes of Auvers-sur-Oise and its colorful community. Rather than focusing on a hermetic act of creation and a small cast of players, *Van Gogh* offers a carnivalesque bounty of activities, settings, and situations. At the closing awards ceremony, the two films found decidedly different receptions. Rivette received the Grand Prix du Jury; Pialat emerged from the festival prizeless.

Portrait of a Village Community

In crafting an exhilarating portrait of "temps retrouvé," Pialat relished the opportunity to paint the age in which Vincent Van Gogh lived. *Van Gogh* celebrates the vibrancy of cinema and, for more than two hours, demonstrates how vital the art of film can be, how alive and complexly connected to nature, human destiny, and empirical existence. After *Under the Sun of Satan* was awarded the Palme d'Or in 1987, Pialat first discussed his next film project with the patron of the arts and collector Marin Karmitz at a dinner arranged by Daniel Toscan du Plantier (his former producer at Gaumont). The collaboration with Karmitz would ultimately not come to pass, but on that evening Pialat decided that he wanted to offer a fresh portrait of the legendary painter.[38] From the figure of the artist inscribed in the popular imagination, however, the French filmmaker would retain very little: some gestures, a hand (ironically, Pialat's own) tracing a touch of blue on the screen-canvas, for instance, or the making of "Marguerite Gachet," the portrait of the bourgeois young woman as a piano player. Otherwise such heritage cinema touches are rare; they intimate what the film could have looked like, but did not become. "This *Van Gogh* is his own!/ Ce *Van Gogh* est le sien!"[39] Forgoing the familiar tics and anecdotes, Pialat offers an original and powerful portrait of a legend.

Upon his arrival in Auvers-sur-Oise, Vincent Van Gogh (Jacques Dutronc) rents a modest room at Ravoux's, the local inn. The "crazy Dutchman," as he is called by Adeline Ravoux (Leslie Azzoulai), quickly settles into the village's community. Following the recommendation of his brother Théo (Bernard Le Coq) and in the hope of curing the malady that led to an extended stay at the Saint-Rémy Hospital, he seeks out Doctor Gachet (Gérard Séty), a connoisseur who takes great pride in his collection of paintings which includes works by Cézanne, Renoir, and Seurat. Van Gogh paints a portrait of the physician's daughter, Marguerite (Alexandra London), despite the young woman's initially dismissive response to this enterprise. Traveling to the neighboring village, he visits old friends, pimps, and prostitutes, among them Cathy (Elsa Zylberstein). One Sunday, his brother Théo, with his wife Jo (Corinne Bourdon) and their little son Vincent, spend a day in the country at Dr. Gachet's; a long lunch is followed by a leisurely walk along the river, where Van Gogh confesses to Jo that he hates being a burden on his brother and family. Vincent's subsequent trip to Paris occasions an argument with art critics as well as an altercation with Théo. A lively night in the Montmartre cabaret follows, during which he is joined by an enamored Marguerite. At the end of the party, he returns to Auvers-sur-Oise where he is confronted by Gachet, who is infuriated that his daughter has spent the night with the painter. Vincent rejects Marguerite and shoots himself in the stomach. The film closes on Marguerite who remarks to a passing painter that Van Gogh was "her friend."[40]

Pialat's portrait of an artist in the midst of a community altogether unaware that this eccentric man might be a genius differs markedly from that of Rivette, who prefers a more schematic arrangement and does not dwell on class relations.

Pialat's characters, on the other hand circulate in flux, caught between social positions, always at a distance from their origin.[41] The film documents the life of a community, with its big events and secondary dramas, of which Van Gogh is more a spectator than the main protagonist. The camera sticks rigorously to the present. Indeed, the images are painstaking in their presentness; they are not the historic representations of a documentarist which foreground the actual state of things in comparison to what has been reconstituted from paintings, photographs, and documents. Pialat does not believe that cinema is a machine that can travel back in time and discover the truth of past existence.[42] At the same time, he fastidiously reconstitutes the period setting.[43]

For Pialat Van Gogh's life is not the stuff of legends, his film has other stakes. Above all, the filmmaker wants to make the lived details of the world that the painter inhabits palpable to the spectator. This explains why his camera devotes more attention to an innkeeper's household mishap than to the artist's simultaneous suicide. It is in the same vein that we understand the film's last scene, Marguerite's affectionate words about a man who was her friend being directed at a young artist painting the church in Auvers, as if Van Gogh's painting did not exist. There is an undeniably ironic tension between the contemporary viewer's awareness of the myths about Van Gogh as well as the artist's grand posthumous reputation and Pialat's understated and restrained depiction of the character.

Major elements that romanticized Van Gogh's figure (and which play a prominent role in Vincente Minnelli's 1956 *Lust for Life*), such as the dismembered ear, the epileptic seizures, the bouts with mental illness, are mentioned only in passing. After a physical examination, Dr. Gachet concludes that Van Gogh works too much and needs to rest. The prostitute Cathy's remark that one can barely see any traces of the wound on the ear conspicuously understates the famous act of disfigurement. The figure of the artist is emptied of its tragic dimension, and the film sets out to follow the unextraordinary story of a man's everyday life. *Van Gogh* is a tapestry, not a portrait; it shows a painter and the people around him, the community he inhabits, and the world in which he works. Pialat privileges and lingers on what might seem to be extraneous details: dining guests singing *Le Temps des cerises*, the cook Madame Chevalier mentioning in passing that her son has perished in the Paris Commune, or the piano teacher singing *Lakmé* at the Sunday dance. Particularly during the film's set piece that presents a day in the country, Pialat celebrates the glories of nature and the pleasures of human encounters. Vibrant with life and liveliness, colors and sounds, the film is in stark contrast with Artaud's alienated portrait of the painter.[44]

The Artisan through an Auteurist Prism

Pialat's resentment about never being recognized as a prominent French filmmaker as well as his vendetta against the Nouvelle Vague directors can easily be projected onto Van Gogh, a painter who only sold one painting in his lifetime and who would not gain recognition until after his death. Pialat's refusal to reenact the legend occasioned attacks by critics and may well explain why the film did not receive prizes at Cannes and that year's *César* ceremony. This experience of rejection caused much pain and bitterness; Pialat would return to filmmaking only one more time. When Van Gogh agrees with Marguerite Gachet that his portrait of her is only "a pile of mud," one is tempted to see the scene as an anticipation of the critical dismissal that would lead Pialat to believe that his film was a failure. When *Van Gogh* later (much later, for it was fifteen years after its first screening) was chosen for the French program of the prestigious *agrégation*, the institutionalization of the film seemed both belated and ironic in light of the negative response it had faced upon its release. Today *Van Gogh* is considered one of the masterpieces of French cinema, and Pialat, in some quarters at least, is called "the most important post-1960 French filmmaker, Godard being Swiss."[45]

Pialat's professional trajectory parallels that of Nouvelle Vague filmmakers, but in crucial ways deviates from it. Slightly older, he would have to wait a decade after the film breakthroughs of Godard, Truffaut, and Chabrol to complete his debut feature. Despite this temporal discrepancy, both of age and career path, critics nonetheless have often written Pialat and his films into the success story of the famous movement.[46] This is both curious and strange; in fact, it is downright misleading, as would be the attempt to position *Van Gogh* as an extension of the Nouvelle Vague and a celebration of an artist genius as a surrogate filmmaker. An auteurist reading of *La Belle Noiseuse,* as we have seen, allows one to recognize the persistence of themes and understand yet another example of a mise-en-abyme structure in Rivette's work as a whole. The approach that critics have so often and avidly employed in commentaries on Nouvelle Vague productions, however, does not serve so well in trying to make sense of Pialat's work. Nor does the resolutely anti-theoretical and non-cinephilic director provide the kind of cues that one might expect from a Rivette or a Rohmer.

Is there such a thing as a Pialat "style," attributes that would make the director recognizable in a given shot or a specific sequence? The difficulty in identifying a distinctive signature in his work derives not so much from the lack of motifs and recurrent signs as from his vehement refusal to be formulaic or systematic. He prefers the long take and avoids unnecessary technical fussiness. The marks of personal writing are largely absent; we find no prominent motifs, no distinct mannerisms. The Pialat "method" is not striking or conspicuous like that of other filmmakers. His method manifests itself both in the preparation of the films and during the shooting, but the "author" remains discreet and throughout does not leave bold traces of enunciation. If we compare *Van Gogh* to *Under the Sun of Satan*, none of the privileged themes recur. To *Satan*'s tenebrous struggle, *Van Gogh* offers the everyday palette of a small town, a slice of life à la Lumière Brothers. To the north of the country depicted in *Satan*, *Van Gogh* opposes the provincial ambience of Auvers-sur-Oise.

From painting, he borrows some basic elements, like the fixity of shots and perspective. The correlation between the shot envisioned in its duration, as well as in its spatial openness, allows Pialat to bring the full texture of life to the screen. "My ideal," he declared in an interview, "is the unique take that expresses the point of view of the instant as it is happening. Once one cuts, once one fragments or goes back, this original truth escapes precisely because one restarts a process that by definition cannot take place a second time."[47] Because Pialat prefers "life" to "art" and wants to capture the "fugitive moment of truth,"[48] he will always prefer (and use) technically imperfect shots over neat images that are carefully composed. As Jean Eustache once noted, Pialat purposely destroys the "beauty" of the film; it is as if he wanted to hide the production values.[49] Pialat's world is one of aperture rather than formal closure; it opposes the luminosity of the image to empirical immediacy, preferring to capture reality rather than shape what is into something else. The director refuses to let an aesthetic filter stand between the screen and the discharge of truth.

Van Gogh proves that a film about a cultural icon need not become just another exercise in the tradition of quality or heritage cinema; instead Pialat showed how this artistic legend might be appropriated and made anew. Pialat's film is not a film *about* painting or about art and even less about cinema, unless we embrace the commonplace that every film is a film about its own making. We see no original paintings, nor artistic perorations, at best an occasional ironic reference like the pun on Cézanne / *seize ânes*.[50] Otherwise, what is on view are the artist's wanderings, the hysterical tantrums, the small pleasures and occasional irritations of a difficult man of feeble constitution who spends his days slapping paint onto canvases. Pialat, observes Magny, "naturalizes Van Gogh's character, looks at him as if for the first time, untouched by any mysticism, any idealization or religiosity."[51] The absence of the painting *L'Église d'Auvers* (1890) reflects the film's willful neglect of the religious concern that plays such a strong role in the painter's correspondence. In this way the film also denies "the transfer of spirituality from the man to the œuvre, through an homology between religion and painting."[52]

Nothing in the storyline hints that the painter is a genius—and the understated handling of his demise reinforces this impression. After the buoyancy and exuberance of the long night at a Montmartre cabaret, Vincent returns with Marguerite to Auvers. Nothing awaits him there but a void; there is no hope, all that remains is suicide. Pialat's terse and undernarrated conclusion suggests that art is not an end in itself. Marguerite's closing words—"He was my friend"—do not evoke the reputation of the artist or praise his genius; rather they express, in a most unadorned but for that reason all the more intense and sincere manner, his young lover's sorrow.

The country, the dance, the prostitutes: Pialat relishes the sensuality of landscapes and bodies basking in the light and celebrating for moments the lightness of being, filming what Renoir (the father), Seurat, Toulouse-Lautrec or Van Gogh captured in their paintings. Pialat recreates the end of a century and a lost way of living, not by imitating paintings from the time, but by sharing the Impressionists' desire to seize fugitive moments and in so doing, he forges a cinema driven by a manic desire for veracity. If some shots from the Sunday walk evoke Seurat's *Dimanche à la Grande Jatte* or if Jo's toilette reminds us of Degas's *La Toilette*, these are not perfunctory or precious references, but rather the serendipitous coincidence of sensibilities separated by a century. The true painter at work in *Van Gogh* is Pialat rather than his legendary character. This is not an instance of filmed painting, but rather a painter's film.[53]

In this film about a painter, Pialat makes no great fuss about the visual construction, the frame, the composition, light or texture. The light is not the painter's, but the filmmaker's; the texture and the materiality of light attests to this, for instance in the scene where he paints Marguerite's portrait. She sits at the piano, in the living room, while the canvas is mounted outside the room's big open window. The camera goes back and forth through the window and in the continuity of the shots, we cannot help but notice the lighting: outside a stunning saturation of colors, the green of trees; inside the subdued shadows of the living room space.[54]

The framing and lighting of films about legendary painters have become so codified as to be predictable; Minnelli (*Lust for Life*), Huston (*Moulin Rouge*), and even Renoir (*French Cancan*) place their characters in natural or reconstituted decors that consciously evoke famous paintings. At times the spirit of reconstitution takes over; the screen becomes a master's canvas, the cinematic image a mere copy of images produced by a docile artisan, the scenes proceeding from the *tableau vivant*, the characters moving around like in a museum. Pialat eschews such approaches; he wants his film to vibrate with life, and to avoid at all costs any sense that what we see comes from a museum. "What could have the image of the painter's hand painting added to the film?" asks Mérigeau. "Nothing, the artist's grasp on the world, on the matter, cannot be captured this way, and then reconstituted in the editing room." *Van Gogh* is not a film "about" painting, "c'est un film de vie."[55]

Pialat is not one to focus on details. Individual scenes offer compact narrative blocks with few shots, many of which are long takes; sequences unfold chronologically without clear points of connection from one to the next. Marked temporal and spatial gaps abound and render the film, very much like his other work, an extended exercise in ellipsis. A detail here and there, for the film trains the viewer to pay careful attention, might suggest how much time has passed between scenes, ten minutes, a week, half a year. The spectator, for instance, cannot easily determine how much time elapses between Vincent's arrival in Auvers-sur-Oise and his ultimate demise. Pialat's indifference to the elementary rules of storytelling, and his obvious delight in fragmenting the narration, are apparent in his treatment of the material.

For Joël Magny, Pialat's method brings to mind Renoir's metaphor of the filmmaker as a fisherman, who patiently waits for hours, so "that truth comes/happens to his film."[56] Nonetheless, Pialat remains utterly modern since each of his films constitutes the allegory of its own making. This is also true for Rivette who famously once said that "it is always the method of making a film that is its true subject."[57] Rivette's films often focus on artists or artistic communities, more often than not on the theater world, and at once sustain a fiction and display a reflection about the production of meaning. Even seen within such a conception of "modernity," Pialat's *Van Gogh* does not offer a mise-en-abyme of cinema, for self-reflexive moments are all but nonexistent in the film. The compelling artistic impact of *Van Gogh* derives from the fact that it cannot be reduced to an allegory about filmmaking. Instead, Pialat's approach to a topic which is usually treated in a romanticized and mystifying manner demonstrates that the conventional antinomy between the "sacrificial idealism of the artist" and the "calculating materialism of the art world"[58] is spurious and misleading, indeed a false opposition.

Vocational Pursuits

For all their differences, both *Van Gogh* and *La Belle Noiseuse* show us men who paint for a living. The function and place of the work that gives rise to art remain crucial in each case, albeit within quite different settings. The exuberant spectacle of natural panoramas and blooming colors in *Van Gogh* stand in stark opposition to the cold spareness of Frenhofer's studio in *La Belle Noiseuse*. Unlike Rivette's protagonist who is ready to sacrifice everything for the ultimate canvas, Pialat's Van Gogh does not harbor great artistic ambitions. Painting provides the means by which this simple man makes a living. Nonetheless, *Van Gogh* is anything but a straightforward portrait of an artist; the film's impetus brings to mind the crucial distinction between the question of the artist and the question of aesthetic appreciation. In Dominique Chateau's words, "the theoretical role of the artist's status is that it emphasizes the opposition between artistic and aesthetic, between the art object as production within a socio-cultural context, and the aesthetic object as experience of the world where art is only one among several stakes. Art is a controversial issue when the artist becomes a distinct category of social role."[59]

Viewed from Theodor W. Adorno's perspective that posits art in conflict with the dictates of the market and the status quo, authentic art resists domestication by external agencies, even if its very production takes place within a socio-economic field of forces. The true work of art does not protest overtly against these imposing factors, but instead rejects conventional aesthetic solutions that conceal social contradictions. The authentic work of art can only exercise its power negatively, by a will to overcome the ingrained dialectics between the whole and its parts. The dynamics of this approach find partial enactment in both films, especially in the opposition between artists and bourgeois connoisseurs (the art dealer Porbus in Rivette, the collector Gachet in Pialat). According to this model, the autonomy of the work of art can only come about at the price of the artist's sacrifice; the creation of genuinely innovative work is an act of defiance and resistance against a powerful system determined by commerce and controlled by the market. The two films negotiate the functional relationship between art and the market; they also consider the social and economic place of working artists.

For the artist a studio is a vocational domicile; in order to enter it, visitors must be invited or summoned. When Nicolas, Marianne, and Porbus arrive at Frenhofer's residence, he is not there; they will have to wait before his longstanding hesitation to open his studio to "troublemakers" becomes apparent. When he arrives, the absent-minded, unkempt, and disheveled man quickly assumes the controlled ease of the master of the house, who carefully monitors all intrusions into his working space. In fact, the studio is a site with crucial historical connotations. If the institution of art has assumed three primary organizational configurations since the Middle Ages, that is, the Corporation, the Academy, and the market,[60] Chateau argues that one dare not exclude the artist's studio.[61] This locus, at least in terms of its institutional legitimacy, is the equal of the Corporation and the Academy. The introduction of the "studio" during the Renaissance would bring an end to the artist's economic subordination to the Corporation. And the studio would survive the end of the Academy at the close of the nineteenth century. The space represents a "decentralized organizational model of artistic practice," or in the words of Chateau, of "the artist as the center of this practice, which is in the essence the same thing." The studio "inaugurates the magisterium of an individual whose theoretical and practical authority, grounded on the recognized mastering of his art, imposes itself absolutely in the well confined space of his practice." As such, the studio provides the artist with both a working place and a vocational status.[62] In this functional space, notes Chateau, "the artist reigns as the master of the grounds, at once in his social relationship to the visitors, and in his personal relation to his creative work."[63]

The studio thus serves double duty. It is the site of the artist's ongoing personal struggle to expand his own standards, and, at the same time, it confirms the sometimes troubled relationship between "aesthetic" values and the rules of the market, between the making of art and the making of money. The studio shields creative endeavor from the distraction and constraints of the world: "In the studio, the painter is alone. He is focused. The necessity of this concentration, and of the true isolation that it implies, places it far from nature, as well as from the urban agitation, in a still light, the light of the studio."[64] The studio grants artistic practice an institutional space and a semblance of "social roots." At the same time it corresponds, by dint of its isolation and self-enclosure, to the hope for an artistic world free from social alienation. Nonetheless, as *La Belle Noiseuse* makes clear, in offering a distinct space for the professional pursuits of painters, the studio remains tightly bound to institutional priorities and the dictates of the market.

The Work of Art

In quite distinct ways, both *La Belle Noiseuse* and *Van Gogh* portray professional identities and propose new dispositions of artistic endeavor. What links them, in spite of their fundamental differences (be it in regard to such questions as class or their understanding of artistic vocation), is a strong concern with communities, less on the basis of the integration of the artist in a homogeneous group than on that of the organization in a field of work.[65] The films engage with the question of art's place in the social world and the administration of artistic creation in comparison with other sectors of production. It is significant that both films draw on a modern conception of art and the artist which goes back to the nineteenth century,[66] at which time the integration of different socio-economic factors into the artistic sphere led to a definition of art as an "autonomous and individualizing creative practice."[67] Within this framework, individuals invested themselves totally in their artistic work, which in return allowed them access to a social condition where they could enjoy the benefits of their autonomy.

In updating Balzac's story, Rivette replicates a conceptual framework bound to the Romantic definition of the artist's place within the community only to problematize and go beyond it. This becomes visible in the characters' interactions in the studio and the well-defined relations between the two painters and the art dealer. As for Pialat, he employs a painterly eye quite sensitive to everyday activities and material determinations, for instance in the scene at Théo's apartment which starts with a conversion between the spouses, before developing into a larger discussion about art that includes agents, dealers, and critics. In *Van Gogh* the work of the artist takes place in and is a part of communities and institutions. Vincent says to a mentally disabled denizen of the town, "You see, the world is well made, there is a place for everyone, even the village idiot." In that way Vincent does not stand out from his contemporaries. The discussions between Théo and Jo, or Théo and Doctor Gachet, for instance, all serve to illustrate that painting is a form of work whose product is a material property. If Van Gogh is not financially "successful," it is not because he lacks creative freedom; on the contrary, the film stresses that his work grants expression to the forces that constitute the essence of his humanity. His work as a painter, although not lucrative, is an extension of his individuality and an expression of his humanity. That does not mean, however, that his work remains free from economic circumstance.

While the two films insist that the preservation of individuality lies at the heart of artistic creation, they also address the question of the division of labor within the realm of the arts. In spite of the artist's individuality, or maybe thanks to it, the idiosyncrasies of artistic professions are apparent in numerous kinds of relationships that range from competition to conflict. Two aspects coexist in a tense relationship: the identification of the artistic activity with the "métier" whose exercise is deeply individual, and a profound professional inequality that governs artistic endeavor. In this way, Rivette and Pialat, as film authors, present a notion of art as "expressive" work that issues from and figures within the realm of labor.[68] But can singularity also serve as the justification for making a distinctive artist a social model? Can the value of originality become a social norm?

The celebration of artistic originality is central to the creation of canons; its centrality has certainly led to the creation of the Nouvelle Vague's pantheon of *auteurs*. But the imperative that each artist be different from his peers, with some artists being better and more valuable than others, is also the very premise of competition. This same principle drives the market in which artistic endeavor circulates; in this way the discourse of singularity mimics, indeed replicates, the very determinants it claims to criticize. The valorization of the special and the unique constitutes the basis of a system similar to the one sustained by the capitalist market with its perpetual quest for profit through innovation and the advantages that come with the successfully new. The dynamic of the village community in *Van Gogh* (and the art community we glimpse during Vincent's visit at Theo's) suggests that the conjunction between authenticity, originality, and freedom is opposed to the utilitarian imperatives and conventions of real life. In Rivette's film, the studio is seen as the site of autonomous creation and a space that confirms the singularity of the artist.

Pialat's Van Gogh appears neither as a "peintre de génie" nor as a worker specialized in art; the models presented in the film are Renoir (whose work sells) or even Gilbert, the amateur at Ravoux's. By deflating the myth of the artist, the director points to the downside of any would-be utopia in which each worker might have his own place. Because "this" individual place leads to the identification of the artist with his work, it also renders this identification a result of the singularity it generates, thus confounding the possibility of an egalitarian social community. In an ideal social world, the authenticity required by this model would grant freedom to each individual, and would celebrate difference and diversity, without falling sway to a competitive dynamic. Self-expression through a chosen form of labor would not be hindered by social conformism nor by social inequality. When every individual has an original way of being human, work can allow for the discovery and expression of the self. The reference to art and artist is in this way essential, for art defined in this way might serve as a model of what Marx called non-alienated labor and as such the "utopian truth of mankind."[69] Pialat's highly evocative film suggests that creative work might forward a radical social and economic critique, but only if this work is integrated in the social structure and not isolated as an individual's atomized pursuit. *Van Gogh* demonstrates how large this "if" is.

Rivette's and Pialat's Cannes entries of 1991 show us painters who are workers and empirical beings, and as such, subject to a variety of imperatives. Both narratives depict, quite painstakingly so, the material and domestic conditions of artists' destinies, showing the spaces they work in, the people they live with, and the institutions they must defer to and rely on, demonstrating how creation, as a form of work, is subject to the social and economic principles that regulate expressive activity. Commentators at the time had little to say about these questions. Indeed, these crucial dimensions became obscured in a critical discourse that transformed these narratives into allegories about endangered *auteurs*. These significant films became pressed into service as further confirmations of a master narrative regarding the end of cinema and with it, the end of cinephilia and personal filmmaking.[70] In this instance, one understands well what Arnaud Desplechin had in mind when he argued that the putative crisis of cinema was nothing more than a crisis of film criticism, which is to say auteurist criticism and its circumscribed understanding of the fields of force that constitute cinematic endeavor. Neither passion plays about the artist genius nor enactments of the "end" of cinema, *La Belle Noiseuse* and *Van Gogh* in fact portray both the ends and aporias of artistic pursuit, which is to say the work of artists.

Notes

1. Kieron Corless and Chris Drake, *Cannes: Inside the World's Premier Film Festival* (London: Faber and Faber, 2007), 5.
2. André Bazin, "Du festival considéré comme un ordre," *Cahiers du cinéma* 48 (June 1955): 6.
3. Corless and Drake, *Cannes: Inside the World's Premier Film Festival*, 49.
4. See Michel Pascal, *Cannes: Cris et Chuchotements* (Paris: Nil Éditions, 1997), 75–79.
5. Quoted in Corless and Drake, *Cannes: Inside the World's Premier Film Festival*, 53.
6. Ibid., 3.
7. In addition to the four French movies in competition (*La Belle Noiseuse*, *Hors la vie*, *Lune froide* and *Van Gogh*), there were numerous French co-productions: Rustam Khamdamov's *Anna Karamazoff*, Danielle Luchetti's *The Yes Man*, Theo Angelopolous's *The Suspended Step of the Stork*, Krzysztof Kieslowski's *La Double Vie de Véronique*, and Peter Greenaway's *Prospero's Book*.
8. See Michel Ciment, "Cannes 91," *Positif* 365–366 (June–July 1991): 73.
9. See Susan Sontag, "The Decay of Cinema," *New York Times Magazine* (25 February 1996); David Denby, "The Moviegoers: Why Don't People Like the Right Movies Anymore?" *The New Yorker* (6 April 1998): 95; Stanley Kauffmann, "A Lost Love," *New Republic* (8 and 15 September 1997): 28.
10. André Gaudreault and Philippe Marion, *The End of Cinema: A Medium in Crisis in the Digital Age*, trans. Timothy Barnard (New York: Columbia University Press, 2015), 12–13.
11. Thierry Jousse and Antoine de Baecque, "Interview avec Arnaud Desplechin," in *Le Retour du cinéma*, ed. Antoine de Baecque and Thierry Jousse (Paris: Hachette, 1996), 99: "Je dirais qu'il n'y a pas tant un malaise du cinéma qu'un malaise de la critique. C'est un échec à la fois intellectuel et pédagogique: la critique ne comprend plus les films, n'arrive plus à les placer les uns en rapport avec les autres, ne parvient plus à les situer dans une histoire ou dans leur contexte présent, et elle ne parvient pas non plus à dire des choses aux spectateurs."
12. Jousse and de Baecque, "Interview avec Arnaud Desplechin," 100.
13. See for example Pascal Bonitzer, *Décadrages: peinture et cinéma* (Paris: Éditions de l'étoile, 1985); Jacques Aumont, *L'Œil interminable* (Paris: Séguier, 1989); Marc Vernet, *Figures de l'absence* (Paris: Editions de l'Etoile, 1990); *Cinéma et peinture: approches*, ed. Raymond Bellour (Paris: Presses Universitaires de France, 1990); and Raymond Bellour, *L'Entr'images: Photo, cinéma, vidéo* (Paris: Différence, 2002).
14. Daniel Morgan, *Late Godard and the Possibilities of Cinema* (Berkeley: University of California Press, 2013), 3.
15. Thomas Elsaesser, "Around Painting and the 'End of Cinema': A Propos Jacques Rivette's *La Belle Noiseuse*," in *European Cinema: Face to Face with Hollywood* (Amsterdam: Amsterdam University Press, 2005), 172.
16. Ibid., 172. Interestingly, Elsaesser does not mention that *La Belle Noiseuse* was made for television and received funding from Arte.
17. Gilles Jacob, *Citizen Cannes: The Man behind the Cannes Film Festival*, trans. Sarah Robertson (London: Phaidon, 2011), 271.
18. Corless and Darke, *Cannes: Inside the World's Premier Film Festival*, 115.
19. See Charles Taylor, *The Malaise of Modernity* (Concord: Anansi, 1991), 69–70.
20. Ibid., 168.
21. *Paris nous appartient* (*Paris Belongs to Us*, 1958–1960) is Rivette's first film, a picture of a restless creative group working on an abortive production of Shakespeare's *Pericles*. An expression

of cinephilia (a three-minute clip from Lang's *Metropolis* testifies to this), and of the amateur passion for film, it stood out for its unconventional narrative, a common place throughout Rivette's heterogeneous filmography. Its long time in the making became a part of the narrative itself, and articulated a theme that will recur, namely that we are victims of a great conspiracy. This "dual motif of plot (as conspiracy and narrative) and performance (often improvised)", in Ginette Vincendeau's terms, provides a reflection on fiction and imagination in his future films, *L'Amour fou* (1967–1969), *L'Amour par terre* (*Love on the Ground*, 1984), *Le Pont du Nord* (1981), or *La Bande des quatre* (1989). Often mixing 35mm sequences and rougher 16mm material in films of uneven length (*L'Amour fou* was 256 minutes, *Out One: Spectre* [1973] is four hours and twenty minutes, *Jeanne la Pucelle* [1994] six hours), Rivette's films had trouble in distribution, and to this day *La Belle Noiseuse* remains his most successful movie, while along with *Céline et Julie vont en bateau* (*Céline and Julie Go Boating*, 1974) *La Religieuse* is his best known, and also his most scandalous. See Ginette Vincendeau, "Jacques Rivette," in *Encyclopedia of European Cinema*, ed. Ginette Vincendeau (London: BFI, 1995), 361.

22. Jacques Rivette and Michel Delahaye, in the presentation of the interview with Roland Barthes entitled "Sur le cinéma" *Cahiers du cinéma* 147 (September 1963), reprinted and translated in Roland Barthes, *The Grain of the Voice: Interviews 1962-1980*, trans. Linda Coverdale (Chicago: Northwestern University Press, 2009), 11: "Film has become a part of our culture like all the others, and all the arts, all interests, must take the cinema into account, as it does them. It is this phenomenon of reciprocal information, at times obvious (these are not always the best cases), often diffuse, that we would like, among other things, to try to examine closely in these conversations."

23. In 1968 Rivette insisted that "all films are about the theater. If you take a subject that deals with the theater to any extent at all, you're dealing with the truth of the cinema. Because that is the subject of truth and lies, and there is no other in the cinema: it is necessarily a questioning about truth, with means that are necessarily untruthful. Taking it as the subject of the film is being frank, so it must be done." This does not mean that cinema has to become the subject of cinema, which for him so often comes across as strained and affectatious. Rather, the cinema considers its possibilities while looking at something else, "not itself but its elder brother. Of course, this is another way of looking at itself in the mirror, but the theatre is the 'polite' version of the cinema. It is the face it assumes when it communicates with the public." Approaching the film crew as a self-enclosed conspiracy, Rivette seeks to capture what he calls "the reality of the conspiracy." See *Rivette: Texts and Interviews*, ed. Jonathan Rosenbaum (London: British Film Institute, 1977), 27.

24. See Rivette's article "Lettre sur Rossellini," *Cahiers du cinéma* 46 (April 1955): 14–26, as well as his intervention in the round table "Hiroshima, notre amour," *Cahiers du cinéma* 97 (July 1959): 1–18.

25. Elsaesser, *European Cinema*, 49.

26. Elsaesser, "Around Painting and the 'End of Cinema'," 172.

27. Nicole Brenez, "Movie Mutations: Letters from (and to) Some Children of 1960: Jonathan Rosenbaum, Adrian Martin, Kent Jones, Alexander Horwath, Nicole Brenez, and Raymond Bellour," in *Movie Mutations: The Changing Face of World Cinephilia*, ed. Jonathan Rosenbaum and Adrian Martin (London: British Film Institute, 2003), 19.

28. Marja Warehime, "Money, Markets, Women and the Death of Art: Maurice Pialat's *Van Gogh* and Jacques Rivette's *La Belle Noiseuse*," *Sites: The Journal of Twentieth-Century/ Contemporary French Studies* 6.2 (2002): 414.

29. Elsaesser, "Around Painting and the 'End of Cinema'," 175.
30. The movie lasts exactly as long as it takes for the painting to be completed; one should also note that the sound reveals the materiality of the process, the scratching of the pen/pencil etc. See Lynda Nead, "Seductive Canvases: Visual Mythologies of the Artist and Artistic Creativity," *Oxford Art Journal* 18.2 (1995): 59–69.
31. Bresson, *Notes*, 41.
32. See Jacques Derrida, "Plato's Pharmacy," *Dissemination*, trans. Barbara Johnson (London: The Athlone Press, 1981), 61–172. See also Jacques Derrida, *Spurs: Nietzsche's Styles*, trans. Barbara Harlow (Chicago and London: University of Chicago Press, 1979).
33. Bresson, *Notes*, 41.
34. Quotations from Laurence A. Rickels, "The King and I—Klaus Theweleit Interview—and Excerpts from *Book of Kings*, Vol. 2," *ArtForum* (September 1994). See http://mccoyspace.com/nyu/10_s/ideas/texts/week12-Theweleit-Interview.pdf (accessed 9 August 2015).
35. Klaus Mladek, "Klaus Theweleit's *Book of Kings*: Excerpts in Translation." See http://nideffer.net/proj/Tvc/reviews/18.Tvc.v9.reviews.Mladek.html (accessed 8 August 2015).
36. Warehime, "Money, Markets, Women and the Death of Art,".
37. Elsaesser, "Around Painting and the 'End of Cinema'," 175–78.
38. Pialat's biographer, Pascal Mérigeau, recounts Pialat's confession: "C'est un type, il est sur le quai de la gare, il prend le train pour Auvers. Il a cent tableaux à peindre, trois mois à vivre, il s'appelle Van Gogh et il n'en a rien à foutre." See Pascal Mérigeau, *Pialat* (Paris: Grasset, 2002), 286.
39. Ibid., 288.
40. Joël Magny, *Maurice Pialat*, (Paris: Éditions de l'étoile, coll. Auteurs, 1992), 107–108.
41. Ibid., 52.
42. Ibid., 46.
43. See Mérigeau, *Pialat*, 293: "Les tiroirs des meubles doivent être remplis de linge ou de vaisselle d'époque, même si jamais ils ne seront ouverts à l'écran. Les wagons de 1ère classe du train sont refaits à neuf, impeccables, comme l'étaient des wagons de 1ère classe. Acteurs et figurants portent leurs costumes quatre, cinq mois avant le début du tournage. ... Aucune perruque, surtout, et le moins de chapeaux. Pour les scènes de dance, tout le monde répète chaque dimanche, en costume, musiciens également: cinq danses sont prévues. C'est pratiquement un village entier qui est reconstitué, dans le respect de la vérité d'alors."
44. See Antonin Artaud, *Van Gogh, le suicidé de la société* (Paris: Gallimard, 1990 [1947]).
45. De Baecque and Jousse, *Le Retour du cinema*, 101.
46. Vincent Amiel offers an insightful characterization of Pialat's relation to the Nouvelle Vague. The "tradition of quality" was criticized for its reliance on easy subjects and prominent characters, its production of overrated and mediocre fare devoid of stylistic allure and formal daring. The filmmakers of the Nouvelle Vague noticed important changes in cinema's socio-economic status, and in response they undid the hierarchy of subjects and genres, employing newly affordable technology to counter the hierarchy of the production system (in the process granting cineastes the status of authors). The recognition of the filmmaker as the center of the cinematic project went hand in hand with the new relationship between reality and its filmic representation. See Vincent Amiel, *'Van Gogh' de Maurice Pialat* (Neuilly: Atlande, 2006), 22–25.
47. Stéphane Levy-Klein and Olivier Eyquem, "Trois rencontres avec Maurice Pialat," *Positif* 159 (May 1974): "Mon idéal, c'est le plan unique dans lequel s'exprime un point de vue sur une

chose qui se produit à l'instant même. Dès que l'on découpe, que l'on fragmente, que l'on revient en arrière, cette vérité se dérobe puisque l'on recommence ce qui par définition ne se produit qu'une fois."

48. Magny, *Maurice Pialat*, 117.
49. Ibid., 25.
50. The 2013 DVD edition provides a selection of scenes that were shot but not included.
51. Magny, *Maurice Pialat*, 110.
52. Heinich, *L'Élite artiste*, 66. See also Nathalie Heinich, *The Glory of Van Gogh: An Anthropology of Admiration*, trans. Paul Leduc Browne (Princeton: Princeton University Press, 1996).
53. Olivier Kohn, "Deux ou trois choses sur *Van Gogh*, un film de Maurice Pialat," *Positif* 369 (November 1991): 10–11.
54. See Jean-Pierre Jeancolas, "Le Tub de Madame Théo," *Positif* 369 (November 1991): 12–13.
55. Pascal Mérigeau refers to Pialat's comments on the relationship between painting and cinema, his love for the first, eternal, continuous, and his hate for the second, flawed by multiple rewatchings that only reveal the imperfections. See Mérigeau, *Pialat*, 302.
56. Magny, *Maurice Pialat*, 113.
57. Quoted in Alain Bergala, "Roberto Rossellini et l'invention du cinéma moderne," in Roberto Rossellini, *Le Cinéma révélé*, ed. Alain Bergala (Paris: Éditions de l'étoile, 1984), x.
58. Pierre-Michel Menger, *Portrait de l'artiste en travailleur: Métamorphoses du capitalisme* (Paris: Seuil, 2002), 9.
59. Dominique Chateau, *Qu'est-ce qu'un artiste* (Rennes: Presses Universitaires de Rennes, 2008), 11.
60. Raymonde Moulin, *Art et humanisme à Florence au temps de Laurent le Magnifique* (Paris: PUF, 1961), 21–22.
61. Dominique Chateau, "La Visite de l'atelier dans *La Belle Noiseuse*," *Études cinématographiques* 63 (1998): 127–41.
62. Accounts of the motif of the studio in representations of painters focus on the vocational dimension of artistic endeavor. See Lynda Nead, "The Artist's Studio: The Affaire of Art and Film," in *Film, Art, New Media: Museum without Walls?*, ed. Angela Dalle Vacche (New York: Palgrave, 2012), 23–38.
63. Chateau, "La Visite de l'atelier dans *La Belle Noiseuse*," 128–29.
64. René Passeron, *L'œuvre picturale et les fonctions de l'apparence* (Paris: Vrin, 1980), 101: "À l'atelier, le peintre est seul. Il se concentre. La nécessité de cette concentration, et du véritable isolement qu'elle implique, la place aussi loin de la nature que de l'agitation citadine, dans une lumière immobile, la lumière de l'atelier."
65. Ibid., 29.
66. See Heinich, *L'Élite artiste*.
67. Dominique Chateau, "Portrait de l'artiste en artiste," *Figures de l'art* 7 (January 2004), 146.
68. Ibid., 22.
69. Menger, *Portrait de l'artiste en travailleur*, 13.
70. Michel Guérin, *L'Artiste et la toute-puissance des idées* (Aix-en-Provence: Publications de l'Université de Provence, 2007). See also Sontag, "The Decay of Cinema."

Conclusion

Let us in closing return to our point of departure, the argument that the dominant theory of film authorship, whose impetus goes back to the *politique des auteurs*, fails to include and account for crucial dimensions of authorial endeavor. Even though its oversights have been often noted, it still enjoys wide currency as a critical practice. Indeed, dramatic challenges have been issued, but have failed to bring about fundamental changes, much less have a lasting impact. Despite claims, for instance, that the author is dead and that the source of any film's meaning is the viewer, film scholars to this day continue to invoke authorship and, despite their better knowledge, at the very least to hold séances. This unresolved discrepancy between critical practice and theoretical misgiving animated the belief that gave rise to this book, namely that film authorship, for all the scholarship devoted to it, deserves reconsideration and further study.

The previous chapter has suggested that the current crisis of cinema may above all be a crisis of film criticism, i.e., a way of thinking about and conceptualizing cinema and the film experience. In her influential polemic of 1996, Susan Sontag spoke of "the decay of cinema" and lamented how great movies were being superseded by bloated, witless, and derivative commercial fare. "The reduction of cinema to assaultive images, and the unprincipled manipulation of images (faster and faster cutting) to make them more attention-grabbing," she complained, "has produced a disincarnated, lightweight cinema that doesn't demand anyone's full attention." Once celebrated as the art of the twentieth century, cinema in Sontag's estimation has become "a decadent art." Gone are the days of arthouses, art films, and dazzling features made by implacable filmmakers. Cinephilia, that special love that came in the wake of going to films and talking and thinking about them, also becomes a thing of the past in an "era of hyperindustrial films."[1] Sontag's intervention is, I think, above all useful as a symptom, a recognition that a certain way of conceiving of and thinking about cinema which we have come to know as auteurism and which has gained wide credence in the guise of classical cinephilia may well have run its course or, at the very least, has become unviable and, as such, in need of updating.

Or, perhaps such a claim is harsh and too hasty. Indeed, the key premise of my study has not been that auteurism is altogether wrong or mistaken; it simply stops too short and does not go far enough in accounting for the complex workings of film authorship. Nor, as Sontag's intervention makes clear, does it seem flexible enough to account for changed circumstances and new possibilities. Singular *auteurs* have existed and continue to exist, but to stress their singularity is to overlook the commonality of circumstance they share with other film professionals and to underestimate the collective dimension of their endeavors. Directors can be seen as creative forces, but why should we not also see them as workers and, as such, as individuals subject to institutions, agencies, and market forces, as members of communities that span generations and different sensibilities? As a whole this study has sought to augment our apprehension of film authorship by considering auteurism's blindspots and, in that endeavor, filling in some crucial blanks in order to extend and nuance our understanding. It is surely not the first study to take issue with the idea that the author is a stable or sole source of meaning. It does, however, represent a concerted endeavor to confront discourses on film authorship with wider discourses on authority, both within the humanities as well as the social sciences.

In my interrogation of auteurism, I traveled back in time and reviewed how a certain approach to cinematic creativity emerged from a national legacy of authorship that stretches over many centuries. As such, the analysis assumed an archeological resolve so that we might appreciate the wide range of meanings that have been invested in French discussions about authorship. Such a focus also made the circumscribed quality of the *politique des auteurs*' appropriation quite visible, especially in its insistent valorization of a singular directorial style and unique signature. This more expansive archeological view is also salubrious insofar as it allows us to revive dimensions of authorship lost in its auteurist codification and probe their continuing pertinence and use value.

To apprehend the discourse of authorship has meant to fathom its history and to reconsider its workings, both in the making of films and in writing about films. My account of the Bressonians was not meant to be a definitive and fine-grained historical study of three filmmakers and some of their contemporaries. Rather this ensemble provided a point of focus and a site of exposition within a larger conceptual enterprise. It is my hope that this book will encourage further study of other Bressonians like Chantal Akerman, Claire Denis, Bruno Dumont, Philippe Garrel, and Jacques Rozier, all of whom we might think of within the transdiscursive constellations explored in this book. Likewise, it might well lend itself to productive discussions that account for Bressonianism in other national contexts, for instance in the output of the Berlin School or the work of Béla Tarr, Apichatpong Weerasethakul, and Luo Li.

This investigation has sought to grant film authorship—as well as discussions of film authorship—a new impetus, a renewed suggestiveness, and a wider range of application. The *auteur* in this understanding is not so much a master of time and space as an animating force for heightened appreciation and different experience among both filmmakers and filmgoers. The lasting power of films made by Bresson and the Bressonians does not lie in their explanations of the world, but rather in their invitations to see it anew and in that way widen our sense of what is real and what is possible.

Notes

1   Sontag, "The Decay of Cinema." Noël Burch, a witness to the development of *Cahiers*' cinephilia, published an acerbic critique in 2007. He assailed "the establishment of a pantheon as proof for the artistic legitimacy of cinema, the cult of films (*œuvres*) removed from socio-historical contingencies," claiming that such gestures "institute cinephilia as a cultural practice that is masculine, individualist and elitist." See Noël Burch, "Cinéphilie et Masculinité," in *De la beauté des latrines: Pour réhabiliter le sens au cinéma et ailleurs* (Paris: L' Harmattan, 2007), 86. In 2009, Laurent Jullier, an advocate of a more inclusive "postmodern" cinephilia, waged a renewed attack against *Cahiers* auteurism. See Laurent Jullier and Jean-Marc Leveratto, *Cinéphiles et cinéphilies: Une histoire de la qualité cinématographique* (Paris: Armand Colin, 2010). Jullier sought to rekindle awareness that "there is still the cult of Great Men (the *auteurs*), esotericism, aestheticism, sexism and especially 'a disgust for the taste of others' in the words of Pierre Bourdieu." He took exception to Jean Douchet's petition in support of the *Cahiers du cinéma* during the journal's acute financial crisis, in which the latter wrote that "the cinema concerns us all in a pressing way: artists, philosophers, writers, filmmakers, critics, actors, directors of festivals." The statement, asserted Jullier, "lacks only one category of people: those who are not part of this 'little world,' that is to say, common mortals!" He went on to say that "one sees it clearly when one talks to a Parisian critic: they still conform to the Baudelairian model of *the one who knows* (how to appreciate modernity), who stands apart from the *vulgar taste* of the public." See Laurent Jullier, "Philistines and Cinephiles: The New Deal," *Framework* 50.1–2 (Spring/Fall 2009): 202.

Bibliography

Adorno, Theodor W. *The Language of Authenticity*. Trans. Knut Tarnowski and Frederic Will. Evanston: Northwestern University Press, 1973.
———. "Transparencies on Film." Trans. Thomas Y. Levin. *New German Critique* 24/25 (Winter/Spring 1981–1982): 199–205.
Agel, Henri. *Sept ans de cinéma français (1945-51)*. Paris: Éditions du Cerf, 1953.
Ajame, Pierre. "Le Cinéma selon Bresson." *Les Nouvelles littéraires* (26 May 1966): 1–13.
Amengual, Barthélemy. "Une vie récluse en cinéma ou l'échec de Jean Eustache." *Études cinématographiques* 153 (1986): 45–124.
Amiel, Vincent. *Le Corps au cinéma: Keaton, Bresson, Cassavetes*. Paris: Presses Universitaires de France, 1998.
———. *'Van Gogh' de Maurice Pialat*. Neuilly: Atlande, 2006.
———. *'Lancelot du Lac' de Robert Bresson*. Lyon: Presses Universitaires de Lyon, 2014.
Andrew, Dudley, ed. *Opening Bazin. Postwar Film Theory and Its Afterlife*. Oxford, New York: Oxford University Press, 2011.
Andrews, David. "No Start, No End: Auteurism and the Auteur Theory." *Film International* 60 (2012): 37–55.
Arnaud, Philippe. *Robert Bresson*. Paris: Cahiers du cinéma, 1986.
———, ed. *Robert Bresson: Éloge*. Paris: Cinémathèque Française/Mazzotta, 1997.
Artaud, Antonin. *Van Gogh, le suicidé de la société*. Paris: Gallimard, 1990 [1947].
Ascoli, Albert Russell. *Dante and the Making of the Modern Author*. London, Cambridge: Cambridge University Press, 2008.
Assayas, Olivier. "Que d'auteurs, que d'auteurs! Sur une politique." In *La Politique des auteurs: Les Textes*, ed. Antoine de Baecque and Gabrielle Lucantonio. Paris: Cahiers du cinéma, 2001, 172–83.
———, Claire Denis, Cédric Kahn, and Noémie Lvovsky. "Quelques Vagues plus tard." *Cahiers du cinéma* (Special Issue, 1998), 67–77.
Astruc, Alexandre. "La Naissance d'une nouvelle avant-garde: la caméra-stylo." In *Du stylo à la caméra. Écrits 1942-1984*. Paris: L'Archipel, 1992, 324–328.
Aumont, Jacques. *L'Œil interminable*. Paris: Séguier, 1989.
———. *Les Théories des cinéastes*. Paris: Nathan Cinéma, 1999.
Ayfre, Amédée. *Conversion aux images? Les Images et Dieu, les images et l'homme*. Paris: Éditions du Cerf, 1964.
Baby, Yvonne. "Le Domaine de l'indicible." *Le Monde* (14 March 1967).
———. "Entretien avec Robert Bresson." *Le Monde* (11 November 1971).

Balázs, Béla. *Schriften zum Film.* 2 vols. Ed. Helmut H. Diederichs and Wolfgang Gersch. Munich: Hanser, 1984.
Barot, Emmanuel. *Caméra politica: dialectique du réalisme dans le cinéma politique et militant.* Paris: Vrin, 2008.
Barthes, Roland. *Image, Music, Text: Essays.* Trans. Stephen Heath. New York: Hill and Wang, 1977.
——. *The Grain of the Voice: Interviews 1962–1980.* Trans. Linda Coverdale. Chicago: Northwestern University Press, 2009.
Bazin, André. "Du festival considéré comme un ordre." *Cahiers du cinéma* 48 (June 1955): 54–56.
——. *What Is Cinema?* 2 vols. Ed. and trans. Hugh Gray. Berkeley: University of California Press, 1967.
——. "De la politique des auteurs." In *La Politique des auteurs: Les Textes,* ed. Antoine De Baecque and Gabrielle Lucantonio. Paris: Cahiers du cinéma, 2001, 99–117.
Bellour, Raymond, ed. *Cinéma et Peinture: Approches.* Paris: Presses Universitaires de France, 1990.
——. *L'Entr'images: Photo, Cinéma, Vidéo.* Paris: Différence, 2002.
Bénichou, Paul. *Le Sacre de l'écrivain: 1750–1830. Essai sur l'avènement d'un pouvoir spirituel laïc dans la France moderne.* Paris: José Corti, 1996.
Bennett, Andrew. *The Author.* London: Routledge, 2005.
Bergala, Alain. "Maurice Pialat, un marginal du centre." *Cahiers du cinéma* 354 (1983): 20.
——. "Roberto Rossellini et l'invention du cinéma moderne." In Roberto Rossellini, *Le Cinéma révélé,* ed. Alain Bergala. Paris: Éditions de l'étoile, 1984, 5–18.
Bernanos, Georges. *Œuvres romanesques suivies de "Dialogue des Carmélites".* Paris: Gallimard, Bibliothèque de la Pléiade, 1991.
——. *Mouchette.* Trans. J.C. Whitehouse. New York: New York Review Books, 2006.
Biagioli, Mario, and Peter Galison, eds. *Scientific Authorship: Credit and Intellectual Property in Science.* New York: Routledge, 2003.
Bickerton, Emilie. *A Short History of Cahiers du Cinéma.* London: Verso, 2009.
Blatt, Ari. "Thinking Photography in Film, or The Suspended Cinema of Agnès Varda and Jean Eustache." *French Forum* 36.2–3 (Spring/ Fall 2011): 181–200.
Bloom, Harold. *The Anxiety of Influence: A Theory of Poetry.* Oxford, New York: Oxford University Press, 1973.
Bonitzer, Pascal. *Décadrages: peinture et cinéma.* Paris: Éditions de l'étoile, 1985.
——. *Eric Rohmer.* Paris: Éditions de l'étoile, 1991.
Boozer, Jack, ed. *Authorship in Film Adaptation.* Austin: University of Texas Press, 2008.
Bordwell, David. *On the History of Film Style.* Cambridge: Harvard University Press, 1997.
Brenez, Nicole. *De la figure en général et du corps en particulier: L'invention figurative au cinéma.* Paris: DeBoeck Université, 1998.
——. "Movie Mutations: Letters from (and to) Some Children of 1960: Jonathan Rosenbaum, Adrian Martin, Kent Jones, Alexander Horwath, Nicole Brenez, and

Raymond Bellour." In *Movie Mutations: The Changing Face of World Cinephilia*, ed. Jonathan Rosenbaum and Adrian Martin. London: British Film Institute, 2003, 1–35.

———, et al. "Robert Bresson—A Symposium." In *Robert Bresson (Revised)*, ed. James Quandt. Toronto: TIFF Cinémathèque, 2011, 595–627.

Bresson, Mylène, ed. *Robert Bresson par Robert Bresson: Entretiens, 1943–1983*. Paris: Flammarion, 2013.

Bresson, Robert. *Notes sur le cinématographe*. Paris: Gallimard, 1975.

———. *Notes on the Cinematograph*. Trans. Jonathan Griffin. London: Quartet Books, 1986.

Briot, René. *Robert Bresson*. Paris: Éditions du Cerf, 1957.

Burch, Noël. *De la beauté des latrines: pour réhabiliter le sens au cinéma et ailleurs*. Paris: L'Harmattan, 2007.

Burke, Séan, ed. *Authorship: From Plato to the Postmodern. A Reader*. Edinburgh: Edinburgh University Press, 1995.

———. *The Death and Return of the Author: Criticism and Subjectivity in Barthes, Foucault and Derrida*. Edinburgh: Edinburgh University Press, 1998.

Burnett, Colin. "Bresson in the 1930s: Photography, Cinema, Milieu." In *Robert Bresson (Revised)*, ed. James Quandt. Toronto: TIFF Cinémathèque, 2011, 203–25.

Caughie, John, ed. *Theories of Authorship*. London: Routledge & Kegan Paul, 1981.

Cérisuelo, Marc. "Mes petites amoureuses." In *Le Dictionnaire Eustache*, ed. Antoine de Baecque. Paris: Léo Scheer, 2011, 190–93.

———. *Fondus enchaînés: Essais de poétique du cinéma*. Paris: Seuil, 2012.

Charensol, Georges. *Panorama du cinéma*. Paris: Éditions du Sagittaire, 1930.

Chartier, Roger. "Foucault's Chiasmus: Authorship between Science and Literature in the 17th and 18th centuries," in *Scientific Authorship: Credit and Intellectual Property in Science*, ed. Mario Biagioli and Peter Galison. New York: Routledge, 2003, 13–31.

Chateau, Dominique. "La Visite de l'atelier dans *La Belle Noiseuse*." *Études cinématographiques* 63 (1998): 127–41.

———. "Portrait de l'artiste en artiste." *Figures de l'art* 7 (January 2004): 145–60.

———. *Qu'est-ce qu'un artiste*. Rennes: Presses Universitaires de Rennes, 2008.

Ciment, Michel. "The Poetry of Precision." *American Film* (October 1983): 70–73.

———. "Cannes 91." *Positif* 365–366 (June–July 1991): 71–97.

———. "I Seek Not Description But Vision: Robert Bresson on *L'Argent*." In *Robert Bresson (Revised)*, ed. James Quandt. Toronto: TIFF Cinémathèque, 2011, 707–19.

Cléder, Jean, ed. *Eric Rohmer: évidence et ambiguïté du cinéma*. Paris: Éditions Le Bord de l'eau, 2007.

Compagnon, Antoine. *Qu'est-ce qu'un auteur? Cours de M. Antoine Compagnon*. Paris: Cours de Licence LLM 316 F2, Université Paris IV—Sorbonne, 2012. http://aphelis.net/wp-content/uploads/2012/03/Compagnon-Auteur.pdf

Corless, Kieron, and Chris Drake. *Cannes: Inside the World's Premier Film Festival*. London: Faber and Faber, 2007.

Corrigan, Timothy. *Cinema without Walls: Movies and Culture after Vietnam*. New Brunswick, New Jersey: Rutgers University Press, 1991.
Crofts, Stephen. "Authorship and Hollywood." In *American Cinema and Hollywood: Critical Approaches*, ed. John Hill and Pamela Church Gibson. New York: Oxford University Press, 2000, 84–98.
Culler, Jonathan. *Structuralist Poetics: Structuralism, Linguistics and the Study of Literature*. London: Routledge, 1975.
Cunneen, Joseph. *Robert Bresson: A Spiritual Life in Film*. New York, London: Continuum, 2003.
Dahan, Danielle. *Robert Bresson: Une téléologie du silence*. Heidelberg: Winter, 2004.
Dalle Vacche, Angela, ed. *Film, Art, New Media: Museum without Walls?* New York: Palgrave, 2012.
De Baecque, Antoine. *La Cinéphilie: Invention d'un regard, histoire d'une culture—1944–1968*. Paris: Fayard, Hachette, 2003.
———, ed. *Le Dictionnaire Pialat*. Paris: Léo Scheer, 2008.
———, ed. *Le Dictionnaire Eustache*. Paris: Léo Scheer, 2011.
——— and Noël Herpe. *Eric Rohmer: Biographie*. Paris: Stock, 2014.
——— and Thierry Jousse, eds. *Le Retour du cinéma*. Paris: Hachette, 1996.
——— and Gabrielle Lucantonio, eds. *La Politique des auteurs: Les textes*. Paris: Cahiers du cinéma, 2001.
De Sutter, Laurent. *Théorie du trou: Cinq méditations métaphysiques sur 'Une sale histoire' de Jean Eustache*. Paris: Léo Scheer, 2013.
De Valk, Marijke, and Malte Hagener, eds. *Cinephilia: Movies, Love and Memory*. Amsterdam: Amsterdam University Press, 2005.
Delahaye, Michel, and Jean-Luc Godard. "La Question: Entretien avec Robert Bresson." *Cahiers du cinéma* 178 (May 1966): 26–35. Reprinted in translation as "The Question." In *Robert Bresson (Revised)*, ed. James Quandt. Toronto: TIFF Cinémathèque, 2011, 635–665.
Delavaud, Gilles, and Jean-Pierre Esquénazi, eds. *Godard et le métier d'artiste*. Paris: L'Harmattan, 2001.
Delluc, Louis. *Le Cinéma au quotidien: Écrits cinématographiques*. Paris: Cinémathèque française/Cahiers du cinéma, 1990.
Denby, David. "The Moviegoers: Why Don't People Like the Right Movies Anymore?" *The New Yorker* (6 April 1998).
Derrida, Jacques. *Spurs: Nietzsche's Styles*. Trans. Barbara Harlow. Chicago, London: University of Chicago Press, 1979.
———. *Dissemination*. Trans. Barbara Johnson. London: The Athlone Press, 1981.
Devisch, Ignaas. *Jean-Luc Nancy and the Question of Community*. London: Bloomsbury, 2013.
Doniol-Valcroze, Jacques, and Jean-Luc Godard. "Entretien avec Robert Bresson." *Cahiers du cinéma* 104 (February 1960), 1–8.

Dubois, Colette. *'La Maman et la putain' de Jean Eustache*. Paris: Yellow Now, coll. Long Métrage, 1990.
Duca, Lo. "Un acte de foi." *Cahiers du cinéma* 1 (April 1951): 1.
Durham, Scott. "On the Authenticity of Jargon: From Barthes and Adorno to Godard." *The World Picture*, 2008.
Elsaesser, Thomas. *European Cinema Face to Face with Hollywood*. Amsterdam: Amsterdam University Press, 2005.
Epstein, Jean. "On Certain Characteristics of *Photogénie*." Trans. Tom Milner. *Afterimage* 10 (1981): 1–23.
Esquénazi, Jean-Pierre, and Gilles Delavaud, eds. *Politique des auteurs et théorie du cinéma*. Paris: L'Harmattan, 2012.
Estève, Michael. *Robert Bresson: La Passion du cinématographe*. Paris: Albatros, 1983.
———. "Jean Eustache présenté par Michel Estève." *Études cinématographiques* 153 (1986): 1–4.
Fabre, Daniel. "Le Corps pathétique de l'écrivain." *Gradhiva* 25 (1999).
Fassbinder, Rainer Werner Fassbinder. *The Anarchy of the Imagination*. Ed. Michael Töteberg and Leo Lensing. Trans. Krishna Winston. Baltimore: Johns Hopkins University Press, 1992.
Fieschi, Jean-André, Jean-Louis Comolli, Michel Mardore, André Téchiné, Gérard Guégan, and Claude Ollier. "Vingt ans après: Le cinéma américain, ses auteurs et notre politique en question." *Cahiers du cinéma* 172 (November 1965): 18–31.
Fontanel, Rémi. *Formes de l'insaisissable, le cinéma de Maurice Pialat*. Lyon: Aléas, 2004.
Forbes, Jill. *The Cinema in France: After the New Wave*. Bloomington and Indianapolis: Indiana University Press, 1992.
Foucault, Michel. "What is an Author?" Trans. Donald F. Bouchard and Sherry Simon. In *Language, Counter-Memory, Practice*, ed. Donald F. Bouchard. Ithaca, New York: Cornell University Press, 1977, 113–38.
———. *The Order of Things: An Archeology of Human Sciences*. London, New York: Routledge, 1989.
———. *The Archeology of Knowledge*. Trans. A.M. Sheridan Smith. New York: Vintage Books, 2010.
Frappat, Hélène. *Jacques Rivette, secret compris*. Paris: Cahiers du cinéma. Coll. Auteurs. 2001.
Frodon, Jean-Michel. *Robert Bresson*. Paris: Cahiers du cinéma, 2007.
Gallop, Jane. *The Deaths of the Author: Reading and Writing in Time*. Durham: Duke University Press, 2011.
Gaudreault, André, and Philippe Marion. *The End of Cinema: A Medium in Crisis in the Digital Age*. Trans. Timothy Barnard. New York: Columbia University Press, 2015.
Gauthier, Christophe. *Cinéphiles, ciné-clubs et salles spécialisées à Paris de 1920 à 1929*. Paris: AFRHC, 1999.
——— et al., eds. *L'Auteur de cinéma: Histoire, généalogie, archéologie*. Paris: AFRHC, 2013.
Gelmis, Joseph. *The Film Director as Superstar*. Garden City, NY: Doubleday, 1970.

Gerstner, David A., and Janet Staiger, eds. *Authorship and Film*. New York: Routledge, 2003.
Gimello-Mesplomb, Frédéric. *Objectif 49: Cocteau et la nouvelle avant-garde*. Paris: Séguier, 2013.
Grant, Barry Keith, ed. *Auteurs and Authorship: A Film Reader*. Oxford: Blackwell, 2008.
Guérin, Marie-Anne. "Numéro zéro." In *Le Dictionnaire Eustache*, ed. Antoine de Baecque. Paris: Léo Scheer, 2011, 215–17.
Guérin, Michel. *L'Artiste et la toute-puissance des idées*. Aix-en-Provence: Publications de l'Université de Provence, 2007.
Guiguet, Jean-Claude. "Entretien avec Françoise Lebrun." In Colette Dubois, *'La Maman et la putain' de Jean Eustache*. Paris: Yellow Now, coll. Long Métrage, 1990.
Gunning, Tom. *The Films of Fritz Lang*. London: British Film Institute, 2000.
Haneke, Michael. "Terror and Utopia of Form Addicted to Truth: A Film Story about Robert Bresson's *Au hasard Balthazar*." In *Robert Bresson (Revised)*, ed. James Quandt. Toronto: TIFF Cinémathèque, 2011, 385–93.
Hanlon, Lindley. *Fragments: Bresson's Film Style*. Rutherford: Farleigh Dickinson University Press, 1986.
Heath, Stephen. "Comment on 'The Idea of Authorship'." *Screen* 14.3 (Autumn 1973): 86–91.
Heinich, Nathalie. *La Gloire de Van Gogh: essai d'anthropologie de l'admiration*. Paris: Minuit, 1991.
———. "Godard, créateur de statut." In *Godard et le métier d'artiste*, ed. Gilles Delavaud, and Jean-Pierre Esquénazi. Paris: L'Harmattan, 2001, 305–13.
———. *L'Élite artiste: excellence et singularité en régime démocratique*. Paris: Gallimard, 2005.
———. *De la visibilité: excellence et singularité en régime médiatique*. Paris: Gallimard, 2012.
Henry, Pierre. "L'Évolution de l'art de l'image animée." *Ciné pour tous* 55 (17 December 1920): 5–6.
Hess, John. "La Politique des auteurs (Part One): World View as Aesthetics." *Jump Cut* 1 (May–June 1974): 19–22.
———. "La Politique des auteurs (Part Two): Truffaut's Manifesto." *Jump Cut* 2 (July–August 1974): 20–22.
Hill, John, and Pamela Church Gibson, eds. *American Cinema and Hollywood: Critical Approaches*. New York: Oxford University Press, 2000.
Hillier, Jim, ed. *Cahiers du cinéma, the 1960s: New Wave, New Cinema, Reevaluating Hollywood*. Cambridge: Harvard University Press, 1986.
Hinderliter, Beth et al., ed. *Communities of Sense: Rethinking Aesthetics and Politics*. Durham: Duke University Press, 2009.
Hobbes, Thomas. *Leviathan*. London: Penguin, 1995.
Ince, Kate, ed. *Five Directors: Auteurism from Assayas to Ozon*. Manchester: Manchester University Press, 2008.

Jacob, Gilles. *Citizen Cannes: The Man behind the Cannes Film Festival*. Trans. Sarah Robertson. London: Phaidon, 2011.
Jardonnet, Evelyne. *Poétique de la singularité au cinéma: Une lecture croisée de Jacques Rivette et Maurice Pialat*. Paris: L'Harmattan, 2006.
Jay, Martin. *Downcast Eyes: The Denigration of Vision in Twentieth-Century French Thought*. Berkeley and Los Angeles: University of California Press, 1994.
Jeancolas, Jean-Pierre. "Le Tub de Madame Théo." *Positif* 369 (November 1991): 12–13.
———. Jean-Jacques Meusy, and Vincent Pinel. *L'Auteur du film: description d'un combat*. Paris: SACD; Arles: Actes Sud, 1996.
Jones, Kent. "Adieu." *Cahiers du cinéma* 543 (February 2000): 32–33.
———. "Critical Condition: From the *Politique des Auteurs* to the *Auteur* Theory to Plain Old *Auteurism*. How Clear of a Picture of Actual Movies Are We Receiving?" *Film Comment* 50.2 (March–April 2014): 40–45.
Joubert-Laurencin, Hervé. *Le Sommeil paradoxal: Écrits sur André Bazin*. Paris: Éditions de l'œil, 2014.
Jousse, Thierry. "Bresson souffle où il veut." *Cahiers du cinéma* 543 (February 2000): 30–31.
Jullier, Laurent. "Philistines and Cinephiles: The New Deal." *Framework* 50.1–2 (Spring/Fall 2009): 202–205.
———, and Jean-Marc Leveratto. *Cinéphiles et cinéphilies: Une histoire de la qualité cinématographique*. Paris: Armand Colin, 2010.
Kael, Pauline. *I Lost It at the Movies*. Boston: Little, Brown & Co., 1965.
Kauffmann, Stanley. "A Lost Love." *New Republic* (8 and 15 September 1997).
Keathley, Christian. *Cinephilia and History, Or The Wind in the Trees*. Bloomington: Indiana University Press, 2006.
Kessler, Frank. *Mise-en-scène*. Montréal: Caboose, 2014.
Klawans, Stuart. *Film Follies: The Cinema Out of Order*. London: Cassell, 1999.
Kohn, Olivier. "Deux ou trois choses sur *Van Gogh*, un film de Maurice Pialat." *Positif* 369 (November 1991): 10–11.
Kojève, Alexandre. *The Notion of Authority (A Brief Presentation)*. Ed. François Terré. Trans. Hager Weslati. London, New York: Verso, 2014.
Kozloff, Sarah. *The Life of the Author*. Montréal: Caboose, 2014.
Le Maître, Barbara. *Entre film et photographie: Essai sur l'empreinte*. Saint-Denis: Presses Universitaires de Vincennes, 2004.
Leblanc, Gérard, and David Faroult, *Mai 68 ou le cinéma en suspens*. Paris: Éditions Syllepse, 1998.
Lefranc, Albert. *L'amour la gueule ouverte: Hypothèses sur Maurice Pialat*. Paris: Hélium, 2015.
Lever, Maurice. *Beaumarchais, A Biography*. Ed. Jean-Pierre Thomas. Trans. Susan Emanuel. New York: Farrar, Straus and Giroux, 2009.
Lévi-Strauss, Claude. *The Savage Mind*. Trans. George Weidenfeld. London: Nicholson, 1966.

Levy-Klein, Stéphane, and Olivier Eyquem. "Trois rencontres avec Maurice Pialat." *Positif* 159 (May 1974): 2–15.
MacCabe, Colin. "The Revenge of the Author." In *Film and Authorship*, ed. Virginia Wright Wexman. New Brunswick, NJ: Rutgers University Press, 2003.
Macé, Arnaud. "Politique des auteurs, politique de l'écriture: Éléments pour une histoire des discours critiques." *Cahiers du cinéma* 592 (July–August 2004): 32–33.
Magny, Joël. *Maurice Pialat*. Paris: Éditions de l'étoile, 1992.
Malle, Louis. "Avec *Pickpocket* Bresson a trouvé." In *Robert Bresson: Éloge*, ed. Philippe Arnaud. Paris: Cinémathèque Française/Mazzotta, 1997, 35–37.
Mary, Philippe. *La Nouvelle Vague et le cinéma d'auteur: Socio-analyse d'une révolution artistique*. Paris: Le Seuil, 2006.
Menger, Pierre-Michel. *Portrait de l'artiste en travailleur: Métamorphoses du capitalisme*. Paris: Seuil, 2002.
Mérigeau, Pascal. *Pialat*. Paris: Grasset, 2002.
Merleau-Ponty, Maurice. *The Prose of the World*. Trans. John O'Neill. Evanston: Northwestern University Press, 1973.
Mladek, Klaus. "Klaus Theweleit's *Book of Kings*: Excerpts in Translation." See http://nideffer.net/proj/Tvc/reviews/18.Tvc.v9.reviews.Mladek.html (accessed 8 August 2015).
Monod, Roland. "En travaillant avec Robert Bresson." *Cahiers du cinéma* 64 (November 1956): 16–20.
Morgan, Daniel. *Late Godard and the Possibilities of Cinema*. Berkeley: University of California Press, 2013.
Morin, Didier. Interview with Isabelle Weingarten in "Les 40 ans de *La Maman et la putain*." *Mettray* (September 2013), n.p.
Moulin, Raymonde. *Art et humanisme à Florence au temps de Laurent le Magnifique*. Paris: Presses Universitaires de France, 1961.
Moullet, Luc. "Blue Collar Dandy." *Film Comment* 36.5 (September/October 2000): 38–43.
Nancy, Jean-Luc. *The Inoperative Community*. Ed. Peter Connor. Minneapolis: University of Minnesota Press, 1991.
——— and Federico Ferrari. *Iconographie de l'auteur*. Paris: Galilée, 2005.
Narboni, Jean. "The Critical Years: Interview with Eric Rohmer." In *The Taste for Beauty*. Trans. Carol Volk. Cambridge: Cambridge University Press, 1989, 1–18.
———. *La Nuit sera noire et blanche. Barthes, 'La Chambre claire,' le cinéma*. Paris: Les Prairies ordinaires et Capricci, 2015.
Naremore, James. "Authorship and the Cultural Politics of Film Criticism." *Film Quarterly* 44.1 (Fall 1990): 14–23.
Nead, Lynda. "Seductive Canvases: Visual Mythologies of the Artist and Artistic Creativity." *Oxford Art Journal* 18.2 (1995): 59–69.
———. "The Artist's Studio: The Affaire of Art and Film." In *Film, Art, New Media: Museum without Walls?*, ed. Angela Dalle Vacche. New York: Palgrave, 2012, 23–38.

Neupert, Richard. *A History of the French New Wave Cinema*. Madison: The University of Wisconsin Press, 2002.
Pascal, Michel. *Cannes: Cris et Chuchotements*. Paris: Nil Éditions, 1997.
Passeron, René. *L'Œuvre picturale et les fonctions de l'apparence*. Paris: Vrin, 1980.
Paxton, Robert. *La France de Vichy*. Paris: Seuil, 1973.
Penrose, Antony. *Roland Penrose, the Friendly Surrealist*. Munich, New York: Prestel, 2001.
Perkins, V.F. "Film Authorship: The Premature Burial." *CineAction!* 21/22 (November 1990): 57–64.
Philippon, Alain. *Jean Eustache*. 2nd edn. Paris: Éditions de l'étoile, 2005.
Pialat, Maurice. *À nos amours: scénario et dialogue du film*. Paris: L'Herminier, 1984.
Pipolo, Tony. *Robert Bresson: A Passion for Film*. Oxford: Oxford University Press, 2010.
Polan, Dana. "Auteur Desire." *Screening the Past* 12 (March 2001): www.latrobe.edu.au/www/screeningthepast/firstrelease/fr0301/dpfr12a.htm
Powrie, Phil. *The Cinema of France*. London: Wallflower Press, 2006.
Prédal, René. *Robert Bresson: L'Aventure intérieure*. Paris: L'avant-scène cinéma, 1992.
Price, Brian. *Neither God Nor Master: Robert Bresson & Radical Politics*. Minneapolis: University of Minnesota Press, 2011.
Provoyeur, Jean-Louis. *Le Cinéma de Robert Bresson*. Paris: L'Harmattan, 2003.
Quandt, James, ed. *Robert Bresson (Revised)*. Toronto: TIFF Cinémathèque, 2011.
———. "Framed: James Quandt on Robert Bresson's *L'Argent*." *Artforum* 51.3 (November 2012): 250–52.
Quignard, Pascal. *Sur l'idée d'une communauté de solitaires*. Paris: Arléa, Diffusion Seuil, 2015.
Rancière, Jacques. "The Aesthetic Revolution and its Outcomes: Emplotments of Autonomy and Heteronomy." *New Left Review* 14 (March–April 2002): 133–51.
———. *The Politics of Aesthetics: The Distribution of the Sensible*. Trans. Gabriel Rockhill. New York: Continuum, 2004.
———. *Film Fables*. Trans. Emiliano Battista. Oxford: Berg, 2006.
———. *Aesthetics and Its Discontents*. Trans. Steven Corcoran. Cambridge: Polity, 2009.
———. "Contemporary Art and the Politics of Aesthetics." In *Communities of Sense: Rethinking Aesthetics and Politics*, ed. Beth Hinderliter et al. Durham: Duke University Press, 2009, 31–50.
———. *Les Écarts du cinéma*. Paris: La Fabrique Éditions, 2011.
———. *The Intervals of Cinema*. Trans. John Howe. London: Verso, 2014.
Reader, Keith. *Robert Bresson*. Manchester: Manchester University Press, 2000.
Reilhac, Michel. *Plaidoyer pour l'avenir du cinéma d'auteur: Entretiens avec Frédéric Sojcher*. Paris: Klincksieck, 2009.
Rivette, Jacques. "Lettre sur Rossellini." *Cahiers du cinéma* 46 (April 1955): 14–26.
———. *Texts and Interviews*. Trans. Amy Gateff and Tom Milne. Ed. Jonathan Rosenbaum. London: British Film Institute, 1977.
Rohmer, Eric. *Six Contes Moraux*. Paris: Éditions de l'Herne, 1974.

———. *The Taste for Beauty*. Trans. Carol Volk. Cambridge, New York: Cambridge University Press, 1989.
Rosenbaum, Jonathan and Adrian Martin. *Movie Mutations: The Changing Face of World Cinephilia*. London: British Film Institute, 2003.
Roubaud, Alix-Cléo. *Journal 1979-1983*. Paris: Seuil, 1984.
Sadoul, Georges. *Dictionnaire des cinéastes*. Paris: Seuil, 1982.
Sarris, Andrew. "The Director's Game." *Film Culture* 22–23 (Summer 1961): 68–81.
———. *The American Cinema*. New York: Dutton, 1968.
———. "The Auteur Theory Revisited." *American Film* 2.9 (July–August 1977): 49–53.
———. "Auteurism Is Alive and Well and Living in Argentina." *Film Comment* 26.4 (July–August 1990): 19–22.
Sayad, Cecilia. *Performing Authorship: Self-Inscription and Corporeality in the Cinema*. London: Tauris, 2013.
Schilling, Derek. *Eric Rohmer*. Manchester: Manchester University Press, 2007.
Schrader, Paul. *Transcendental Style in Film: Ozu, Bresson, Dreyer*. New York: Da Capo, 1988.
———. "Robert Bresson: In Memoriam." *The Village Voice* (11 January 2000).
Screening the Past. "Auteurism 2001." Special issue no. 12 (2001).
Sellier, Geneviève. *Masculine Singular: French New Wave Cinema*. Trans. Kristin Ross. Durham: Duke University Press, 2008.
Sellors, C. Paul. *Film Authorship: Auteurs and Other Myths*. London: Wallflower, 2010.
Sémolué, Jean. *Bresson, ou l'acte des métamorphoses*. Paris: Flammarion, 1993.
Shapin, Steven. "The Ivory Tower: The History of a Figure of Speech and Its Cultural Uses." *The British Journal for the History of Science* 45.1 (March 2012): 1–27.
Shaviro, Steven. *The Cinematic Body*. Minneapolis: University of Minnesota Press, 1998.
Silverman, Kaja. "The Author as Receiver." *October* 96 (Spring 2001): 17–34.
Sloan, Jane. *Robert Bresson: A Guide to References and Resources*. Boston: Hall, 1983.
Smith, Alison. *French Cinema in the 1970s: The Echoes of May*. Manchester: Manchester University Press, 2005.
Sontag, Susan. *Against Interpretation*. New York: Farrar, Straus & Giroux, 1966.
———. "The Decay of Cinema." *New York Times Magazine* (25 February 1996): 60.
Staples, Donald E. "*La politique des auteurs*: The Theory and Its Influence on the Cinema." *Language and Style* 3 (1970): 303–11.
Steimatsky, Noa. "Incoherent Spasms and the Dignity of Signs: Bazin's Bresson." In *Opening Bazin: Postwar Film Theory and Its Afterlife*, ed. Dudley Andrew. Oxford, New York: Oxford University Press, 2011, 167–76.
———. "On the Face, in Reticence." In *Film, Art, New Media: Museum without Walls?*, ed. Angela Dalle Vacche. New York: Palgrave, 2012, 159–77.
Stillinger, Jack. *Multiple Authorship and the Myth of the Solitary Genius*. Oxford: Oxford University Press, 1991.
Taubin, Amy. "Remembering a Master of Precise Gesture and Cinematic Emotion." *The Village Voice* (4 January 2000).

Taylor, Charles. *The Malaise of Modernity*. Concord: Anansi, 1991.
Taylor, Greg. *Artists in the Audience: Cults, Camp and the American Film Criticism*. Princeton: Princeton University Press, 2001.
Toffetti, Sergio, and Aldo Tassone. *Maurice Pialat, l'enfant sauvage*. Turin: Lindau, 1992.
Toubiana, Serge. *Maurice Pialat: Peintre et cinéaste*. Paris: Cinémathèque française, 2013.
Truffaut, François. "Crise d'ambition du cinéma français." *Arts* (30 March–5 April 1955).
Vernet, Marc. *Figures de l'absence*. Paris: Éditions de l'étoile, 1990.
Vincendeau, Ginette. *Encyclopedia of European Cinema*. London: BFI, 1995.
Warehime, Marja. "Money, Markets, Women and the Death of Art: Maurice Pialat's *Van Gogh* and Jacques Rivette's *La Belle Noiseuse*." *Sites: The Journal of Twentieth-Century/Contemporary French Studies* 6.2 (2002): 414–23.
———. *Maurice Pialat*. Manchester: Manchester University Press, 2006.
Watts, Philip. *Le Cinéma de Roland Barthes*. Trans. Sophie Queniet. Paris: De l'incidence éditeur, 2015.
Wexman, Virginia Wright, ed. *Film and Authorship*. New Brunswick, NJ: Rutgers University Press, 2003.
Weyl, Daniel. *Robert Bresson: De la plume médiévale au cinématographe*. Paris: L'Harmattan, 2014.
Wiazemsky, Anne. *Jeune fille*. Paris: Gallimard, 2007.
Wiles, Mary. *Jacques Rivette*. Urbana: University of Illinois Press, 2012.
Willemen, Paul. *Looks and Frictions*. Bloomington: Indiana University Press, 1994.
Wollen, Peter. *Signs and Meaning in the Cinema*, 3rd rev. edn. Bloomington: Indiana University Press, 1972.
———. "The Auteur Theory." In *Theories of Authorship*, ed. John Caughie. London: Routledge & Kegan Paul, 1981, 138–51.
Wood, Robin. "Authorship Revisited." *CineAction!* 21/22 (November 1990): 46–56.
Woodmansee, Martha. *The Author, Art, and the Market: Rereading the History of Aesthetics*. New York: Columbia University Press, 1994.

Index

A
A Man Escaped, 32, 35, 61
À nos amours, 101, 102, 118, 189
adaptation, 36, 43, 66–71, 105–6
Adorno, Theodor W., 12, 66, 83n30, 83–4n42, 168
Amengual, Barthélémy, 39, 54n94, 54n96 117n37
Amiel, Vincent, 77–78, 175n46
Amour, l'après-midi, L', 139, 149n73
Amour existe, L', 102
Anges du péché, Les, 24, 43, 47
artisan, 17, 45–46, 155, 164–8
artist as genius, 2, 6–7, 13, 17, 23, 26, 27, 38, 40, 45, 154–5, 159, 161, 162, 164, 166, 172
artist as saint, 15, 17, 25, 27
artistic sovereignty, 4, 28, 123, 158
Assayas, Olivier, 7, 20, 58
Association des Auteurs de Films (AAF), 41, 43
Astruc, Alexandre, 6, 41, 71, 120
Au hasard Balthazar, 30–31, 35, 37–38, 64, 68, 69, 71, 77
Aumont, Jacques, 49, 66,
authenticity, 3, 7, 11, 171, 172

B
Balázs, Béla, 66
Balzac, Honoré de, 51n47, 154, 156, 170
Barthes, Roland, 8, 120, 144–5, 154
Bazin, André, 39, 41, 42, 61, 69–70, 134–5, 143, 150
Beaumarchais, 3–4
Belle Noiseuse, La, 17, 152, 153, 154, 155–72
Bergala, Alain, 101, 176n57
Bernanos, Georges, 16, 64–75, 80–84, 105–13
Bloom, Harold, 88
Bonitzer, Pascal, 141–42, 173n
Bonnaire, Sandrine, 105
Bordwell, David, 63–64
Brenez, Nicole, 24, 25, 26, 28, 81, 91, 93
Bresson, Robert
  cinematographic writing, 28, 67–69, 76–80
  fragmentation, 16, 58, 66, 68, 73, 76, 78, 100, 104, 109
  maniac of truth, 10, 28, 38, 45, 124
  metteur-en-ordre, 78
  model, 31–38, 65, 71, 72, 73, 75, 79, 86, 90, 94, 100, 104, 114
  obituaries, 23–25, 58, 61
  painter, 33–34, 70, 101
Burch, Noël, 179n1
Burke, Séan, 49, 120

C
Cahiers du cinéma, 6, 17, 29, 32, 37, 58, 59, 86, 118, 120, 121, 134, 154, 156
camera-stylo, 6, 36, 41, 71, 120
Cannes, 41, 150, 151, 153–156, 164, 172
Chartier, Roger, 4
Chateau, Dominique, 168, 169
Ciment, Michel, 9, 33, 59, 151
cinephilia, 25–26, 42, 48, 101, 150, 172, 177
Claire's Knee. See *Genou de Claire, Le*
Clouzot, Georges, 158
Cocteau, Jean, 30, 34, 42, 46, 139
community
  aesthetic, 11, 80, 81, 115
  of authors, 5, 10, 14, 18, 37, 44, 36, 58–64
  professional, 13, 18, 45, 48, 170

D
De Baecque, Antoine, 118n46, 173n11
De Sutter, Laurent, 128
death of the author, 2, 8, 9, 14, 16, 115, 119–21, 144, 145, 157
Depardieu, Gérard, 105, 111, 113
Desplechin, Arnaud, 152, 172
Diary of A Country Priest. See *Journal d'un cure de campagne*
Douchet, Jean, 115n3, 127, 179n1

E

end of cinema, 2, 14, 17, 23, 115, 145, 151, 157, 172
Enfance nue, L', 95, 101, 102
Eustache, Jean
    authorship, 10, 16, 114, 122–25, 127
    biography, 86, 88, 116n8, 126
    cinephile, 86, 97
    iconography, 15, 88
    relation to Nouvelle Vague, 86, 101, 122
    style, 59, 90–92, 94–100, 114, 123–33
    truth, 11, 115, 144, 145

F

Femme de l'aviateur, La, 140–1
Foucault, Michel
    archeology, 7, 114
    author-function, 8, 9, 12
    What is an Author?, 8–12, 114
Four Nights of a Dreamer. See *Quatre nuits d'un rêveur*

G

Gaumont, 17, 162
Genou de Claire, Le, 137, 139–140, 142, 144
Giraudoux, Jean, 41, 43
Godard, Jean-Luc, 6, 9, 10, 27, 37, 42, 48, 49, 59, 101, 121, 134, 151, 152, 159, 164

H

Haneke, Michael, 31, 79
Heinich, Nathalie, 48–49, 184n52

I

influence, 9, 14, 49, 59, 61, 80, 91–100,

J

Jacob, Gilles, 85n59, 154
Jones, Kent, 1, 23, 58, 59, 63
Journal d'un curé de campagne, 61, 69–70, 71, 73, 76, 78, 111
Jousse, Thierry, 58, 59,

K

Kojève, Alexandre, 114–5

L

Lancelot du Lac, 26, 31, 77
Léaud, Jean-Pierre, 92
Lebrun, Françoise, 89, 90, 116n16, 129
Lévi-Strauss, Claude, 120, 154
Lhomme, Pierre, 89
Loulou, 102
Lumière Brothers, 9, 101, 112, 118n55

M

Maison des bois, La, 101
Maman et la putain, La, 80, 86–92, 94, 123, 126, 129
Ma nuit chez Maud, 137, 139
Marx, Karl, 59, 172
Menger, Pierre-Michel, 176n58
Mépris, Le, 151, 159,
Merleau-Ponty, Maurice, 79, 82n19
Mes petites amoureuses, 80, 88, 91, 92–100, 114, 126, 146n23
Minnelli, Vincente, 158, 163, 167
mise-en-scène, 1, 2, 13, 17, 32, 33, 37, 38, 58, 60, 71, 83n32, 80, 91, 92, 96, 120, 127, 133, 137, 139
montage, 15, 65–66, 72, 76, 78–80, 90–92
Montaigne, Michel de, 45, 76, 78, 85n65
Mouchette, 35, 64–77, 88, 91, 92, 104

N

Nancy, Jean-Luc, 10, 60, 81
naturalism, 28, 103
Notes on the Cinematograph, 28, 29, 34, 43, 46, 63, 76, 78, 150, 159
Nous ne vieillirons pas ensemble, 102
Nouvelle Vague, 6, 9, 11–14, 16, 17, 40–46, 86, 100–102, 122, 136, 146n17, 151–52, 164, 171

O

objectivity, 135
ontology, 122, 132, 135, 146n26

P

Pagnol, Marcel, 41, 43, 88, 101
painting, 11, 33–34, 39, 46, 49, 69, 101, 153, 155–61, 165, 166, 168
Père Noël a les yeux bleus, Le, 92, 94, 126, 146n23
Photos d'Alix, Les, 124–26

Pialat, Maurice
    adaptation of Bernanos, 105–12
    authorship, 10, 15, 59, 112, 115, 122, 164–68, 171
    ellipsis, 16, 80, 104, 167
    naturalism, 95, 103
    painter, 101, 154, 170, 172
    relation to Nouvelle Vague, 100, 101, 102, 122, 154, 164
    style, 103, 112, 113, 164–68
    truth, 11, 12, 103, 111, 112, 113, 115, 118n59
    work with actors, 80, 102, 104, 111, 112, 113
Pickpocket, 30, 35, 37, 43, 63, 65, 80, 89, 92, 98, 99
Pipolo, Tony, 27, 68
Police, 102
politique des auteurs, 1, 6–7, 9, 13, 14, 17, 29, 35–40, 48, 49, 62, 119, 121, 122, 151, 154, 177, 178
Prédal, René, 25–26

Q
Quandt, James, 24, 35,
Quatre nuits d'un rêveur, 80, 86, 89

R
Rancière, Jacques, 2, 15, 69–72, 81, 106
Renoir, Jean, 5, 7, 9, 10, 37, 42, 59, 89, 95, 100, 101, 139, 167, 171
Rivette, Jacques
    critic, 6, 17, 18, 121,
    filmmaker, 17, 101, 115n4, 152–61
Rohmer, Eric
    critic, 6, 16, 17, 39–40, 61–62, 133–5
    filmmaker, 17, 42, 101, 122, 136–43, 144, 145, 165
Rosière de Pessac, La, 123, 126
Roubaud, Alix-Cléo, 125
Rozier, Jacques, 10, 100, 179

S
Schilling, Derek, 6, 148n65
Schrader, Paul, 23–27, 103
signature, 6, 10, 11, 13, 14, 15, 24, 46, 59, 62, 71, 79–80, 112–13, 120, 121, 152, 155, 165
singularity, 2, 4, 7, 10, 13, 15, 17, 18, 27, 28, 37, 45, 48, 61, 62, 81, 114, 153, 171–72, 178
Société des Auteurs et Compositeurs Dramatiques (SACD), 41

Société du droit d'auteur cinématographique, 40
social realism, 95
Sontag, Susan, 27, 176n70, 177, 178
Sous le soleil de Satan, 16, 80, 102, 105–13, 154, 161, 165
Steimatsky, Noa, 75, 83n41
style, 2, 4, 10, 11, 13, 14, 15, 24, 36, 47, 58, 60–64, 78–80, 122, 165, 186

T
transdiscursivity, 8–10, 15, 59, 179
Truffaut, François, 6, 10, 42, 92, 95, 101, 134, 151, 164

U
Under the Sun of Satan. See *Sous le soleil de Satan*
Une femme douce, 32
Une sale histoire, 126–32, 144

V
vocation, 11–12, 14, 26, 45–48, 155, 168–70
Van Gogh, 17, 102, 152, 153, 154, 161–72

W
Watts, Philip, 149n80
Weingarten, Isabelle, 80, 86, 88, 89, 90, 91

www.ingramcontent.com/pod-product-compliance
Lightning Source LLC
Chambersburg PA
CBHW071344080526
44587CB00017B/2950